PSYCHOLOGY & PSYCHIATRY
TODAY

PSYCHOLOGY &

PSYCHIATRY TODAY

A MARXIST VIEW

BY

JOSEPH NAHEM

INTERNATIONAL PUBLISHERS New York

Library of Congress Cataloging in Publication Data

Nahem, Joseph, 1917-
    Psychology and psychiatry today.

    Includes bibliographical references and index.
    1. Psychology—Philosophy.   2. Psychology—Method-
ology.   3. Psychiatry—Philosophy.   4. Psychiatry—
Methodology.   5. Marx, Karl, 1818-1883.   I. Title.
[DNLM: 1. Communism.   2. Psychiatry.   3. Psychology.
4. Socialism.   WM 100 N153p]
BF38.N28   150'.1'8   81-680
ISBN 0-7178-0581-6   AACR2
ISBN 0-7178-0579-4 (pbk.)

To Cathy, Gregory and Beladee

Contents

PSYCHOLOGY & PSYCHIATRY TODAY

Preface

For a number of years, there has been a need for a more active Marxist presence in the fields of psychology and psychiatry. Particularly in the seventies, there was a flood of new therapies, variants on old therapies, and popular psychiatric fads and psychological fripperies. There have also been some healthy developments in these fields. A Marxist appraisal and critique should take its place in the arena of discussion, especially in view of the ideological role which is played by both psychology and psychiatry.

This book does not claim to be a comprehensive analysis of these fields. Instead, it deals with a selected number of areas from a Marxist viewpoint. An introductory chapter presents the general Marxist approach in psychology and psychiatry. The book then divides into three parts; each part opens with a brief comment. The three parts contain eleven chapters and are followed by a brief conclusion.

A straight reading of the book will give a better understanding of Marxism and psychology and psychiatry. However, each chapter was written as an independent analysis of a specific subject and may be read separately and in any order.

It is hoped that the book has achieved a scholarly but non-technical level so that both professionals and non-professionals may gain a clear grasp of the subject matter. Although the material and analyses are set forth by the author with conviction and documentation, there may well be incompleteness or one-sidedness since many of the topics are being handled from a Marxist perspective for the first time. In any case, it is hoped and expected that the book will furnish material for fuller discussion.

There is a continuing need for a Marxist analysis of many topics not discussed or just touched upon in this book, such as psychotherapy, aggression, workers and mental health, human sexuality, marriage and family life, unconscious processes, community psychiatry, family therapy, education, and learning disabilities. It is hoped that this book will stimulate Marxist writings in these areas.

Introduction

Psychology is the science which studies the human mind. Like all other sciences, psychology must discover the laws which govern the origin, development and functioning of the specific area it studies, i.e., the human mind. Psychology is, perhaps, the most complex of any science. Its complexity is shown by its need to deal with the following major features.

Psychology must study the human mind in both its normal and its abnormal state. It is therefore closely linked to and dependent in part upon psychiatry.

The human mind is based upon and produced by the brain and the central nervous system, which function according to certain physical, chemical, biological, and physiological laws. Particularly important for psychology is the study of the physiological laws relating to neurological activity. Hence, essential for psychology is the study of unconditioned and conditioned reflexes, excitation and inhibition, analysis and synthesis, generalization, dynamic stereotype, first and second signal systems, etc.

Since human beings are a product of evolutionary development, as Darwin demonstrated, the study of animal behavior sheds important light on human psychological functioning. Animal psychology, therefore, is allied to the science of human psychology.

The human mind is a reflection of the external natural and social world. This reflection is produced for individuals in the course of their activity in the world. Since human activity is basically social, the dependence of human psychology on the social world and on the social activity of the individual is profoundly significant. Indeed, psychology cannot be truly scientific unless it elaborates the laws governing the relationship of human psychology to human society.

In order to discover this relationship, a scientific analysis of society is vital. The roles of class, race, sex, work, family life, and marriage in each society must be analyzed and understood. The nature of production and of ideology must be grasped. The essential quality or nature of the society must be identified and its laws must be understood—different for a capitalist society than for a feudal or socialist society.

Human reflection is not a passive reflection of the environment and of society. It is produced in the course of human activity and guides behavior. Hence, the study of human activity and behavior in its many forms is a psychological necessity.

The human psyche has its own laws and its own psychological phenomena. These include sensation, perception, consciousness, conception, memory, attention, learning and intelligence. Study of these categories is central for psychology.

Human beings function on both a conscious and an unconscious level. Human consciousness is decisive in understanding the human psyche. However, the role of unconscious mental processes must also be scientifically delineated.

Human beings are not just thinking and acting beings—they also have feelings and emotions. These feelings enter into and interact with thought and behavior. The study of human affect is indispensable for psychology.

The psychology of the individual is determined by that individual's psychological history and social relationships. Psychology must, therefore, study the formation and the present state of the individual's mind in the light of that individual's society, community, national and racial background, sex, religion, economic status, family, upbringing, education, work activity, peer relationships, love and marital history, class consciousness, organizational ties, views and attitudes, and philosophic outlook. Psychology requires a social-historical-cultural approach to the individual mind and behavior.

The complexity of psychology as a science is thus indicated by its ed to study evolutionary development, animal psychology, physiology and psychiatry, sociology and social psychology, along with the specific laws of human psychological functioning, including cognition, emotion and behavior, and the laws of individual psychological development.

Psychology is not only a complex and many-sided science—it is a young science. Psychology emerged as an independent science in the latter part of the nineteenth century. In certain areas, particularly those related to the natural sciences such as physiology, psychology has made significant progress. Important advances also have been made in the study of sensation, perception, and memory. The role of speech and language has been more satisfactorily understood recently. However, relatively slow progress has been made in areas such as personality, social psychology, learning, emotion, the nature of unconscious processes, and the nature and treatment of mental illness. Because of its complexity and its youth, psychology has had an uneven development. But psychology's progress has been crucially affected—mainly in a negative way—by social and class forces. Psychology arose and developed in capitalist society, a class society. In all class societies, the dominant social, cultural and political views are those of the dominant class.

Under capitalism, the dominant capitalist class develops an ideology to serve its interests. Since the social and behavioral sciences exercise a powerful influence on the thinking of people, these sciences are strongly co-opted to serve the ideological interests of capitalism. In the United States, we find the history of psychology rife with unscientific theories and practices regarding working people, Black people, national minorities, women, and the nature of human beings. Racism, chauvinism, sexism, and anti-working-class ideas have occupied a major position in psychology and psychiatry.

Further, the study of crucial psychological areas, such as intelligence, behavior, motivation, the unconscious, social activity, emotions, and mental illness, are distorted and falsified by powerful class and racist influences. Although there is no such scientific split as "capitalist psychology" and "Marxist psychology", Marxism has a considerable contribution to make to the development of the sciences of psychology and psychiatry, and to the understanding their social role and significance.

The contributions of Marxism to psychology are to be found in four areas: 1. The Marxist dialectical materialist approach to science in general and to psychology and psychiatry specifically. 2. The Marxist historical materialist approach to the development of human beings and to society. 3. The Marxist critique of psychology in the United States. 4. The contributions of Marxism and of Marxist psychologists to the science of psychology.

Dialectical Materialism and Psychology

Scientists, including psychologists and psychiatrists, are either indifferent to philosophy or adopt a philosophy without considering its relevance to their scientific work. Frederick Engels, the co-founder of Marxism, remarked about this phenomenon:

> Natural scientists believe that they free themselves from philosophy by ignoring it or abusing it. They cannot, however, make any headway without thought and for thought they need thought determinations. But they take these categories unreflectingly from the common consciousness of so-called educated persons, which is dominated by the relics of long obsolete philosophies, or from the little bit of philosophy compulsorily listened to at the university (which is not only fragmentary, but also a medley of views belonging to the most varied and usually the worst schools), or from uncritical and unsystematic reading of philosophy of all kinds. Hence, they are no less in bondage to philosophy, but unfortunately in most cases to the worst philosophy, and those who abuse philosophy most are slaves to precisely the worst vulgarized relics of the worst philosophers.[1]

Philosophy, of course, does not and cannot replace science. Each science, including psychology, must study its specific area with scientific methods in order to uncover the basic laws governing the phenomena in that area. However, philosophy exercises a strong influence on the nature of the research carried out, the construction of new hypotheses, the interpretation of scientific results, and the development of theories. Darwin's theory of evolution was arrived at only after Darwin began to question the Biblical story of Creation and constructed a different hypothesis from a materialist viewpoint. Thereafter, Darwin was able to correctly interpret the scientific data he accumulated and to develop a scientific theory which disproved the Biblical theory.

Philosophy also influences the methodology used in scientific research. In the United States, most behavior research is dominated by the methodology of Research Design and Statistical Probability. This methodology arose from Operationalism, which is rooted in subjective idealist philosophy.*

*See Chapter 10 on Behavior Research for full discussion of Operationalism.

Science, above all, is guided by a philosophy of science, an overall view of nature, the universe and human society. Such a philosophy must include two aspects: a theory of the world and a method of approach to studying reality. More specifically, science operates, overtly or covertly, with a materialist or idealist view of the world, and with a dialectical or mechanical approach to reality.

Illustrative of the materialist v. idealist theory of the world is the story that, when Napoleon asked the French astronomer Laplace where God fit in his theory of the solar system, he replied, "I had no need of that hypothesis, Sire." Laplace's theory was based only on natural law, not on the Biblical story of Creation.

The dialectical v. mechanical approach is exemplified in Pavlov's rejection of the mechanistic view that all animals, including human beings are like machines. Pavlov identified the *qualitative* difference between humans and animals in the possession by humans of a second signal system, i.e., speech, which was "the latest acquisition in the process of evolution."[2]

Marxism is rooted in the philosophy of dialectical materialism. Its materialist viewpoint excludes religious, supernatural or idealist views. Thus, in psychology, it excludes the idea of a supernatural soul as explanatory of human behavior.

Materialism itself has been the basis for scientific development throughout history. Materialism was the philosophy which was openly espoused by science in its rapid development after the Middle Ages. Marxism founded its overall theory and philosophy on the materialist tradition.

Marxist dialectics were developed by Marx and Engels as the most general laws of nature, society and human thought.[3] These general laws, which were derived from science and its specific laws, call for seeking the laws of change, both quantitative and qualitative, and for the uncovering of the relationships and interdependence of phenomena. Further, the unity and contradiction in phenomena must be ascertained. Engels called for the pursuit of truth by the positive sciences "and for the summation of their results by dialectical thinking."[4]

Marxism believes that science has advanced by fighting off religious-idealist views and mechanical-metaphysical approaches. Marxists believe that science would benefit if it *consciously* adopted dialectical materialism as the philosophy of science and as a methodology for research.

There is a special link between philosophy and psychology. This link is found in that special area of philosophy known as epistemology, or the theory of knowledge. Epistemology deals with, among other things, the origin of consciousness and the mind, the relationship of mind and body, the nature of thought, language and logic, abstract and concrete thought, and the influence of society and social labor on individual and social thinking. It is obvious that these general philosophical areas are also major areas of scientific psychological study. Indeed, it can be stated that psychology provides the scientific basis for certain major features of epistemology, while epistemology generalizes the specific scientific findings of psychology.

Psychology, like all sciences, has been the battleground between materialist and idealist viewpoints throughout history. Before its separation from philosophy as an independent science, psychology had a long materialist tradition rooted in the views of the ancient Greek materialist philosophers, and in the materialist philosophy of Bacon, Hobbes and Locke in seventeenth century England and Diderot, Helvetius and d'Holbach in eighteenth century France. Marxism derived and built its materialist theory of knowledge on that materialist foundation.

The fundamental propositions set forth by this materialist epistemology are: that matter is primary and that mind and consciousness are secondary and derivative; that mental processes and consciousness itself are products of specially organized matter in the form of the brain and nervous system. Thus, Marxist materialism holds that psychological theories which separate the mind from the brain, or which deny the primacy of the brain and nervous system are unscientific. The work of Pavlov and others in physiology is viewed as a confirmation of materialist epistemology since it confirms the reliance of mental processes on physiological processes.

Psychology has also had to fight the battle between mechanical and dialectical approaches. Marx and Engels overcame mechanical, static materialism by combining materialism with dialectics. They held that the world is to be comprehended as a complex of *processes* which go through an uninterrupted change of coming into being and passing away. Further, science must study phenomena in their unity and conflict and in their interrelation and interdependence. All phenomena must be seen, they maintained, in their quantitative change leading to qualitative change.[5]

From this dialectical viewpoint, behaviorism in psychology, such as the theories of J.B. Watson or B.F. Skinner,* must be criticized as mechanical, as the reduction of the *psychological* process of human functioning to the *physiological* process of behavior alone. Behaviorism, carried to extremes, has led to unscientific—and reactionary—theories, such as Behavior Modification which uses unethical and even brutal means to change behavior.**

On the other hand, we have the metaphysical theory of Freudianism, which focuses on an unconscious mind, divorced from social and individual reality and consciousness, which is seen as the basic source determining human affect, attitude and behavior.*** Scientific psychology must reject the general theories of both Behaviorism and Freudianism. It must seek to show the dialectical relationship between social and individual reality, between thought, consciousness, unconscious processes, emotion, attitude and behavior.

Along with the contributions of Marxist dialectical materialism in the field of epistemology, Karl Marx also provided a significant contribution to psychology in his development of the concept of human alienation. Marx rooted alienation in the very process of capitalist production itself.[6] Marx saw the worker as alienated from the product of his labor and from work itself because, since the product belongs to the capitalist, his work is "forced labor . . . not his own, but someone else's."[7] Further, workers are estranged from their true nature as *human* beings because their work and its product are alien to them. They cannot feel a oneness with nature and society. Alienation is, therefore intrinsic to capitalism and the private ownership of the means of production. Hence, the basis for its elimination, in the long run, is the replacement of capitalism by socialism.

Even under capitalism, however, Marx saw that workers could combat alienation through associating together to fight for their class interest:

> (T)he most splendid results are to be observed whenever French socialist workers are seen together. Such things as smoking, drinking, eating, etc., are no longer means of contact or means that bring together. Company,

*See Chapter 2 on B.F. Skinner's behaviorism.
**See Chapter 3 which deals with Behavior Modification.
***See Chapter 1 on Freudianism.

association, and conversation, which again has society as its end, are enough for them; the brotherhood of man is no mere phrase with them, but a fact of life, and the nobility of man shines upon us from their work-hardened bodies.[8]

Marxism is based upon science. Its philosophy is derived from science and provides a basis for the evaluation and interpretation of scientific theories, areas of research, and methodology. Dialectical materialism has particular importance for psychology since epistemology and psychology are intertwined. Marxist epistemology can be a valuable guide and approach for the science of psychology.

Historical Materialism and Psychology

Historical materialism is the application of dialectical materialism to the origin, development and functioning of human society. Marx and Engels adopted an historical approach to the investigation of the origins of life, of human beings, and of human society.[9] They supported the view, rooted in materialist philosophy, that life arose from inanimate matter as a new and qualitatively different mode of existence of matter. Evolutionary development, as confirmed by Darwin, led to the appearance of multifarious species of plants and animals, proceeding from lower to higher stages of living organisms.

With the appearance of primates, who had the ability to make and utilize tools for the production of the necessities of life, a new stage of development occurred. Cooperative social labor with tools led to the development of articulate speech as a means of communication and thought. Thus, social labor based upon tool-making and tool-using produced speech and language. Human consciousness and mind, based upon speech and language, are seen as produced through the development of social labor and material production.[9] As Marx and Engels placed it: "The premises from which we begin are . . . real individuals, their activity and the material conditions under which they live. . . . Men can be distinguished from animals by consciousness, by religion or anything you like. They themselves begin to distinguish themselves from animals as they begin to *produce* their means of susbistence . . . "[10]

Marxist historical materialism analyzed the development of human society as proceeding from the primitive communism of the first stage of human development, through the societies of slavery, feudalism, capitalism and socialism.[11] Society is, hence, not static and repetitive, but changes dialectically throughout its history.

Such changes in human society are the result of changes occurring in social being. The mode of production consists of the productive forces and the social relations of production, i.e., how people are related to each other in production—as classes or in communal relations. Changes in society are due to changes in the productive forces, which then lead to changes in the relations of production. Thus, the feudal mode of production had certain productive forces and class relations of production made up of the landlord feudal master and the exploited serf producer.

With the development of the productive forces, especially the tools and instruments of production, new classes, the capitalists and the exploited workers, arose and changed the feudal relations of production to capitalist relations of production through revolution (e.g., the French Revolution of 1789).

The materialist conception of history further holds that there arises an ideological superstructure on the economic foundation of society. Thus, the capitalist production relations produce a capitalist ideological superstructure, which serves the interests of the capitalist economic foundation. Similarly, a socialist foundation produces a socialist superstructure. Thus, social consciousness does not produce nor explain social being, but vice versa. As Engels wrote: "From this point of view the final causes of all social changes and political revolutions are to be sought, not in men's brains, not in man's better insight into eternal truth and justice, but in changes in the modes of production and exchange."[12]

In class society, the dominant views, ideology and philosophy are those of the dominant class. Since the social and behavioral sciences are of great influence in the formation of the ideology and beliefs in capitalist society, these sciences cannot be viewed as pure sciences, separated from social or class interests. They must be analyzed as being also shaped, influenced, and distorted by the class which controls the government, the educational and university system, the commercial media, and the wealth to subsidize specific views and ideology. Hence, psychology cannot be viewed as a neutral science, unaffected by class interests. A racist theory such as that of psychologist Arthur Jensen,* which concludes that Black people are genetically inferior in intelligence to white people, can be understood as an instrument of a capitalist class for continued superexploitation of

*See Chapter 7 on Jensenism.

Black working people and as a major means of dividing white and Black people.

Psychology, from the viewpoint of historical materialism, must be seen as playing an ideological role in the capitalist superstructure. Its scientific role continues alongside its ideological role but such a scientific role is limited and underdeveloped because of the class nature of capitalism.

Socialism, like all societies, also produces its own superstructure. However, since socialist relations of production are classless, there is no dominant class to control and distort psychology. Under socialism, psychology plays a role of advancing socialist society through its own scientific development. Obstacles to such development are, hence, not of a class nature, but are due to the youth and complexity of psychology as a science.

Historical materialism provides for psychology a materialist approach to human and social development. It provides a scientific analysis of the class role that psychology plays under capitalism. It emphasizes the class character of capitalism and the importance of class status for the psychology of individuals. It analyzes the psychological effect of class ideology on human thought, attitude and behavior. It gives paramount importance to human consciousness as opposed to the role of unconscious processes in individual functioning. It explains alienation, not on an existentialist basis of loneliness and social isolation, but on the precise process of capitalist production. Psychology can, indeed, benefit from an historical materialist approach.

The Marxist Critique of Psychology

The science of psychology has made important progress in various areas. However, as previously discussed, psychology has been hindered or distorted in its development by idealist or metaphysical philosophical views and theories. It has been dominated by an unhistorical and undialectical view of the development of human society and its relation to individual development. Moreover, the ideological superstructure of capitalism has developed major features that have saturated the social and behavioral sciences. These features have penetrated and shaped much of the development of psychology. They include the following:

1. *Anti-working-class ideology.* Capitalist ideology has always de-

picted workers as unintelligent, unwashed, crude, simple-minded, and inferior. The social and behavioral sciences have mainly ignored the true reality of working people, their positive traits, their social and class struggles, their mutual support of each other, and their social strivings. With certain exceptions, when studies have been made of working people, they arrive at conclusions which support the capitalist stereotype of the coarse, stupid, passive, selfish individual. It is no accident that a central feature of the massive fraud perpetrated by psychologist Cyril Burt upon the psychological world, was that he had "proved" that workers were inferior in intelligence to middle and upper class people.*

In psychiatry, working people are considered to be difficult patients because they lack the awareness and insight of "higher" classes. In public education in the United States, a complex system of tracking exists, whose main purpose and effect have been to prevent working people, Black people and national minorities from gaining advanced education. Educational tracking sets up different tracks (classes) for children: bright, average, slow, disturbed, hyperactive, etc.

The result of such tracking has been to provide an uneducated pool of working people, Blacks, Hispanic, and other minorities for dirty, menial and superexploited jobs or for a reserve army of unemployed. Many psychological theories have been developed to justify such an educational tracking system: homogeneous classes, career opportunity (for dishwashing, clerical, housekeeping work), environmental deprivation, cultural disadvantage, Black matriarchy.

2. *Racism.* The early development of capitalism in our country was marked—and marred—by slavery and by the ideology of the slaveowners. After the Civil War and the freeing of the slaves, racism became a major and basic ideological instrument for capitalist super-profit and division of working people. Psychology has served these venal class interests by providing racist theories of the inferiority of Black people. Thus, Jensen's theory of Black genetic intellectual inferiority is a stain on the science of psychology. Daniel Moynihan's theory of psychiatric disturbance of Black children due to "the Black matriarchy" has done its racist dirty work in the field of psychiatry. Psychological testing instruments, such as the standardized IQ Tests (Stanford-Binet and WISC), are used for racist assignment of Black

*See Chapter 7 on Jensenism for discussion of Burt's anti-working-class and racist fraud.

children to classes for retarded, brain-damaged and emotionally disturbed, in hugely disproportionate numbers.* Racism has soaked through the entire fabric of psychology and psychiatry.

3. *National chauvinism.* Since working people in the United States include many national minorities, especially large numbers of Chicanos, Latino and West Indian people, national chauvinist theories and practices abound in our country. Rather than a "Melting Pot", our ideological superstructure has fostered harsh prejudices and discrimination against foreign-born working people and against most national minorities.

Psychology has played a divisive role in many instances by providing the rationalization for such prejudices and their accompanying discriminatory practices. Thus, the Wechsler Intelligence Scale for Children (WISC) is routinely used to test Hispanic children, although it is culturally and linguistically inappropriate and heavily penalizes bi-lingual children. It is an educational fact that Hispanic children are disproportionally placed in special classes, to their serious educational harm. The same psychological theories used against Black children—disadvantaged, deprived, sensorily immature, a fatherless home—are also applied to national minorities, especially to the poor and to working people.

4. *Sexism and male supremacy.* Division of working people along sex lines is also a basic feature of U.S. capitalist ideology. This ideology of the inferiority of women corresponds to and justifies the unequal economic, social and political status of women in our country.

Sexism in psychiatric theory and practice is rife. Freud's basic theory is male supremacist to the extreme: women are hysterical, passive, strange, filled with penis envy, hyperemotional, more neurotic, and have weaker personalities, according to Freud.**

Black women are victimized by both racism and sexism in both psychology and psychiatry. Children's problems are systematically blamed on the mother. Therapy is used to lead the woman to accept the destiny provided by her anatomy.*** Although the surge of the

---

*See Chapter 7 on Jensenism for discussion of the Stanford-Binet and the WISC and the California Court decision barring use of those tests for assignment of Black children to classes for mentally retarded.

**See Chapter 9 on Women and Psychiatry

***Freud stated about women: "Anatomy is destiny." ("Some Psychological Consequences of the Anatomical Distinction between the Sexes," *International Journal of Psychoanalysis,* 1927.)

women's Liberation movement has mounted a counteroffensive against sexism in psychology and psychiatry*, psychological theory and practice are still dominated by sexism, and psychology has only made a beginning in the scientific understanding of women in our society.

5. *Human Nature*. The ideological superstructure in the United States is shot through with theories that human nature is fixed and unchanging, that it is greedy, selfish, aggressive, untrustworthy, warlike, prejudiced, lustful and lazy. Psychology and psychiatry provide the high-sounding theories to justify such a judgment of human nature. Witness the theory of Freud that we have a warlike and destructive drive (thanatos) in our biological inheritance.** The theory of Stanley Milgrim that we will knowingly and willingly inflict pain on others falls into the same category.*** B.F. Skinner puts down human beings by considering them to be on the same level as animals, responding only to response-reward programming of their entire lives.**** Konrad Lorenz achieved fame through his theory of innate human aggressiveness,[13] while Edward Wilson attributes animal behavior and instincts to human beings in his theory of sociobiology.[14]

If human nature is both evil and unchanging, then racism, aggression, poverty and war are basically inevitable and cannot be attributed to the social system. Thus, this theory of fixed and evil human nature has a class basis which has negatively influenced psychology.

6. *Individualism and Subjectivism*. Capitalist ideology is filled with individualism and subjectivism. This ideology has flooded the social sciences, including psychology. Freudianism is a prime example of a subjective, non-social approach to the human mind and behavior: biological instincts operating through drives, complexes, defences and unconscious motivation, isolate each individual from his social existence and explain normal and abnormal behavior in subjective fashion.***** The Human Potential movement has carried individualism and subjectivism to extremes. The individual is thrown back on feelings and attitudes, divorced from their social context. "Est" is an openly subjective idealist theory which ends up with each

*See Chapter 9 on Women and Psychiatry
**See Chapter 1 on Freudianism
***See Chapter 10 on Behavior Research for discussion of Milgrim.
****See Chapter 2 on Skinner.
*****See Chapter 1 on Freudianism.

individual creating the world and merely experiencing this subjective world at the present moment.*

This latest onslaught on human reason, on collective action, on consciousness and knowledge is a reflection of capitalism in its decaying state. Est is the most exaggerated version of the capitalist thrust to compel people to accept the world as it is, to consider it perfect and to be happy doing just what they are doing.

Captalism also utilizes individualism to "blame the victim." Thus, we find theories in psychology that the poor provide their own environment of poverty, so *they* are to blame.**

7. *False or one-sided theories.* The history of science is filled with false theories, such as the theory that the sun moves around the earth, or that bleeding a physically ill patient will be beneficial. Some false theories may be considered a natural feature of young and developing sciences. The proving of a scientific theory requires careful observation, correct experimentation, accurate interpretation and valid conclusions. Speculation and hypothesizing are necessary for constructing and proving—or disproving—a theory. In this complex process of arriving at confirmed theories regarding a complex reality, false and one-sided theories arise.

However, in class society, many theories are put forth, not in order to prove a scientific theory, but because they serve the interest of the dominant class. Thus, false theories regarding working people, Black people, women, national minorities and human nature are false propaganda, and unscientific. The famous example of Galileo being forced by the Inquisition to disown his correct scientific theory about the movement of the earth around the sun is illustrative of this deliberate misuse of science.

One-sided theories in psychology and psychiatry are the rule and not the exception in capitalist society. Even the common definition of psychology as "the science of behavior" is one-sided since it leaves out thought, emotion, relations, activity, and individual history. The common term for mental disturbance is "emotional illness", when, of course, mental illness also affects cognition, behavior, attitude, work ability, and relationships. The behaviorism of Skinner centers on only one feature of functioning: behavior. Sensitivity training focuses on

*See Chapter 5 on est.
**See Chapter 7 on Jensenism.

"the here-and-now", to the unscientific exclusion of the "then-and-there."* Skinner hypostasizes positive reinforcement, while ignoring thought, judgement, feeling.**

False theories and one-sided theories are due to both class influence and to narrow and undialectical approaches in psychology and psychiatry in the United States.

The Contributions of Marxism

The contributions of Marxist dialectical and historical materialism to psychology and psychiatry and the Marxist critique of these sciences in a class society have already been presented. Marxism has a number of features and emphases that it believes will help advance the science of psychology:

1. Marxism rejects as invalid and unscientific all theories of intellectual, emotional or behavioral inferiority of race, class, sex or national minority. It emphasizes the crucial importance of studying *human* development in the concrete reality of its existence, social and individual.

2. Marxism approaches the human mind and consciousness as a product of the brain and central nervous system. It highlights the highly significant role of language as a means of communication, thought, and regulation of behavior. The work of Soviet psychologists Lev Vygotsky and Alexander Luria on the role of language has helped to advance psychological knowledge in this area.[15]

3. Marxism stresses the important relationship of the individual to society. The psychology of individuals in the United States must be examined in the context of a class society with a specific—capitalist—superstructure. The effects of the ideological superstructure on the individual's psychology is of vital significance in psychological study. Similarly, the changes in the psychology of individuals in a socialist society must be seen within the context of the many changes occurring in the transformation of capitalist society to socialist society.

4. Marxism sees the science of psychology as playing an important role in advancing human development. The uncovering of laws of human psychological development can be of great value to education, to human personality, to the formation of character, and to the expansion of human abilities.

*See Chapter 5 on Sensitivity Training.
**See Chapter 2 on Skinner's theories.

5. Marxism emphasizes that psychology and psychiatry are sciences which need to be advanced through careful, meticulous, comprehensive scientific work. The scientific work being carried out under socialism is exemplified in the volume *A Handbook of Contemporary Soviet Psychology*[16] which contains articles on progress attained in areas of developmental, abnormal, and social psychology, general experimental psychology, and higher nervous activity.

6. Science is international in scope and requires the best efforts of scientists in all countries for its full progress. International cooperation in the fields of psychology and psychiatry is of vital importance for these sciences. Such cooperation is particularly important for scientists in socialist and capitalist countries, since they have much to learn from each other.

7. Marxism believes that science advances through struggle, both scientific and social. Healthy controversy and debate within the field is necessary and welcome and can contribute towards the rejection of false theories and the correction of one-sided theories. Social struggle against racist and reactionary ideology in the guise of scientific psychological theories can lead to their exposure.

8. Marxism believes that a socialist society can produce great changes in people's psychological health and welfare. The provision of full, comprehensive, available, free health and mental health care is guaranteed under socialism. Likewise, the guarantee of employment, social security, education, equal opportunity, facilities for working mothers, equal pay, and an ever-expanding economic and social system provide psychological security for people under socialism.

PART ONE

THEORIES, THERAPIES AND FADS

Two theories have had the most powerful effect on psychology and psychiatry in the United States. The first is the theory and practice of psychoanalysis, stemming principally from the work of Sigmund Freud and later refined by the neo-Freudians. The second is the behaviorism of John B. Watson, which has culminated in the contemporary theory and practice of B.F. Skinner.

Two popularized and attention-getting variations of Freudianism are Primal Scream Therapy and Transactional Analysis. Skinner's behaviorism has spawned Behavior Modification and Behavior Therapy.

The 1970s saw the emergence of a staggering number of therapeutic fads and fantasies. The search for identity, for honesty in human relations and for genuine human communication produced Sensitivity Training and Encounter Groups. "Instant personal growth" was promised to the lonely, the alienated and the rebellious by Gestalt Therapy on through the impressive-sounding Erhard Seminar Training (est). Further, psychedelic drugs, eastern religions, transcendental meditation, consciousness alteration, and communes offered their own versions of pleasure and satisfaction.

1

Freudianism and Neo-Freudianism

In an article entitled "Oh! What a Lovely War!", editorial columnist Anthony Lewis wrote: "Stuart Hampshire, the English philosopher, wrote recently of the impact of Freud's demonstration that human behavior is governed less by conscious than by unconscious thoughts and feelings... The significance of that understanding is of course not only for neurotics; the most normal man is moved by forces of which he may be unaware... We must rely on some such view of men to help explain war."[1]

Lewis was trying to explain the immoral war in Vietnam, but his statement reveals several significant features of psychology and ideology under capitalism: that neurosis is determined by "unconscious thoughts and feelings"; that war can be explained only by such unconscious forces; that there are no rational explanations of individual and social behavior.

The use of Freudianism and neo-Freudianism to explain the normal abnormality of capitalist society (war, violence, oppression, racism) is commonplace in the United States. Further, the struggle of masses against these evils must also be explained away. Here we find Dr. Bruno Bettelheim, the Vienna-born disciple of Freud, stating to the U.S. House Special Subcommittee on Education that militant student leaders are "emotionally fixated at the age of the temper tantrum." In customary Freudian fashion, Dr. Bettelheim dismissed the splendid actions of young people who organized sit-in demonstrations against racism and war by declaring: "Big in size and age, those who sit-in feel like little boys with a need to 'play big' by sitting in papa's big chair."[2]

Freudian Theory

Freudianism has made its most powerful impact on psychology and ideology by its development of the concept of "the unconscious." As Heinz Hartmann puts it: "Explanations of human behavior in terms of propositions about unconscious mental processes have been an essential part and one characteristic feature of psychoanalysis."[3]

Taking this basic principle—that human behavior is explained by unconscious mental processes—Sigmund Freud elaborated (in purely speculative fashion) a full-scale theory of the human psyche and of psychic development. He split the psyche into three parts: the dominant *id* with its two innate basic instincts of eros (libido) and thanatos (death and destructive drive); the unimportant *ego,* a window on reality; and the *superego,* which moderates between the wild primitive id (the unconscious) and the ego (consciousness) in dealing with reality.*

Human psychic development, for Freud, consisted of three infantile psycho-sexual stages (oral, anal and genital), plus the Oedipus complex: the innate and inevitable libidinal attachment of the child to the parent of the same sex, and hostility and hatred for the parent of the opposite sex. The Oedipus complex was accompanied by a castration complex (males) and penis envy (females). The dynamic of this psychic development was, of course, id-directed and unconscious to the individual.

The abnormal psyche, i.e., neurosis, was explained by Freud as based upon repressed unconscious infantile memories of perverted

---

*Although Freud, in his earlier works, used the *unconscious,* along with the *ego* and the *superego,* as one of the three mental provinces, he replaced the *unconscious* with the *id* in 1932: "The superego, the ego and the id—these, then, are the three realms, regions, provinces, into which we divide an individual's mental apparatus, and with the mutual relations of which we shall be concerned in what follows." (*New Introductory Lectures on Psychoanalysis,* Norton, New York, 1965, p. 72.)

sex impulses toward father, mother, sister or brother. These infantile sexual memories, existing in the id, cause regression when real-life problems cannot be met, resulting in neurosis. Treatment for neurosis, according to Freud, must be through psychoanalysis and its techniques: dream analysis (as "the royal road" to understanding the patient's unconscious), free association, transference, resistance, mistakes, nonverbal behavior. The aim of psychoanalytic treatment was to achieve insight on the part of the patient into unconscious mental processes, or, as Freud put it, "the analyst enters into an alliance with the ego of the patient to subdue certain uncontrolled parts of the id, i.e., to include them in the synthesis of the ego."[4]

Freud thus combined a psychological (normal) and psychiatric (abnormal) approach to the psyche in his psychoanalytic theory. Had he limited his theory to the sphere of these two sciences, it could have been dealt with (refuted and rejected) in the area of science. But Freud claimed that psychoanalytic theory had universal application: to history, society, groups (youth, women, neurotics, children), culture and daily living.

A striking and dramatic example of the application of psychoanalytic theory to a major social phenomenon took place in 1932 when Albert Einstein wrote to Freud to ask for his participation in preserving peace. In an open letter, Freud replied that "it (war) seems quite a natural thing, no doubt it has a good biological basis and in practice it is scarcely avoidable." Freud further explained to Einstein that "the aggressive or destructive instinct . . . is at work in every living being and is striving to bring it to ruin and to reduce life to its original condition of inanimate matter."[5]

Freud made other sweeping generalizations regarding civilization (due to sublimation of repressed unconscious drives), women (victims of penis envy), and resistance to authority (due to Oedipal rebellion against the father figure).

Today we find that other theorists are buttressing capitalist ideology with Freudian-like theories. Konrad Lorenz speaks of "the aggressive instincts common to all higher animals."[6] Robert Ardrey trumpets his thesis that humans are hostile and competitive by instinct.[7] However, Freud's original theory is still powerful, and is utilitarian for an exploiting class: it fits snugly into the "slaves-of-instincts-and-drives" theory of human behavior.

The Modernizing of Freudianism

Classical Freudianism could not and did not remain unchanged in a world undergoing massive social change and scientific growth. While preserving Freud in the original for those who could still accept it, the more unscientific and regressive aspects had to be eliminated to make Freudianism palatable to those influenced by science and social struggle.

Experimental psychology had made great strides in the study of perception, memory, learning, psycho-motor functioning—in those very areas discounted as unimportant by Freud. Ego psychology had to be made more prominent in Freudian theory: Heinz Hartmann constructed a more scientific-appearing theory in this area of what Freud called "the secondary processes of the ego." Anna Freud also came to her father's "scientific" rescue by introducing the mechanisms of defense of the ego: reaction formation, regression, repression, undoing, isolation, projection, introjection, reversal, and turning against the self.

Further, rising social struggle based upon class and national consciousness, together with major anthropological findings on the effects of culture on human behavior, made necessary the removal of Freud's concept of a universal, unchanging "racial unconscious" (exploited more fully—and even more unscientifically—by Jung as "the collective unconscious"). Revisers of Freud such as Franz Alexander and Abram Kardiner helped to perform this surgery.

Freudianism, purged of "the racial unconscious" and placing more emphasis on the role of the ego, now presented a more modern and scientific appearance. But these changes were insufficient to give it a truly progressive posture. It needed the look of cultural responsiveness, of social consciousness—it needed neo-Freudianism.

The Emergence of Neo-Freudianism

Leading anthropologists such as Margaret Mead, Ruth Benedict, Cora DuBois and Franz Boas had amassed evidence to disprove the claimed universality of such basic Freudian assumptions as the sex and death instincts, innate infantile sexual stages, and the Oedipus complex. Further, a number of these concepts had been experimentally tested and found to be false. Summing up and evaluating these experimental findings in his *Survey of Objective Studies of Psychoanalytic Concepts*,[8] Robert Sears came to the following conclusion:

By the criteria of the physical sciences, psychoanalysis is not a *good* science ... few investigators feel free to accept Freud's statements at face value. The reason lies in the same factor that makes psychoanalysis a bad science—its method. Psychoanalysis relies upon techniques that do not admit of the repetition of observation, that have no self-evident or denotative validity, and that are tinctured to an unknown degree with the observer's own suggestions ... When the method is used for uncovering psychological facts that are required to have objective validity, it simply fails.[9]

Another strong impetus for streamlining classical Freudianism came from the militant, conscious movement of workers, youth, farmers, and Blacks beginning with the catastrophic economic crisis of the thirties and continuing through today. The static, childhood-based, instinctual, sex-oriented psychoanalytic theory could not satisfactorily explain these conscious movements which responded to specific social phenomena. A new look was needed—and neo-Freudianism emerged.

Led by Karen Horney, Erich Fromm and Harry Stack Sullivan, the neo-Freudians set about excising the more grotesque features of classical Freudianism. The sex and death instincts, the infantile sexual stages, the Oedipus complex—all were cast overboard. Calling their sleek new theory "the cultural psychoanalytic approach," they claimed to relate the psyche to the culture and society in which the individual lives. They stated that mental illness was due to sociocultural factors. They even called for basic changes in society to reduce mental illness, e.g. Fromm explicitly calls for socialism, albeit his own version.

This skillful neo-Freudian approach attracted many progresives, and even Marxists—for do not Marxists ascribe many basic human problems to the socio-cultural sphere?

Recent Developments in Psychoanalytic Theory

Psychoanalytic theory and practice has been under severe attack in the past two decades. Its dominance has been challenged by Behavior Therapy. The Self-Help movement has attracted many former adherents of psychoanalysis. Impatience with the expensive, long-term, often unproductive analytic treatment has mounted. John E. Gedo, in the Preface to his book *Beyond Interpretation: Toward a Revised Theory of Psychoanalysis,* sees the need for a response to the widely felt sense of crisis in contemporary psycho-analysis. The analytic community is in disfavor with a public beguiled by a smorgasbord of alternatives advertised as quick, cheap and palatable. . . . Perhaps more serious . . . is a crisis of confidence on our part concerning the effectiveness of psychoanalysis as therapy and the adequacy of our theories as a valid psychology.[10]

The major response by psychoanalysis has been a greatly increased emphasis on the ego or the self. Leaders in this movement have been Heinz Kohut,[11] Arnold Goldberg and Marian Tolpin.[12] Other thrusts have been on object relations, counter-transference, and identity.

Despite these efforts to refurbish psychoanalysis and to bring it closer to the world of individual and social reality, the basic Freudian principles and techniques remain fundamentally unchanged.

Identity of Freudianism and Neo-Freudianism

Freud had made one concept the cornerstone of his psychoanalytic theory: "The unconscious is the true psychic reality . . . "[13] It is this concept that is crucial both to the general theory and to the psycho-analytic technique. The scheme of instincts, infantile sexuality and Oedipus complex which Freud built on the concept of the *uncon-scious* was only the clothing on the body. The neo-Freudians dis-carded the old-fashioned clothing and then dressed the same body with stylish and seductive finery (strivings for safety and satisfaction, interpersonal relations, mechanisms of escape, etc.).

Thus, we find Ruth Munroe, in her sympathetic work *Schools of Psychoanalytic Thought* stating: "Horney retains, with modification, the Freudian concepts of anxiety, repression and conflict, and she strongly emphasizes the role of unconscious processes as such, elim-inating only their relationship to the infantile libido."[14]

Fromm, in his *Escape From Freedom* writes: "Only a psychology which utilizes the concept of unconscious forces can penetrate the confusing rationalizations we are confronted with in analyzing either an individual or a culture."[15]

Hence, the neo-Freudians are as one with the Freudians in attribut-ing human behavior to the operation of the unconscious. Further, they also attribute mental illness to the dynamics of unconscious processes. Like Freud, the neo-Freudians retain the concepts of repression and resistance, and use the very same psychoanalytic techniques invented by Freud: dream analysis, free association, trans-ference, etc.[16]

Here we have the identity of Freudianism and neo-Freudianism (and the newer "self" psychoanalysts): in their common focus on the unconscious as the compeller of human behavior, in their adherence to the role of repression, and in their common use of psychoanalytic techniques. Common to both is also their cultural and social analyses based upon the unconscious. Capitalist ideology is infinitely adept in offering the same ideological food with different sauces. Neo-Freudianism covers Freud's main dish of the unconscious with the sauce of "social-cultural responsiveness."

Like Freud, the neo-Freudians apply their theory to both mentally ill and normal people. Karen Horney states: "The difference (of the neurotic) from the normal is merely quantitative."[17] Erich Fromm poses the question "whether the study of individuals who are commonly labeled neurotic can be of any use in considering the problems of social psychology." Answering in the affirmative, he says: "The phenomena which we observe in the neurotic person are in principle not different from those we find in the normal."[18]

The erasing of the *qualitative* difference between normal people and mentally sick people is an essential feature of psychoanalytic theory. It enables both the Freudians and the neo-Freudians to explain sociopolitical actions and events involving normal people in terms of sex repression, instinctual drives or other unconscious mechanisms. Fromm, for example, is constantly devising new—but psychoanalytically-based theories of reforming society and achieving his brand of socialism. He evaluates human action and mass movements as "mechanisms of escape (which) are the driving forces in normal man."[19] These Frommian "mechanisms of escape" include masochistic and sadistic strivings, withdrawal from the world, destructiveness, and automaton conformity. Of course, these mechanisms operate unconsciously, below the level of awareness, in "the deeper layers of personality."[20]

Fromm devotes all of Chapter 5 of *Escape From Freedom*[21] to explaining the "Psychology of Nazism." While recognizing certain objective political and economic factors which led to the rise of Nazism, Fromm attributes the success of Hitlerism to the character structure and the sadomasochistic strivings of the German people.

We can compare such an explanation of Hitler's success by the neo-Freudian Fromm to the explanation of the political role of President Woodrow Wilson by the original Freudian, Freud himself. *The New*

York Times[22] announced the publication of the book *Thomas Wood-row Wilson: A Psychological Study,*[23] written by Freud jointly with the American diplomat, William C. Bullitt, and stated: "According to the Freud-Bullitt view, Wilson was an emotionally troubled man who had been dominated by his father and protected by his mother, who lacked the masculine will to carry out his policies and who came to believe he was a savior who could 'lay down the law of God to the nations'."[24] It was Wilson's "severe personality problems that thwart-ed his efforts to win a lasting peace after World War I," according to Freud and Bullitt.

Such are the explanations offered for a Nazi dictator and for a predatory imperialist. Class struggle and historical forces are ignored (Freud) or given a back seat (Fromm). The mighty unconscious is the key to historical events for psychoanalytical theory.

Psychoanalysis and Ideology

In analyzing the nature and role of capitalist ideology as the superstructure of a capitalist base, one is struck by certain ideological components which function in many spheres, which, so to speak, soak through the whole ideological superstructure. Psychoanalysis has that kind of ideological liquidity. "The Go-Between," winner of the grand prize at the 1971 Cannes Film Festival opens in New York City and the *New York Times* film critic calls it "a classical Freudian case history about the traumatized adolescent, and about the sterile adult he becomes."[25]

Eugene O'Neill's play, *Mourning Becomes Electra,* is put on at Stratford, Conn., and critic Walter Kerr speaks of it as "this adapta-tion of the Greek legend of the House of Atreus to O'Neill's simplistic Freudian purposes and to America's Civil War." The three leading American playwrights—Arthur Miller, Edward Albee and Tennessee Williams—write works shot through with psychoanalytic symbolism and Freudian motivation along with existentialist guilt and despair. Films like Fellini's "8½" reek with dream symbols and Freudian themes.

One must admit that psychoanalytic theory offers strikingly dra-matic material to writers and dramatists: sex, patricide, incest, perver-sion, sadomasochism, dream symbolism, insight, and unconscious motivation. It offers, one must sadly conclude, everything but psycho-logical truth.

For historians, a new technique is reported: "Perhaps the fastest growing of the new techniques (of historians) is psychohistory. Analysts and historians with psychoanalytic training have adapted Freudian analysis in the search for the hidden psychological forces that have motivated men." Applying Freudian "psychohistorical" analysis to Richard Nixon, historian Bruce Mazlich of Massachusetts Institute of Technology writes that Nixon has had "a serious problem with death wishes and anxiety: in relation to his brothers, himself and Eisenhower".[26] So much for the man who daily killed babies and other humans in Indochina!

Instances of psychoanalytical penetration of all fields can be multiplied endlessly, but the comment of the *New York Times*[27] about the July 1971 meeting of the International Psychoanalytic Association sums it up: "The principle of the turbulent unconscious and its crucial importance in human behavior has been employed in many allied fields, among them the arts and literature, comparative religion, ethics, sociology, anthropology, economics and social work."

Psychoanalysis and Mass Struggle

Not only is history mutilated by the psychoanalytic theory of universal, unconscious, compulsive behavior, but the role of workers, Blacks, women and youth in the class struggle is either negated or distorted. Psychoanalyst Herbert Hendin writes of the students who demonstrated against Nixon's policies: "These young radicals have suffered in families . . . which ignored and frustrated their personal needs and continue to be blind to them as people . . . Identification with the poor and the oppressed permits these radical students to react to poverty and oppression without having to face how personally impoverished, victimized and enraged they feel."[28]

In an article highlighting Freud's psychoanalytical theory, of women Richard Gilman points out that Freud ascribed every conceivable trait of inferiority to them: hysterical, masochistic, childlike, passive, vain, envious, unreliable. Gilman further points out: "Freud's disciples and successors, as well as the psychoanalytical heretics (the neo-Freudians—J.N.) have for the most part left his basic views on women unchanged."[29] Is it strange then that the women's liberation movement in the United States rejects most Freudian and neo-Freudian views on women?

Frequent attempts are also made to Freudianize the Black liberation movement. A book of this genre[30] by two psychiatrists met this rebuff by Black reviewer Janet Saxe in *The Black Scholar:* "*Black Rage*" is a collection of commonly held assertions about Black people strung on the thin thread of Freudian psychoanalysis and clasped together with interestingly tragic anecdotes about a few unusually unfortunate Black people."[31]

One need hardly refer to the Freudian and neo-Freudian stereotype of militant workers and Communists as rebels against authority (the father figure) due to Oedipal conflict (Freud), or externally expressing their inability to deal with their unconscious internal emotional conflicts (neo-Freudians).

Psychoanalytic theory thus buttresses the effort by the ruling class to "blame the victims" for their victimization by capitalist society, and to turn workers, Blacks, women and youth inward into their own psyche rather than outward against the real causes of their oppression.

The magazine *Psychology Today* gives the most telling evidence of the unscientific and reactionary character of psychoanalysis. In its advertisement giving seventeen reasons why you should buy it, we find: "The inferiority feelings of men who seek corporate power; Why political leaders are in constant danger of insanity; Are 'hawks' sexually repressed?; Why Asians make better politicians than Westerners; Why are today's students attracted to violence?; What your daydreams reveal about your ethnic background; Are campus activists rebelling against the system—or their parents?"[32]

The "Merger" of Freud and Marx

One of the most pernicious offshoots of Freudianism is the attempt to merge Freud with Marx. Leaders in this effort have been Erich Fromm, Herbert Marcuse and Wilhelm Reich. Although a fullscale critique of their views is not possible, some flavor of their efforts must be given.

Fromm sought to merge Marx with Freud by eliminating several basic principles of Marxism: that humans are rational; that the working class could bring about socialism; and that socialization of the means of production was the essence of genuine socialism. In their place, Fromm substituted "the irrational forces in man which make him afraid of freedom, and which produce his lust for power and his destructiveness." Further, Marx "did not see that a better society could not be brought into life by people who had not undergone a moral change within themselves."[33] Finally, it "is not ownership of the means of production, but participation in management and decision-making" which is needed when Fromm's "Humanistic Communitarian Socialism" is achieved. This, indeed is the kind of merger that the cat makes with the mouse: Fromm and Freud swallow up Marx.

With Herbert Marcuse, the late philosopher of the New Left, we find an ardent defense of the original Freudian theory as socially radical, together with a slashing attack against neo-Freudianism. In his *Eros and Civilization: A Philosophical Inquiry into Freud,* Marcuse develops what might aptly be called "The Erotic Theory of Revolution." He centers on what he calls "surplus sexual repression . . . which is that portion of repression which is the result of specific societal conditions sustained in the specific interest of domination."[34] It is not a mere witticism to suggest that Marcuse substitutes surplus repression for Marx's surplus value. Stating that Freud's original and basic theory was radically critical of society, Marcuse arrives at this conclusion: "And this critical sociological function of psychoanalysis derives from the fundamental role of sexuality as a 'productive force'; the libidinal claims propel progress toward freedom and universal gratification of human needs . . . "[35]

Thus, revolution comes not through working-class struggle (Marcuse, we know, ignores this), but through the libido and its gratification. If confirmation of this Marcusean theory of revolution through sexuality is needed, Marcuse himself furnishes it by his criticism of Wilhelm Reich, another daring "fuser" of Freud and Marx. Marcuse writes: "He (Reich) emphasized the extent to which sexual repression is enforced by the interests of domination and exploitation, and the extent to which these interests are in turn reinforced and reproduced by sexual repression. However, Reich's notion of sexual repression remains undifferentiated; he neglects the historical dynamic of the sex instincts and of their fusion with the destructive impulses . . . Consequently, sexual liberation *per se* becomes for Reich a panacea for individual and social ills."[36]

A Marxist can only cry out at this quarrel between Marcuse and Reich: "A plague on both their sexual houses!"

Descent into Mysticism

One further point should be made regarding Erich Fromm. Lenin pointed out that subjective idealist philosophy always opens the way to spiritualism and mysticism. William James, the father of Pragmatism ended up believing in table-tipping, seances, etc. Freudianism is subjective idealism applied to the mind, it is "mentalism", i.e., the divorce of the psyche from its physiological base and from objective social reality. Dissatisfied with his earlier attempts to reform Freud (and Marx), Fromm descended into the ideational abyss of Zen Buddhism and religious mysticism.[37]

One of the alleged curative features of psychoanalysis is the achievement by the patient of "insight": "All psychoanalytic schools emphasize the importance of 'insight' in effecting the profound change in the organization of the personality which is considered a true psychoanalytic cure . . . The limitation caused by *unconscious* fears, goals, and attitudes is removed."[38]

Fromm discovers in Zen Buddhism the concept of "satori", the sudden awakening, the enlightenment. Now Fromm makes a genuine merger—unlike his merger of Freud and Marx—the merger of Freudian "insight" with Zen Buddhist "satori." He can now offer a glittering and seductive goal: the achievement of inner peace and true happiness to those dissatisfied with the capitalist "vale of tears." Fromm has gone the long road from the speculative and socially reactionary Freudian theory to the mystical and unattainable "satori" of Zen Buddhism.

As part of the ideological superstructure, both varieties of Freudianism play a dual role: they distort and misrepresent human thought, emotion and behavior, and they psychologize social processes. What could be more pleasing to a dominant class than to convince people that their problems are due to their unconscious conflicts? And what could pay off more handsomely than the idea that human history today, with its wars, racism and oppression, is due to unconscious, destructive and libidinous forces and not to capitalism?

Psychoanalysis forces the individual to look within the mind for the cause of personal and emotional problems. It prevents the individual from joining with others in real struggle against the real causes.

There is a rising tide of opposition to Freudianism in philosophical and scientific circles. At a symposium on psychoanalysis, the following were among the comments on Freudianism made by professors of philosophy:

"It is the most sophisticated form of metaphysics ever to enjoy support as a scientific theory." (Michael Scriven)

"But on the Freudian theory itself, as a body of doctrine for which factual validity can be reasonably claimed, I can only echo the Scottish verdict: Not proven." (Ernest Nagel)

"Freudian doctrine ... provides a language for saying silly things in an impressive way." (Charles Frankel)

"A theory which explains everything, which cannot be contradicted by any sort of facts, does not deserve to be called a scientific theory." (Raphael Demos)[39]

These criticisms are valid and are to be welcomed. But it is Marxism which makes the most comprehensive and effective critique of Freudianism.

The Struggle Against Psychoanalysis

Discussing the gathering of Freudian analysts in Vienna, the *New York Times*[40] wrote that "the principle (of the turbulent unconscious and its crucial importance in human behavior) has penetrated psychology, psychiatry, nursing, pedagogy, criminology, and medicine. It is the basis for most efforts to deal with emotional and personality disorders that do not rely on drugs, including such recent phenomena as psychodrama, group therapy, sensitivity clinics, and encounter sessions."

It was Lenin, in his talks with Clara Zetkin in 1920, who made this penetrating criticism of Freudianism: "The extension of Freudian hypotheses (to the sexual question) seems 'educated,' even scientific, but it is ignorant, bungling. Freudian theory is the modern fashion. I mistrust the sexual theories of the articles, dissertations, pamphlets, etc., in short, the particular kind of literature which flourishes luxuriantly in the dirty soil of bourgeois society. I mistrust those who are always contemplating the sexual question, like the Indian saint his navel. It seems to me that these flourishing sexual theories . . . are mainly hypothetical, and often quite arbitrary hypotheses . . . There is no place for it in the Party, in the class conscious, fighting proletariat."[41]

Since this statement by Lenin, psychology has made great strides in gaining knowledge of psychological functioning. A fully scientific psychology (and psychiatry) must uncover the laws of higher nervous activity. Here, Pavlov and his followers have literally established the science of higher nervous activity. The role of language in human behavior is another major area of psychology—Alexander Luria, Kurt Goldstein, and others have gone far in developing scientific knowledge of this crucial area. The forms and treatment of mental illness must also be understood—Pavlov made important beginnings while significant work is being carried on in the Soviet Union, the United States, and other countries along non-Freudian lines. The laws of learning are also vital for scientific psychology—fine work is being carried out in this field in many countries by scientific researchers such as Sokolov, Bruner, and Luria. Finally, the area of sociology and social psychology required scientific foundation. Here, only Marxism-Leninism could provide the general basis for the specific study of social phenomena.

In every one of these major areas of psychology, psychoanalysis has failed to provide any scientific laws. The very nature of psychology was distorted into a study of unconscious processes. Scientific psychology studies the human reflection of the objective world. This reflection is fundamentally and decisively a conscious one, i.e., one which is clothed in language. Pavlov proved through his laws of higher nervous activity that this human reflection (the psyche) is produced by the brain and nervous system in the course of the individual's activity in the surrounding world. Conditioned reflexes developing on the basis of unconditioned reflexes, along with language and society play an indispensable role in human adaptation to reality.

Marx and Engels had held that human consciousness had developed on the basis of language which, in turn, arose when the higher anthropoids began to use tools for labor.[42] It remained for Pavlov to show that language was a second signal system which only humans possess, in addition to the first (sensory) signal system which both humans and animals possess.

For scientific psychology, social activity by the individual is the central and decisive feature in the formation of each individual's psyche (reflection). The role of parents, family, school, peer groups, unions, fellow workers, and mass struggle is vital in shaping the ideas, emotions, attitudes, behavior, outlook and personality of the individual.

Hence, rather than an innate (Freudian) or an acquired (neo-Freudian) unconscious which compels behavior, human consciousness as a reflection of social reality is the true psychic reality and plays the dominant role in human behavior. Rather than a mind which functions internally, basically isolated from daily reality, as the psychoanalysts see it, the mind is formed by and operates in daily reality, precisely to enable the individual to behave in adaptive fashion.

Scientific psychology can not and does not reject the existence of unconscious mental processes. These processes exist in non-verbalized, automatic activity. They are central to the concept of psychological set as developed in the theory of set of D.N. Uznadze.[43] They play a role in motivation and in the affective life of children and adults.[44] The approach of Soviet psychology to such unconscious processes is indicated by Soviet writer Alexander Petrov: " . . . Soviet science does not reject Freud's theory of the unconscious, but it disagrees with his conclusions, notably, the domination of the sexual urge in man, his inborn aggressiveness and the endless battle between the conscious and the unconscious. The problem of the unconscious is of considerable applied importance, for instance, in the treatment, education and contacts of people in the collective. It is widely discussed in scientific circles the world over, the USSR included. Our country is getting ready to publish a two-volume monograph written by a group of authors, entitled: *The Unconscious: Its Nature, Functions and Methods of Research.* On the Soviet Union's initiative, an international symposium on the problem of subconscious psychic activity will take place in the capital of Soviet Georgia, Tbilisi, in 1979."[45]

It must not be concluded that psychology has become a fully-rounded, comprehensive science. In 1909, Pavlov stated: "One can truthfully say that for the first time since the days of Galileo the irresistible march of natural science has been held up quite perceptibly before the study of the higher parts of the brain, the organ of the highly complex relationship between the animal and the external world."[46]

It is this complexity, not just of the brain but also of the relationship of the individual to society, which must be emphasized. Much has been accomplished in the more than sixty years since Pavlov made this statement. But many major problems remain. The field of personality is little developed; emotions and feelings need much more intensive study; and social psychology is just beginning to be recognized as an important science.[47] What is important, however, is the thrust, the direction that the science of psychology follows. Psychoanalysis follows the road of the unconscious which has led to a dead end.

Further, it has served as a major ideological instrument. Scientific psychology is on the road leading to fuller knowledge of individual and social development.

Marxist Philosophy and Scientific Truth

In one of his earliest works (1894), Lenin wrote: "He, the scientific psychologist, discarded all philosophical theories of the soul and set about making a direct study of the material substratum of psychical phenomena—the nervous processes—and gave, let us say, an analysis and explanation of such and such psychological processes."[48]

How was Lenin able to perceive that it was this very study of "the nervous processes" which was required to develop the science of psychology? Lenin was a Marxist philosopher, a profound dialectical materialist. Philosophically, he understood the relationship of the mind to the brain, of thought to matter. He understood the theory of reflection of Marx and Engels (he developed it more fully in *Materialism and Empirio-Criticism*).[49] With such philosophical equipment, Lenin could point out the materialist road that psychology must follow. Here, we see graphically the role of philosophy in science generally and in psychology specifically.

Every science must have its specific laws and facts. A scientific psychology must develop the specific laws and facts of its subject matter—the human mind. But there are two giant forces which determine whether any science will move towards greater and greater knowledge or be lost in the shallows and shoals of mysticism, speculation and irrationality. The first force is that of society and its needs. A progressive or socialist society will seek to advance science. A capitalist society will use science to serve its needs for profit and for deceiving the masses. Psychology, as a behavioral science, cannot be permitted full, unfettered growth by the dominant class. It is often used to mislead and divide the masses. Thus, we find a foul and racist theory of genetic intellectual inferiority of Black people being promulgated by a leading American psychologist, Arthur Jensen.[50] So, too, as has been pointed out, Freudianism serves precisely the interests of reaction in the ideological sphere.

But there is a second major force which shapes the direction of each science—its philosophy. Every science bases itself, knowingly or unknowingly, on a philosophical view, on its philosophy of science. Here, bourgeois psychology bases itself, in the main, on idealist and mechanistic views. Freudianism is idealist in essence. It separates thought from matter, the psyche from the brain and nervous system. It also isolates the living, active individuals from their social environment and makes them the passive puppet of their unconscious. It is also mechanistic in failing to relate the development of the psyche to the many-sided, dialectical reality in which it operates. Freudianism ends up in true idealist fashion: with a timeless, nonlogical, nonreflective, symbol-laden unconscious, divorced from social reality, and compelling behavior. Freudianism can be traced back to the idealist views of the unconscious of Schopenhauer and Nietzsche.

With scientific psychology, these same two giant forces impel its progress and shape its study. Socialist society, with its elimination of profit-fixated capitalism need not distort truth in any science. Further, its philosophy of dialectical materialism helps to place science on the right road and can aid it in evaluating its findings. Under capitalism, the working class and progressive strata must struggle for a genuine science. Marxist psychology, with its Pavlovian base, its historical materialist viewpoint and its concern for truth can only reject Freudianism in its various forms.

Unlike Freudianism, scientific psychology stresses consciousness, its growth and development, its expansion, and its adaptive functioning. Unlike the ugly Freudian model of driven, conflicted, neurotic and helpless humans, scientific psychology is optimistic. It joins with Pavlov in saying: "The chief, the strongest and the lasting impression gained from the study of the higher nervous activity by our method is the extraordinary plasticity of this activity, its immense potentialities; nothing is immobile, unyielding; everything can always be attained, changed for the better, if only the proper conditions are created."[51]

Such "proper conditions" for realizing the "immense potentialities" of human beings exist in socialist society. Here in the United States, the struggle against psychoanalysis as a "science" and as a social theory is a part of the necessary ideological struggle we must wage if we, too, are to achieve those "proper conditions" here. Given those conditions, given socialism, we can then realize the essence of what Hamlet said about humankind: "What a piece of work is man! How noble in reason! How infinite in faculties! In form and moving, how express and admirable! In action, how like an angel! In apprehension, how like a god! The beauty of the world! The paragon of animals!"

2

Skinner's
Brave New World

B. F. Skinner has been called "perhaps the most catalytic contemporary figure in the science of human behavior."[1] Members of the American Psychological Association named him as the psychologist who has contributed most to twentieth century psychology—Freud placed second.[2]

It is, therefore, not surprising that Skinner's book *Beyond Freedom and Dignity*[3] became an immediate best seller and was the subject of heated controversy in the social and behavioral sciences and in popular discussion. For Skinner's book is a dramatic plea to utilize his system of "Behavioral Engineering" to control the behavior of everyone in our country with the goal of eliminating war, violence, prejudice, and all social evils. Since Marxism has a similar goal, an analysis of his proposal is called for. At the same time, the book offers the opportunity to evaluate Skinner as a psychologist and theoretician.

Skinner's Work
B. F. Skinner has won fame as a psychologist through his experimental work with animals and, more recently, with autistic and severely retarded children. He has centered his efforts around operant

conditioning, i.e., the conditioning of behavior by the reinforcement (reward) of a behavioral response. As Skinner puts it, "Behavior is shaped and maintained by its consequences."[4] That is, animals and humans will begin to behave in a certain way if they are rewarded for that behavior, and they will continue the same behavior if the reward is continued.

Skinner's classical example, demonstrated live on the speaker's platform, is his shaping of a hungry pigeon's pecking behavior with food pellets so that it ends up pecking an exact, pre-designated spot on a wooden board. Skinner has also done work on the conditioning of escape and avoidance behavior, i.e., behavior to escape or avoid pain or punishment.

Skinner has influenced school education as the father of programmed learning, more popularly known as "teaching machines." His influence has spread into psychiatry through the Behavior Therapy movement and his "Token Economies" in mental hospitals: mentally ill patients are rewarded with tokens for specified behavior, the tokens being exchanged for cigarettes, food, privileges, etc.*

Skinner is also the moving force in the Behavior Modification movement, which has strongly affected psychology, education, child rearing, prison control, and psychiatry.**

In all these areas, Skinner has developed principles and techniques which have serious limitations and inadequacies, and often result in serious harm. Throughout his work, Skinner has ignored or brushed aside fundamental laws of psychological development. He has reduced animal and human functioning to mechanical responses to rewards and punishments. His entire experimental and theoretical work rests on that flimsy foundation.

Criticism of Skinner could well have remained within the field of psychology if he had limited his principles and techniques to the subjects of his experiments: animals and severely impaired human beings. But Skinner jumps off from a system developed from limited work with such subjects to an application of his Behavioral Engineering to every individual, to society as a whole, to all social problems, and to the entire future of humanity.

*See Chapter 6 on Behavior Therapy.
**See Chapter 3 on Behavior Modification.

Skinner's New Society

The Marxist philosopher Howard Selsam spoke ironically of three kinds of reasoning: inductive, deductive and *seductive*. Skinner's plan for a new society is certainly of the seductive kind. Taking his single principle of shaping behavior by reinforcement, he projects an ideal world in which the behavior of every individual will have been programmed to be socially desirable behavior.

Skinner is a rigid environmentalist of a special kind. He maintains that all behavior is due to the environment which rewards, punishes or ignores animal and human behavioral responses. He writes: "A scientific analysis (of behavior) shifts the credit as well as the blame to the environment . . . "[5] It is, thus, simple for Skinner to arrive at the conclusion that it is only the environment which needs proper manipulation to achieve whatever behavior is desired.

Skinner's "Technology of Behavior" consists precisely of such manipulation of the environment through reinforcement or non-reinforcement. Through programming the life of each individual, he claims he can shape the appropriate "repertoire of behavior" to eliminate all anti-social acts. His Behavioral Engineering will design a culture which will be the best of all possible worlds.

Skinner and Human Psychology

Perception, emotions, memory, personality, will, consciousness, mind, thinking, judgment, behavior: these are major areas of study for the science of psychology. What does our behavioral technologist say about their role in the building of his "Brave New World?" With a single exception, they have no role for Skinner because they do not exist: only behavior exists.

With regard to perception, Skinner states that this is merely a way of behaving: "We change the way a person looks at something . . . we do not change something called perception."[6]

Emotions and feelings are replaced by "contingencies of reinforcement" (systems of rewards): "The same advantages are also to be found in emphasizing contingencies of reinforcement in lieu of states of mind or feelings."[7] Elsewhere, Skinner says flatly: "There are no psychic feelings. What you feel is merely a by-product of what you do. . . . The main thing to realize is that what you are feeling is your own body."[8]

Memory, for Skinner, is also non-existent: "The environment is often said to be stored in the form of memories. . . . As far as we know, however, there are no copies of the environment in the individual *at any time* . . . "9

Traits of character (personality) likewise meet their doom in Skinner's denial that they are "stored" in a person: "But we call a man brave because of his acts, and he behaves bravely when environmental circumstances induce him to do so. The circumstances have changed his behavior; they have not implanted a trait or a virtue."10

Intention and purpose (will) are also dismissed by Skinner: "(C)ontingencies of reinforcement . . . provide alternative formulations of so-called 'mental processes' (such as) intention and purpose."11

Skinner eliminates mind, calling it "an explanatory fiction."12 Thinking itself is placed on the behavioral chopping block along with consciousness and all cognitive activity: "Perhaps the last stronghold of autonomous man is that complex 'cognitive' activity called thinking."13 The "autonomous man" that Skinner scorns is the individual with mind, thought, feelings, judgment, and dignity: "What is being abolished is autonomous man—the inner man, the homunculus (the little man within a man—J.N.), the possessing demon, the man defended by the literatures of freedom and dignity."14

Skinner has thus reduced human functioning to mere behavioral responses to the environment: " . . . a person does not act upon the world, the world acts upon him."15 The individual is robbed of judgment, choice, and initiative—indeed, of individuality itself. For Skinner, "the operant perspective assumes that the individual is not the originator of anything, but merely 'a locus in which things happen.'"16

Skinner, with his "Technology of Behavior," proposes the programming of every "locus" (locust?), of every group, and of society itself. Scientific psychology cannot accept such a mutilated, deformed, and simplistic theory of human psychological functioning.

Pavlov v. Skinner

A basic criticism of Skinner is that he completely ignores the immensely valuable physiological and psychological work of Pavlov and the neo-Pavlovians. He refers, in a passing sentence, to Pavlov's discovery of the conditioned reflex, only to dismiss it cursorily: "The stimulus-response model (of Pavlov) was never very convincing, however, and it did not solve the basic problem . . . "[17]

The basic problem is, of course, solved for Skinner by his own operant conditioning. Without entering into a full discussion of classical conditioning (Pavlov) and operant conditioning (Skinner), it should be indicated that there are many experimental scientists who maintain that Skinner's operant conditioning is only one form of Pavlov's classical conditioning.[18] In any case, the conditioned reflex is only one of the many significant physiological and psychological laws contributed to science by Pavlov.

Skinner's simplistic theory and his reliance on the sole model of response-reinforcement (behavior-reward) is refuted, in part, by an exposition of Pavlov's experimentally verified laws of excitation and inhibition, analysis and synthesis, generalization and differentiation, dynamic stereotype, etc.

A more devastating refutation of Skinner is Pavlov's profound contribution to psychology by his analysis of speech and language as a second signal system. Animals, Pavlov found, function on a sensory level in response to stimuli (signals), i.e., to sights, sounds, smells, tastes, etc. This he called the "first signal system," which both animals and humans possess. But, unlike animals, humans possess a "second signal system" consisting of words, which come to stand for the first (sensory) signals themselves. Thus, the word "bell" takes the place of the sound of a bell, becomes the signal of a signal, i.e., a second signal.

Pavlov attached enormous significance to the role of speech as a second signalling system: "In this way, a new principle of nervous activity arises—abstraction and at the same time generalization of the countless signals of the first signalling system which is again accompanied by analysis and synthesis of the new generalized signals (words)—a principle which ensures unrestricted orientation in relation to the surrounding world and ensures the highest degree of adaptation, namely, science, both in the form of human universal empiricism and in specialized forms."[19]

Here is posed the behavioral automaton of Skinner versus the complex, conscious, thinking human being capable of full adaptation through science to the surrounding world. But scientific psychology repudiates Skinner's theory in additional ways.

Basing itself on a full-fledged scientific theory, which has been experimentally verified, scientific psychology deals with the complexity and dialectical nature of human psychological functioning. As F. V. Bassin stated, "Man can be understood only as a psycho-physiological entity that reflects the whole complexity and diversity of his countless links with the outside world."[20]

Skinner reduces all human psychology to behavior in response to environmental rewards and punishments. Scientific psychology considers behavior only *one* among numerous features and categories of psychological life. In addition to the physiological basis for mental and behavioral activity, as developed by the science of higher nervous activity, there are the categories so summarily swept away by Skinner.

Perception and memory are fundamental to human adaptive activity. Emotions are vitally involved in our complex responses to a complex, dynamic reality. Personality traits, acquired in the life experience of the individual, permit consistency of response and individuality in coping with reality. Consciousness and thought are, perhaps, the most essential features of human psychology, since they enable us to acquire knowledge, to make judgments and choices, to set goals, and to plan our behavior intentionally and purposefully.

Most decisive in its influence on our thoughts, feelings, and behavior is society and social relations. As Marx stated, "In its reality, it (the human essence) is the *ensemble* of the social relations."[21] Human beings are distinguished from animals by their social labor, their social communication, their social groupings, by their social acquisition and use of language, and by their involvement in the ideas, attitudes, morality and behavior of their society.

Human beings, in the course of their life history and life activity, internalize the beliefs, mores, goals, ideology, and philosophy of the nation, class, family, and social grouping in which they live and function. This "internalized reflection" of their social life, is the basis for their perceptions, feelings, thoughts, judgments, choices, goals and behavior. Behavior is the outcome of this complexity of individual and social processes.

Where Skinner says, "Behavior is shaped and maintained by its consequences," scientific psychology replies, "Behavior is shaped and maintained by sensation, perception, memory, emotions, personality traits, consciousness, thought, knowledge, intention, purpose, society—and its consequences."

Skinner's Rejection of Freedom and Dignity

The strange title of Skinner's book, *Beyond Freedom and Dignity,* is explained most carefully since it provides the rationale for his proposal to "behaviorally engineer" a new society. Skinner states that the concepts of human freedom and dignity are products of a pre-scientific stage of psychology, which believed in "autonomous man" who was capable of thought, judgment and choice, who was responsible for his behavior, who was free to choose, and who could attain dignity through his choices.[22]

Skinner maintains that we have now reached the scientific stage of psychology with his discovery of the "Technology of Behavior." Rejecting the idea of "autonomous man," Skinner also discards the idea of freedom. All behavior is completely and automatically determined by the environment in which it occurs—neither judgment nor choice is involved, Skinner asserts. "Freedom is a matter of contingencies of reinforcement . . . " he writes.[23]

Skinner shows his disdain for people's struggles by stating that "the struggle for freedom can be viewed simply as an example of escape and avoidance behavior."[24]

Dignity, too, is renounced by Skinner as an unnecessary and outmoded concept, since we can neither credit nor blame an individual for behavior produced solely by environmental forces. As Max Black, paraphrasing Shakespeare, satirically wrote, "The fault, dear Brutus, is not in ourselves, but in our reinforcers."[25]

"It is a mistake," writes Skinner, "to suppose that the whole issue is how to free men. The issue is how to improve the way in which he is controlled."[26] We are beyond freedom and dignity—the only issue is how we are to be Skinnerized. Stephen Spender, the British poet, may well be correct when, in a debate with Skinner, he characterized Skinner's ideas as "a kind of fascism without tears."[27]

Marxism and Freedom and Dignity

Skinner abandons freedom and dignity and espouses a rigidly determinist view, a view that Marxism calls mechanical materialism. It was only with the development of Marxism that the full relationship between freedom and determinism could be explained. Materialism needed dialectics to delineate the true meaning of freedom.

For Skinner, human beings are unfree since they are determined in their behavior by the environment. It might be pointed out that the

Existentialists adopt the opposite, and equally incorrect, view that human beings are completely free and not in any way determined by the environment. Marxism believes in determinism, in causality, in laws of motion and development. But, for Marxism, human beings and human society have the potential for freedom and have attained a certain measure of freedom.

It was Marx who distinguished between animal and human activity with regard to freedom. In his *Economic and Philosophic Manuscripts of 1844,* Marx wrote: "The animal is immediately one with its life activity. It does not distinguish itself from it. It is *its life activity.* Man makes his life activity itself the object of his will and of his consciousness. He has conscious life activity. It is not a determination with which he directly merges. Conscious life activity distinguishes man immediately from animal life activity.... Only because of that is his activity free activity."[28]

It is noteworthy that Skinner specifically criticized Marx for holding that consciousness existed and mediated between the environment and behavior.[29] Where Marx based freedom on consciousness— thought, judgment, and choice—Skinner denies consciousness and, with it, freedom.

Engels went beyond the young Marx in developing the dialectical concept of freedom: "Hegel was the first to state correctly the relation between freedom and necessity. To him freedom is the appreciation of necessity. 'Necessity is *blind only insofar as it is not understood.* Freedom does not consist in the dream of independence of natural laws, but in the knowledge of these laws, and in the possibility this gives of systematically making them work towards definite ends.... Freedom of the will therefore means nothing but the capacity to make decisions with knowledge of the subject."[30]

Skinner eliminates both consciousness and knowledge. He thus eliminates the basis for freedom. Marxism links knowledge and freedom by calling for the utilization of natural, social and psychological laws discovered by science to achieve mastery over nature, society and ourselves. Knowledge thus is power—power to be free by utilizing knowledge.

Marxism also combats Skinner's renunciation of dignity. Dignity, of course, involves the responsibility for one's ideas, actions and relationships. The attainment of dignity is based upon thought, judgment and choice leading to dignified action. Dignity is achieved in society or in a social group. It is a fundamental social category which is involved in the concept of freedom. Marxism looks to socialism as a milestone on the road to greater freedom and to the true dignity of equality, economic security, opportunity, and expanding knowledge.

Marxism maintains that there are laws of social development which will lead, through conscious struggle, to a better society, socialism. Skinner believes that his "Behavioral Engineering" will make for a better society. What kind of society will Skinner produce?

Skinner's Utopia: Reinforced Capitalism

The outstanding feature of Skinner's "new" society is that it is the same system of capitalism—he even speaks of "the best kind of wage system that the industrialist may design."[31] Skinner does not wish to change capitalism. He believes that "a culture must be reasonably stable."[32]

What about democracy, limited though it may be in capitalist United States? In an earlier book, *Walden Two,* Skinner made clear that he did not believe in the electoral process nor in the intelligence of the members of our society. His Walden Two utopian society was behaviorally engineered by a *non-elected* Board of Planners—a government of experts.[32] More recently, Skinner stated that control of the population will be relegated to specialists: "to police, priests, owners, teachers, therapists, and so on."[33]

Instead of Plato's reactionary concept of philosopher-kings, Skinner offers us the equally reactionary concept of psychologist-kings, with Skinner as the psychologist-emperor. With a government of the elite, Skinner should have added to the title of his book "Beyond Democracy."

Skinner specifically applies his "contingencies of reinforcement" to the control of youth: "A serious problem arises when young people refuse to serve in the armed forces and desert or defect to other countries, but we shall not make appreciable change by 'inspiring greater loyalty or patriotism.' What must be changed are the contingencies which induce young people to behave in given ways toward their government."[34]

Skinner also specifically seeks to program workers: "We may be disturbed by the fact that many young people work as little as possible, or that workers are not very productive and often absent . . .

but we shall not get far by inspiring a 'sense of craftmanship or pride in one's work' . . . Something is wrong with the contingencies."[35]

Indeed, the characterization of Skinner's "Brave New World" by Max Black is most appropriate: "A world of well-controlled bodies, emitting physical movements in response to secret reinforcements." And Black adds, "It may, after all, be better to be dead than bred—like cattle."[36]

Skinner wishes to homogenize people into unthinking, unfeeling, operantly conditioned robots, controlled from the top by an elite group. Marxism believes in reason, in knowledge, in science, in progress, and in struggle to achieve progress.

Marxism, unlike Skinnerism, believes in living, thinking, feeling, active working people, who will, as they fight for their class interest, gain in class consciousness. No, not holes in a punch card to be computerized into permanent exploitation and oppression, but workers fighting their bosses, Blacks moving towards liberation, women seeking equality, young people organizing for a better life.

Above all, working people seek to rise from the indignity and lack of freedom that exist under capitalism. They hunger for and will seek freedom and dignity. They cannot achieve them through Skinner's scheme. Freedom and dignity will be achieved through their conscious struggles.

3

Behavior Modification

Electric shock. Sensory deprivation. Psychosurgery. Vomiting-inducing drugs. Genetic engineering. Hypnotic suggestion. Electrophysiology. Indeterminate sentences. Electrode implants in the brain. Rewards-and-punishment for behavior. Aversive therapy. Drug conditioning. Behavioral engineering. Social control hardware.

That is behavior modification at work. Dr. James V. McConnell, professor of psychology at the University of Michigan, states: "I believe the day has come when we can combine sensory deprivation with drugs, hypnosis and astute manipulation of reward and punishment to gain almost absolute control over an individual's behavior." Anticipating protest, the learned professor quickly added: "You have no say over what kind of personality you acquired and there is no reason to believe you should have the right to refuse to acquire a new one if the old one is anti-social."[1]

New methods of control of people are being introduced by U.S. monopoly capital. It is adding new techniques to its old methods of repression by force and violence. Commenting on the modernizing of police techniques by the federal Law Enforcement Assistance Administration, (L.E.A.A.), Representative James Scheuer (Democrat, New York) said, "As a result of spin-offs from medical, military, aerospace and industrial research, we now are in the process of developing devices and products capable of controlling violent individuals and entire mobs without injury. We can tranquilize, impede, immobilize, harass, shock, upset, stupefy, chill, temporarily blind, deafen or just plain scare the wits out of anyone the police have a proper need to control or restrain."[2]

But these methods alone have proved inadequate. Monopoly needs more sophisticated, scientific-sounding and comprehensive methods to control the most threatening feature of the activity of people—their *behavior*. Ghetto rebellions and massive antiwar demonstrations stunned the Johnson and Nixon administrations; Native Americans chilled the federal government with their heroic actions at Wounded Knee; politically conscious prison revolts have scared the wits out of the Establishment; women's liberation actions threaten the status quo of women's inequality. And haunting the corporate profiteers like a specter is the growing restiveness of labor as shown in strikes, mounting rank-and-file movements and rising struggle against inflation, speedup, taxes, and inadequate wages.

To control such "undesirable" behavior, the Establishment has taken to its breast an entire system of forming, changing or eliminating specific behavior, a system known as behavior modification.

Why Behavior Modification?

Behavior modification is the unethical and unscientific utilization of any form of electrotherapy, chemotherapy, psychosurgery, psychotherapy, aversive therapy, rewards-and-punishment or other means or devices to alter the mood, behavior, personality or psychic state of an individual or a group. Much of behavior modification is based on psychologist B. F. Skinner's theories. *The New York Times* reported that the L.E.A.A. "gave funds to a Pennsylvania correctional institution for a behavior modification program for youthful offenders based on Dr. B. F. Skinner's reinforcement principles in which a reinforcer, or reward, is given at each stage at which a subject produces the specified behavior."[3]

Added scientific weight is given behavior modification by new drugs, discoveries from brain research, new brain surgery techniques, and new developments in electronics and electrophysiology. An imposing scientific facade can thus be given to behavior modification, making its practice more easily accepted by people.

Equally appealing to the Establishment is its emphasis on direct, straightforward changing of behavior. Flavoring is given to this concoction by the psychiatric-psychological veneer of "treatment," "therapy," and "improving mental health." Further, behavior modification is put forth, practiced and extolled at a time of "crime and violence in the streets," the demand for "law and order," and multiple fears and frustrations of people. It thus has the superficial appearance of a scientific, effective and psychologically proven method of ending violence, crime and socially dangerous behavior. When elevated to the status of "behavioral engineering" and put forth as the New Utopia for U.S. society by Dr. Skinner in his book *Beyond Freedom and Dignity,*[4] it assumes impressive proportions indeed.*

But what is the real nature of behavior modification?

Behavior Modification in Practice

"Nothing arouses the fears of prison inmates more than so-called 'behavior modification' programs, and no wonder," writes Tom Wicker, editorial columnist of *The New York Times.*[5] "Behavior modification is a catch-all term that can mean anything from brain surgery to a kind of 'Clockwork Orange' mental conditioning; it usually includes drug experimentation, and in all too many cases it is aimed more nearly at producing docile prisoners than upright citizens."

Powerful aversive drugs are systematically used in behavior modification programs on the principle of associating pain and nausea with behavior deemed "unacceptable" by prison psychologists and authorities. In an Iowa program, a drug called apmorphine was injected without consent into inmates who violated prison behavior rules: "The inmate was then exercised and within about fifteen minutes he began vomiting. The vomiting lasted from 15 minutes to an hour. There is also a temporary cardiovascular effect which involves some change in blood pressure and in the heart.'"[6] In a suit brought by the prisoners, the U.S. Court of Appeals ruled this to be cruel and unusual punishment and unconstitutional under the Eighth Amendment.

The Bureau of Prisons medical center at Springfield, Missouri, applied sensory deprivation techniques: it placed "troublesome" inmates in "round-the-clock isolation in individual cells without radios or reading material and then, if the inmates met certain behavior rules,

*See Chapter 2 on B. F. Skinner.

moved them progressively to one after another 'level' each with more 'privileges' than the level before."[7]

Prisoners have been held for months and even years in such solitary cages for refusing to become docile robots. Ironically, this Springfield program is known as START (Special Treatment and Rehabilitation Training). What is needed there is STOP (Stop Torture of Prisoners).

In Connecticut, electric shocks are administered to inmates as they watch slides of "undesirable" behavior; this is combined with hypnosis.[8]

The Federal Prisoners Coalition in Marion Federal Penitentiary smuggled out a report to be presented to the UN Economic and Social Council which described "psychotherapy" sessions as follows: "During these sessions, on a progressively intensified basis, the prisoner is shouted at, his fears played on, his sensitiveness ridiculed, and concentrated effort made to make him feel guilty for real or imagined characteristics or conduct. . . . Every effort is made to heighten his suggestibility and weaken his character structure so that his emotional responses and thought-flow will be brought under group and staff control as totally as possible."[9]

At Vacaville Medical Facility in California, the drug anectine makes the "uncooperative" inmate stop breathing for up to two minutes while the "therapist" talks to him about his "misdeeds."[10] The use of the drug prolixin on inmates was protested by La Raza Unida, an organization of Chicano prisoners in the California Men's Colony. In a petition addressed to the California Senate Committee on Penal Institutions, they wrote: "The simple fact that a number of prisoners are walking the yard in this institution like somnambulists, robots and vegetables as a result of this drug should be reason enough to make people apprehensive as to the effect it's having."[11]

The indeterminate sentence (*e.g.,* burglary is one to fifteen years in California) is a powerful instrument for inmate coercion: prison authorities can control the behavior of prisoners by either extending or lessening their sentences. As a sociologist told Jessica Mitford: "The indeterminate sentence can keep a 'dangerous' man in almost indefinitely: political non-conformists, inmate leaders of ethnic groups, prison troublemakers."[12]

Psychological degradation, indeterminate agony, endless isolation, death-threatening drugs—that is behavior modification at work. But if it is thought that behavior modification is limited to the above practices in prisons and to drug therapy in mental institutions, in actuality it has a number of other shocking features and seeks its victims everywhere in the land.

Other Features of Behavior Modification

Ronald Reagan, when governor of California, used public money to set up a Center for the Study and Reduction of Violence. Of course, a more feasible subject for such a study would be the White House and the Pentagon. At Reagan's center, one of the major projects, naturally headed by a man, Dr. Richard Green, was "Violence in Women." Here is what that project studied: "The question of violence in females will be examined from the point of view that females are more likely to commit acts of violence during the pre-menstrual and menstrual periods. . . . Hormonal monitoring will be done . . . the findings will have direct application to medical treatment of potentially violent females."[13] One wonders whether Nixon was having a secret menstrual flow when he carried out the secret bombings of Cambodia.

Equally savage is the increasing use of psychosurgery on Blacks, on women (two-thirds of all cases), on prisoners, and on the poor. Psychosurgery is the destruction or removal of brain tissue for the purpose of altering (modifying) behavior. This procedure has long been outlawed in the Soviet Union. The complex nature of the brain, the necessary working together of different parts—functional systems as they are called by the noted brain specialist, Dr. Alexander Luria—the delicate and irreplaceable tissue that forms the brain: these make psychosurgery nothing but brain mutilation.

Psychosurgery on children is a particularly brutal act. A Dr. Orlando J. Andy of the University of Mississippi School of Medicine operated on the thalamus of a nine-year old boy to "cure" his behavioral disorder. Unsuccessful, Dr. Andy operated *three more times* until "there was a marked improvement in behavior." Several years later, Dr. Andy reported: "Intellectually, however, the patient is deteriorating."[14]

Psychosurgery has these possible side effects: intellectual deterioration, speech impairment, loss of ability for abstract thinking, paralysis, loss of urinary control and epileptic seizures. Nevertheless following the Detroit ghetto rebellion of 1967, a letter entitled "Role of Brain Disease in Riots and Urban Violence" was sent to the *Journal of the American Medical Association* by Drs. Frank Ervin, Vernon

Mark and William Sweet. In this letter, this unholy medical trio recommended "diagnosing the many violent slum dwellers who have some brain pathology and treating them" [with brain surgery].[15]

Drs. Mark and Ervin followed up this outrageously racist proposal with a book *Violence and the Brain*[16] in which they propose psychosurgery ("operating directly on the limbic system") for hyperkinetic children. Hyperkinetic children are mostly overactive children who have nothing organically wrong with them. Their overactivity is usually due to the monotony, poor teaching, racism, irrelevance and lack of purpose in most schools. Given the estimate of Mark and Ervin that there are two and a half million hyperkinetic children, one is justified in characterizing their proposal as barbaric.

Behavior modification is being applied on a wide scale in our school system to so-called hyperactive children, most of whom are bored, restless, resistant to racism, or frustrated with school. "Hyperactivity" has now been labeled a disease to be treated with medication—it is estimated that 200,000 to 300,000 children are being drugged with ritalin to control this "disease."[17] Sociologist Steven Box denounces as "psychological violence" such employment of "medical solutions to school problems which are *essentially* moral, legal and social."[18]

Even more ominous are the proposals of Yale Professor of Medicine Dr. José M. Delgado, put forth in his book with the dread title *Physical Control of the Mind: Toward a Psychocivilized Society*.[19] Using what he calls ESB (electrical stimulation of the brain), Delgado has been working on remote control of humans by computers. These computers will be programmed to inhibit selectively various emotions as they are detected and recorded from brain waves: "A two-way communication system can be established between the brain of a subject and a computer . . . anxiety, depression, or rage could be recognized in order to trigger stimulation of specific inhibitory structures."[20]

Delgado has successfully implanted transceivers with electrodes into the brains of experimental animals to monitor and control their activities. Computers have already been tested by Delgado on subjects in mental hospitals; they are programmed to send out inhibitory instructions to control undesirable behavior. But un-Hippocratic Dr. Delgado does not intend to restrict ESB to animals and mental patients. He predicts that ESB could become the "master control of human behavior by means of man-made plans and instruments."[21] We are all to be *psychocivilized* by Dr. Delgado.

Barton L. Ingraham of Berkeley's School of Criminology joins Delgado in proposing electrophysiology for "complete and continuous" surveillance of a person who has demonstrated "criminal tendencies." Ingraham proposes "automatic deterrence or blocking" by ESB to prevent "criminal" activity.[22]

Latest among the schemes for behavior modification is "genetic engineering." Modification of the genes in certain cells to produce specific behavior, mass genetic screening to identify "genetically defective" people, cloning (producing a replica of an individual from one of the somatic cells)—all these are being researched and considered.

Although not specifically part of the behavior modification movement, the forced sterilization of welfare mothers to prevent "reproductive behavior," the restriction of the education of Blacks proposed by Arthur Jensen,* forced cultural assimilation—"Americanization"—of national groups, and the huge number of programs of human experimentation without consent and through deceit**— all are part of an overall reactionary offensive to modify, repress, or eliminate behavior unwanted by monopoly capital. The smell of the ovens hovers around behavior modification.

Behavior Modification: Extent and Victims

The General Accounting Office of the government has stated that there are tens of thousands of behavioral research projects being financed by government agencies. *Human Events* reported: "A preliminary check turned up 70,000 grants and contracts at the Department of Health, Education and Welfare, 10,000 within the Manpower Administration and thousands of additional projects costing millions of dollars financed by the Defense Department, NASA, and the Atomic Energy Commission."[23]

Many behavior modification programs have been conducted in secret. Indeed, the chief planner for the UCLA center, a Dr. Louis L. West, requested a Nike Missile Base (!), stating: "Comparative studies could be carried out there, in an isolated but convenient location,

*See Chapter 7 on Jensenism
**See Chapter 10 on Behavior Research.

experimental or model programs for the alteration of undesirable behavior."[24]

Testifying before a congressional subcommittee, Norman A. Carlson, director of the federal prison system, stated that behavior modification was an "integral part" of many prison programs. When forced to testify before the same subcommittee, the head of the Law Enforcement Assistance Administration admitted to at least 400 projects on behavior modification, including a grant of $130,000 to the University of Puerto Rico for "neurological research into the correlations between criminal behavior and brain damage."[25]

The C.I.A. is heavily involved in behavior control programs. Basing himself on C.I.A. documents, John Marks, associate of the Center for National Security Studies, revealed a 14-year C.I.A. project for controlling human behavior through the use of chemical, biological and radiological materials. In refuting C.I.A. Director Adm. Stansfield Turner, who had called the agency's activity "a program of experimentation with drugs," Marks stated. "To be sure, drugs were part of it but so were such other techniques as electric shock, radiation, ultrasonics, psychosurgery and incapacitating agents."[26]

Over and beyond federal and state sponsorship, behavior modification has achieved significant influence among psychologists, teachers, social workers, school officials, agency heads and others. Dozens of conferences and conventions have been held, and thousands of parents have been trained in its use.

Estimating that thousands of schools in the United States use behavior modification, Philip J. Hilts, in his book *Behavior Mod,* points out that schools are an ideal environment for its practice since millions of children must attend school five days a week for six hours a day for a minimum of ten years, and that teachers are expected to control or alter children's behavior.[27] According to Richard J. Winnett and Robert Winkler, "It appears that behavior modifiers have been instruments of the status quo, unquestioning servants of a system which thrives on a petty reign of 'law and order' to the apparent detriment of the educational process itself. What is, perhaps, most disheartening is that our procedures seem to work, and thus make the system operate that much more effectively."[28]

Although experimental programs have centered on prisons, mental institutions and schools, behavior modification is intended for broader and more sinister use as a "psycho-social control instrument." B. F

Skinner sees control of the behavior of the population in his "behaviorally engineered society" as being delegated to specialists—"to police, priests, owners, teachers, therapists and so on"—with reinforcement by a system of rewards.[29]

Present victims of behavior modification are prison inmates, mental patients and school children. However, at the UCLA Center study will be made of "the family structure and unrest among the poor." The staff is mandated to develop "models designed to control the activities of individuals and groups, including rioters." One aim of this project is "the demonstration and incorporation of preventive models into public school programs, law enforcement activities, governmental actions, and private organizations."[30]

Reverend Dr. Charles E. Cobb, executive director of the Commission for Racial Justice of the United Church of Christ, has charged that the new federal Butner Center will use behavior modification techniques on prison inmates "to develop methods of controlling others, both inmates *and non-inmates*."[31] Truly, ask not for whom the behavior modification bell tolls; it tolls for thee.

Opposition to Behavior Modification

It is not accidental that the fight against behavior modification has been sparked and maintained by prison inmates and particularly by politically aware Black inmates. The major hunting ground for its practice has been the prisons and the schools, with Blacks singled out as targets. Behavior modification is saturated with racism.

Prisons today, with their disproportionately large Black populations—again due to racism—have become centers for social protest and political struggle. Tom Wicker reported that "START (Special Treatment and Rehabilitation Training) will be discontinued after more than a year of inmate protests, lawsuits, hunger strikes, and the like."[32]

Norman Carlson, Director of the U.S. Bureau of Prisons, was requested by two members of Congress, John Conyers and Don Edwards, to conduct an investigation into "incidents of violence, harassment and enforced deprivation in the long-term control unit at the Marion, Ill. Federal Prison."[33]

The *Daily World* reported that prisoners who were being secretly transported in the dead of night from Jackson State Penitentiary to the Marquette Center in Upper Michigan to undergo behavior modification "treatment" *set fire to the bus* to call attention to their plight.[34]

Further, federal anti-crime money through L.E.A.A. has now been banned for behavior modification, psychosurgery, chemotherapy, and medical research, following protracted active opposition by prisoners and their organizations, supported by other liberal and progressive groups.[35] The Prescription Program, a behavior modification project of New York State prisons, has likewise been pressured into abandonment at the Adirondack Correctional Treatment and Evaluation Center and the Clinton Correctional Facility.[36]

In Detroit, the Ad Hoc Coalition Against Behavior Modification is actively pushing for legislation banning all forms of behavior modification in public institutions in Michigan. Psychiatrists and psychologists are also speaking out against this form of psychological control. Dr. Thomas S. Szasz states: "Most of the legal and social applications of psychiatry, undertaken in the name of psychiatric liberalism, are actually instances of despotism."[37] Dr. Peter R. Breggin, leader of the fight to prohibit psychosurgery, says, "Psychosurgical techniques ... seem especially suited to totalitarian application on a large scale for a wide variety of citizens."[38]

Organizations engaged in battle against behavior modification include the National Conference of Black Lawyers, Psychologists for Social Action, the National Prison Center, the Medical Committee for Human Rights, the United Church of Christ, and the American Civil Liberties Union. In California an investigation of the UCLA Center was undertaken by the NAACP, the Mexican-American Political Association, the National Organization of Women, and the California Prisoners Union, with the statement: "Underlying [our investigation] were grave concerns about the role the proposed center might play in encouraging future behavior modification experiments on political protesters, prisoners, inmates of mental institutions, minorities and women."[39]

The American Civil Liberties Union has instituted legal proceedings to prevent juveniles who are deemed "uncontrollable" from being enrolled in behavior modification programs unless there is a full court hearing with attorneys.[40]

One of the major leaders of the offensive against behavior modification is the National Alliance Against Racist and Political Repression. At its national conference in May 1973, it adopted a resolution which stated: "We view the govermental use of behavior modification techniques as direct and blatant political and racist repression. . . . The spread of behavior modification as a means of crushing politically aware prisoners and movements and controlling women, the poor, and Third World peoples in the areas of prisons, ghettos, schools, methadone maintenance programs, military, and in the population at large, necessitates that the National Defense Organization join with progressive groups and individuals involved in psychiatry, psychology, medicine, sociology, and education to combat legally and politically the use of behavior modification and further to expose its use to the people."[41] Many honest people have been taken in by the scientific coating of "learning theory," "positive reinforcement," and "therapeutic treatment" covering the true character of behavior modification.

Further, exaggerated reports of its successes with limited numbers in specialized areas (autistic children, schizophrenics, mentally retarded) has led well-meaning progressives mistakenly to support it.

Behavior modification of the reward type has had minor success of a limited character with a small number of seriously impaired adults and children. Behavior modification of the type described in this article is a comprehensive, full-scale system, hugely backed by government money and multimillion dollar foundations, designed to alter the behavior of millions of normal, healthy workers, Blacks, Chicanos, children and women by outrageous, unethical and frequently criminal psychological and psychiatric methods and techniques.

This system of psychotorture aims to destroy the emotions and thought processes of working people and leave them solely with robotlike behavior suited to the needs of monopoly rule. By concentrating on behavior and its control, it seeks to eliminate consciousness, judgment and reasoning. These are the main targets of the Skinners and the Delgados, who give emotions, knowledge, and thought processes no importance.

Behavior modification is unscientific. It is mainly an instrument to control people. It is an enemy of the working people. It should be repudiated.

4

Altered Consciousness: Drugs, Meditation And Gurus

Consciousness is the most valuable of human attributes. Formed by human labor, nurtured in society, and qualitatively shaped by language and speech, human consciousness has changed and expanded constantly. From the bare beginnings of human thought, as the higher anthropoids began to make and utilize tools and to communicate in the process of their primitive social production, human consciousness has grown with the growth of technology, productive forces, science, and culture.

Further, as society developed from primitive communal forms to the class forms of slavery, feudalism and capitalism, human consciousness took on a class content in addition to its social content. Human consciousness never remains the same—it changes with changes in technology, culture, class struggle, and social ideology.

World War II, Cold War, hot wars of Korea and Vietnam . . . automation, cybernetics, computers . . . civil rights struggles, strikes, antiwar demonstrations, Black freedom thrust, women's liberation movement—consciousness could not and did not remain the same in such a turbulent social scene.

Consciousness needs and requires further altering and expansion. But how do we alter it and with what goals?

Alternate Roads to Altered Consciousness

Timothy Leary, the high priest of psychedelic drugs, recently turned FBI informer, maintains that LSD, mescaline, marijuana, Yoga, and ESB (electrical stimulation of the brain) can enable us to achieve four levels of consciousness not known to ordinary consciousness. These are, in order of ascending pleasure, "Unconditioned Sensory Delight, Somatic Rapture, Genetic Transcendence, and Neuroelectrical Ecstasy."[1]

Calling it "The Science of Creative Intelligence," the Maharishi Mahesh Yogi states: "Transcendental Meditation is a natural technique to explore the deeper and hidden regions of the mind and thereby unfold the full mental potential."[2]

The fifteen year old guru Maharaj Ji—of whom Rennie Davis said, "I would cross the planet on my hands and knees to touch his toe"[3]— offers a different path: "I can promise you satisfaction of mind. You can experience bliss within."[4]

Zen Buddhism offers "a new truth. . . . Nirvana, the mystical enlightenment... the central perception of unsurpassed singularity."[5]

In his book *The Natural Mind,* Andrew Weill ardently espouses the experiencing of "non-ordinary reality." "Internal reality," he writes, "is a different order of reality that is self-validating. And the most elementary requirement for getting in touch with it is simple withdrawal of attention from sensory attachment to external reality."[6]

Charles Reich, in his popular *The Greening of America,* discovered Consciousness III, which "promises a higher reason, a more human community, and a new and liberated individual."[7]

The commune movement also claims to expand consciousness as a top priority. John Sinclair who helped found a commune with the appealing name of "Trans-love Energies" in Ann Arbor, Michigan, says, "We are a conscious community of artists and lovers who live together, work together and share all things, and smoke dope together."[8]

Many and varied are the roads to "altered consciousness." Drugs, meditation, Eastern religions, communal thinking, "stoned" thinking, Consciousness III—all are bidding for the minds of people, particularly the youth. Why have these specific movements for expanding consciousness arisen? More important, why have they achieved such strength?

Why Altered Consciousness?

Consciousness is a reflection of the real world in which we live. It includes the ideas, beliefs, perceptions, attitudes, and feelings we derive from social living. When our consciousness reflects a society which offers us opportunity, freedom, equality, fulfillment and honest relationships, we treasure our consciousness as a means of self-realization. But the reflection we derive from capitalist United States in the last quarter of the twentieth century is the very opposite: inequality in the form of pervasive racism, poverty for millions, hollow and meaningless education, unemployment, a callous and deceitful government, and a business system which makes honest young people gag.

Alienation and depersonalization are the psychological results of such a society. Powerlessness in a monopoly dominated society leaves apathy and despair. A capitalist culture whose predominant expression is in violence, pornography, hopeless characters, shootouts, pimping and car chases, stifles the minds of people.

But human consciousness is vital, resilient and ever seeking forms of fulfillment and growth. Millions of people—workers, Blacks, women, minorities, and especially youth—have rejected much of the culture and ideology of the Establishment and have sought alternate forms of consciousness and satisfaction. Some have recognized the true nature of capitalism and have joined in the fight to bring about fundamental changes. Many more have joined together to improve and reform major areas of our society as in civil rights, education, and equality of women.

But a large number have turned to other forms for altering or "expanding" consciousness. And these forms have proliferated in bewildering fashion. Many young people go from one form to another in a ceaseless search for self-actualization, a search for a different and better consciousness. Psychedelic drugs and hard drugs, transcendental meditation and eastern religions, communes, "the natural mind" and Consciousness III have all won many adherents for their particular brand of "altered states of consciousness." What do they offer? Should they be accepted?

"Somatic Rapture"—Psychedelic Drugs

LSD—lysergic acid diethylamide—is the most powerful of all popular mind-altering drugs.[9] It is in the class of drugs, along with peyote, psilocybin, and mescaline, known as hallucinogens. The popular use of these drugs for "mind expansion" did not take place till about 1965, after which their use assumed massive proportions.

Users of "acid," as LSD is called, report sudden changes in their physical senses: "Walls may appear to move, colors seem stronger and more brilliant . . . Flat objects seem to become three-dimensional. Taste, smell, hearing and touch seem more acute. One sensory impression may be translated or merged into another: music may appear as a color, and colors seem to possess taste."[10]

Marijuana (also known as pot, grass, and Mary Jane) is classified by scientists as a mild hallucinogenic (hallucination-producing) drug.[11] The smoker becomes "high" or "stoned" in about fifteen minutes, for two to four hours. Sense of time and distance frequently become distorted—a minute can seem like an hour and reactions range from depression to a feeling of excitement.

In *The Healing Journey,*[12] Claudio Naranjo espouses the use of four other psychedelic drugs (MDA, MMDA, harmaline, and ibogaine) as "feeling enhancers" and producers of "peak experiences."

The use of psychedelic drugs is a mass phenomenon in our country today. Although it is particularly widespread among the youth, the middle-class white, professionals and intellectuals, it has affected all groups and classes in our country. These psychedelic drugs act physiologically upon the brain, the nervous system and the sense organs. Through their chemical action, they produce varied, distorted, bizarre, novel and unusual sensations and perceptions in the user. They also produce direct physical effects; for example, "The drug (LSD) increases the pulse and heart rate, causes a rise in blood pressure and temperature, dilated eye pupils, shaking of the hands and feet, cold, sweaty palms, a flushed face or paleness, shivering, chills, a wet mouth, irregular breathing . . . "[13]

In addition to bizarre sensations and perceptions, LSD and other psychedelic drugs do alter consciousness by affecting the emotions, the thinking and the conscious reactions of the user. The actual effects depend upon, in part, the situation, the expectation, the previous psychological state, and the overall general level of consciousness of the individual. Despite claims to heightened imagination, greater creativity, and clearer thinking, most studies fail to bear this out.

On the other hand, the use of psychedelic drugs can have serious physiological, psychological and psychiatric effects. In a book aptly entitled *Utopiates* (opiates which promise Utopia), Richard Blum reports: "About half the people . . . report they have had some unpleasant component in their LSD reaction."[14] Among such unpleasant components were "physical distress, feelings of helplessness, or loss of control . . . raw fear . . . initial horror . . . depression . . . awful energy depletion. . . ."[15] It is further reported that users who suffer "bad trips" undergo temporary or longer-lasting psychosis[16]: " . . . we've all seen the bad reactions that people can have; you know, when they get 'the demons' or 'the terror,'" comments one LSD user.[17]

But beyond the physical and psychological effects of psychedelic drugs are the *social* effects. "Psychedelics offer nothing more than a flight from responsibility and an excuse for total withdrawal," states Keith Melville in his *Communes in the Counter Culture*.[18] Timothy Leary writes: "The basic social issues are always hedonic. War, revolution, politics, technology—all are irrelevant symptoms of the underlying current. Loosen up."[19]

Many radicalized young people who participated in splendid movements for civil rights, free speech in universities, and against the Vietnam War, have been diverted into psychedelics. Melville reports: "In a study of the Berkeley drug colony in 1967, James T. Carey found that the hard-core acidheads had completely rejected the possibility of changing the social order through political action. They had developed 'a distinctive life style which celebrates political disengagement.'"[20]

The altered consciousness provided by psychedelic drugs is a consciousness that provides novel sensory and perceptual effects at the expense of clarity of thought and ability to analyze problems. It is a consciousness which undermines discipline, integrity and the ability to participate in organized movement for social change. Psychedelic consciousness, the "stoned" state, is a psychological state which is highly valued and appreciated by the economic-political rulers of our society.

The Tranquilizing of Society: Psychoactive Drugs
The National Commission on Marijuana and Drug Abuse con-

cluded in its report that one reason for the increased use of tranquilizers and stimulants was that "many persons have come to regard very real and fundamental emotions and feelings as abnormal, avoidable, socially and personally unacceptable, and, worst of all, unnecessary."[21] This process of tranquilizing (or over-exciting) the population, in order to deaden or distort genuine psychological reactions to an exploitative society, is being accomplished with the use of psychoactive drugs.

Discovered in the 1950s, tranquilizers are the basis for an epidemic of *legal* drug abuse. Valium, a multipurpose antianxiety drug, unknown 20 years ago, has become the No. 1 prescribed drug in the United States, with librium, another tranquilizer, in third place. In the first six months of 1973, there were 39 million prescriptions filled for these two drugs at a cost of 132 million dollars.[22]

"What makes a woman cry? A man? Another woman? Three kids? No kids at all? Wrinkles? You name it . . . If she is depressed, consider PERTOFANE." So reads an advertisement published in medical and psychiatric journals. Here is another: "School, the dark, separation, dental visits, monsters. The everyday anxiety of children sometimes gets out of hand. . . . Then she may need your help. Your help may include VISTARIL."

Even more pointed politically is the advertisement showing a worried looking woman college student: "Her newly stimulated intellectual curiosity may make her more sensitive and apprehensive about national and world conditions. Help free her of excessive anxiety . . . LIBRIUM."[23]

The abuse of psychoactive drugs victimizes millions of people, but certain groups are particular victims. In a perceptive and socially conscious article pointedly titled "Drug Abuse—Just What the Doctor Ordered," psychologist J. Maurice Rogers writes: "Women use psychoactive drugs twice as often as men do. Many seek prescriptions for these drugs because they are lonely, anxious, dissatisfied or unhappy; because they are not as popular, thin, vigorous, interesting or beautiful as they have been led to believe they should be."[24]

The treatment of the elderly is among the most notoriously heartless in our heartless society. Tranquilizers are massively used in a "forced pacification program" in nursing homes, according to Nelson H. Cruikshank, former president of the national Council of Senior

Citizens: "Exclusive use of tranquilizers (on patients who do not need them) can quickly reduce an ambulatory patient to a zombie, confining the patient to a chair or bed, causing the patient's muscles to atrophy from inaction, and causing general health to deteriorate quickly."[25]

Perhaps most shocking of all is the use of certain stimulant drugs—Ritalin, Dexedrin, Tofranil—which have the paradoxical effect of calming children. Dr. Rogers writes: "Exuberant children may have Ritalin prescribed primarily because parents want to quiet them down, or because teachers report that they are fidgety and inattentive in the classroom. In Omaha, Nebraska, school officials recently discovered that between 5 and 10 percent of the grade-school children in that city were being given medically prescribed amphetamines to modify their classroom hyperactivity or inattention."[26]

The Food and Drug Administration has warned that drugs like Ritalin are physiologically addictive and must be used with extreme caution—despite this warning and despite serious side effects of these drugs, about 250,000 children take Ritalin daily.[27] A large number of these children are, of course, Black and minority children, whose miseducation would naturally cause them to be restless and overactive in the classroom. Racism is not above the use of drugs on children.

Behind the misuse and abuse of psychoactive drugs are the huge drug corporations who are the most open and criminal of drug pushers. Librium and Valium achieved sales of over one-quarter of a billion dollars in 1973. CIBA Pharmaceutical Company sold 10 million dollars of Ritalin the same year.

Drug companies depend upon this country's 180,000 physicians to sell their prescription drugs, including psychoactive drugs. The drug industry spends over three-quarters of a *billion* dollars each year on advertising directed solely at physicians—over $4,200 per physician per year![28]

Psychoactive drugs act on the nervous system to affect and change consciousness. Anger, frustration, unhappiness, depression, anxiety, resentment—all reactions which are naturally produced by poverty, speedup, bad housing, third-rate education, threat of war, unemployment, as well as by personal problems—are subdued, eliminated and *tranquilized* by psychoactive drugs. Even more important, the clarity of mind and mental alertness necessary to arrive at rational solutions to real social and individual problems are harmfully affected by these drugs.

Richard Blum points out that our social environment condemns "misery as a bad thing, a state in need of correction. For a man to be unhappy is 'wrong'; it can be taken as proof of his own personal fault or weakness."[29]

There is a close connection between the widespread use of illegal drugs—LSD, marijuana, mescaline, heroin, cocaine—and the widespread use of legal psychoactive drugs. With a restive society resisting poverty, exploitation and racism, an excellent pacifying and escapist means of aborting such resistance is drugs, legal and illegal.

Transcendental Meditation

"The Transcendental State of Being lies beyond all seeing, hearing, touching, smelling and tasting—beyond all thinking and beyond all feeling. This state of the unmanifested, absolute, pure consciousness of Being is the ultimate state of life." So states Maharishi Mahesh Yogi, founder of Transcendental Meditation.[30]

Sensationalized by its temporary acceptance by the Beatles, Transcendental Meditation (TM) has had wide impact in the United States as a new form of consciousness. It is estimated that there are half a million devotees (mainly white, middle-class) of TM in this country with 207 TM centers and 5,000 teachers.[31] Fees of $75 to $125 are charged for several one-hour training sessions: "What you get for your money is instruction on sitting in a comfortable, relaxed position and saying the mantra (a specific word or phrase—J.N.) over and over while allowing your mind to float free. Meditators are told to do this for two 20-minute sessions every day."[32]

The Maharishi claims that TM is a fourth state of consciousness, different from waking, sleeping and dreaming: "Transcendental Meditation is a natural technique which allows the conscious mind to experience increasingly subtle states of thought until the source of thought, the unlimited reservoir of energy and creative intelligence is reached."[33] The goal of TM is to achieve "cosmic consciousness, the very source of existence, the Absolute."[34]

As testimony to the effectiveness of TM, Bill Walton, the star basketball player, says it "makes him a better basketball player," while Yale psychiatrist Harold Bloomfield says "it helps him in his practice."[35]

Scientific studies have shown that certain physiological changes occur during TM. Dr. Robert Keith Wallace, Harvard physiologist, reported significant decreases in oxygen consumption and carbon dioxide elimination, cardiac output, heart rate and respiratory rate, with more alpha waves (relaxed yet alert) recorded by the brain during TM.[36]

Is Transcendental Meditation a new and desirable state of altered consciousness? The answer is a resounding "No." TM does achieve a state of relaxation which causes the physiological changes reported. States of relaxation, like sleep, do rest the body and restore physical energy. To the extent that physical and mental fatigue are overcome by physical and mental relaxation, TM can restore the normal state of mental alertness.

Transcendental Meditation claims, however, to go far beyond mere relaxation. In its talk of "cosmic consciousness" and "the Absolute," it becomes mystical and unscientific. Its claims to plumb new depths of consciousness is absurd. Consciousness is not made up of layers which can be penetrated by absence of thought and sensation to achieve the deepest layer. Consciousness is made up of the actual thoughts, ideas, knowledge, emotions and perceptions of the individual and are expressed in speech and behavior. The Maharishi's formula for achieving "creative intelligence" by exploring "the deeper and hidden regions of the mind" is like peeling an onion to get at its core—there's nothing there. The state of pure relaxation is the state of empty consciousness. Of course, individual expectation and the swollen promises of TM may lead an individual to *believe* that he or she has transcended reality through meditation—actually, she or he has merely relaxed.

Beyond the actual physiological consequences—relaxation—and the psychological consequences—empty consciousness—lies the socio-political meaning of TM. The Maharishi shows the nature of his political thinking by his explanation of the causes of war: "From my analysis, it is not the military that creates the wars; it's the civilians who remain frustrated, tense, and worried who are creating an atmosphere of tension."[37] The Pentagon, of course, will readily accept that explanation.

Transcendental Meditation also seeks the elmination of all stress, the achievement of harmony, of "cosmic bliss." Here is a recipe for the ignoring of social evils through escaping into inner relaxation. TM alters consciousness by elminating it.

Mystical Consciousness: Gurus and Zen

Rennie Davis says that he has "a practical way to fulfill all the dreams of the movement of the early sixties and seventies. There's a practical method to end poverty, racism, sexism, imperialism." What is that method? Why, by allowing ourselves to "receive knowledge" from the fifteen-year old guru Maharajah Ji, says Davis.[38]

It is healthy to reject capitalism and its Establishment. But capitalist society can always provide alternatives which are nonthreatening to its existence or rule. The disenchantment with the Establishment which affected millions of people, particularly youth, led some to turn away from all aspects of "Western life" and to seek answers in Eastern religions and ideology.

Gurus ("bringing light [ru] out of darkness [gu]") offer mystical answers to real problems. Harrison Pope, Jr., in his book *The Road East*[39], points out that many who used psychedelic drugs to achieve "instant happiness" have now turned to the "natural high" of eastern religion. "Many young people," says Pope, "are very reluctant to enter mainstream American society because they say it is sterile, mechanized, and on the verge of destruction . . . Eastern religions assume the existence of other levels of reality." Further, the new religions provide a figure to be revered like Meher Baba, or Swami Prabhupada of the Hare Krishnas.

Zen Buddhism is also a mystical form of religion. It seeks the achievement of Nirvana through *satori*—the sudden, mystical enlightenment. It seeks the elmination of everyday consciousness and its replacement by mystical insight. It is a thoroughly subjective, individualistic and escapist ideology. It avoids social involvement: "Man must be untouched by lust and suffering, by profit and loss, rising and falling, concern about others, enjoyment and fear—and he shall not cling to any creature."[40]

Mysticism, as practiced by gurus or Zen Buddhism, escapes from reality into the subjective and the supernatural. As Keith Melville puts it, "The attraction of the occult and the irrational often signals the abandonment of the critical faculties, an attack on reason which is a dangerous development in the youth culture."[41] To alter consciousness so that reason and science are rejected is to paralyze one's consciousness as an instrument for coping with reality.

"Stoned Thinking": The Natural Mind

There are religious gurus and there are psychological gurus. Andrew Weill is a psychological guru whose book *The Natural Mind: A New Way of Looking at the Higher Consciousness*[42] is a call to worship "the non-ordinary consciousness" and to exorcize "straight thinking."

Weill believes that there are two different states of thinking or consciousness: straight thinking which is the ordinary, intellectual, sensory, external way of thinking, and stoned thinking which is nonintellectual and includes dreams, trances, meditation, neurotic and psychotic thinking. Weill believes that stoned thinking is an expression of "the natural mind": "It seems to me that stoned thinking, like daydreaming, is a natural component of consciousness that all of us have available to us all the time. It predominates naturally in states of consciousness other than the ordinary ego-centered waking state. . . ."[43]

Weill structures human consciousness in true Freudian fashion. Straight thinking, for Weill, is based upon consciousness, while stoned thinking has its source in the unconscious mind. Straight thinking, or "intellectation," as Weill calls it, only tells us about the outward forms of things since it is based upon the senses. Stoned thinking enables us to get at the "inner contents" of things because it uses intuition which is a product of the unconscious mind: intuition puts us in direct touch with reality, Weill claims. Hence, we should relegate straight thinking to an inferior, unimportant role, while elevating stoned thinking to a position of dominance.

Having taken the path of the irrational, the anti-intellectual, and the mystical, Weill arrives at a natural conclusion: that neurosis and psychosis are positive forms of directly experiencing reality. Weill writes: "I am almost tempted to call psychotics the evolutionary vanguard of our species. They possess the secret of changing reality by changing the mind; if they can learn to use that talent for positive ends, there are no limits to what they can accomplish."[44] One is tempted to say that Weill leaves no stone unturned in his effort to champion stoned thinking.

Perhaps a critique of Weill should simply state that Weill was "stoned" when he wrote his book. More seriously, Weill's entire approach is subjective and incorrect psychologically. Although so-called straight thinking has often been distorted in our society—forced into a mold and saturated with false ideas—all human advance has been based upon the results of straight thinking: science, technology, culture, decent human relationships, and positive social change are the results of reason supported and moved forward by positive human emotion.

The social logic of Weill's theory is expressed in his proud claim that stoned thinking can accept the ambivalent nature of things, e.g., good and evil.[45] The real essence of stoned thinking is that it turns away from the real world, its problems and its necessary struggles and focuses on the fringe areas of consciousness such as trances or intuition.

Weill titled Part I of his *The Natural Mind,* "Through the Looking Glass." We must agree with him for he has led us through a wonderland of stoned thinking which can only result in the continued existence of the hard social reality of capitalist U.S.A.

Consciousness III—The Greening of America

Sweeping like wildfire through the high schools and the campuses, Charles Reich's *The Greening of America*[46] proclaimed, in trumpetlike fashion, the discovery of *Consciousness III.* "The extraordinary thing about this new consciousness," says Reich in the last two pages of his book, "is that it has emerged out of the Corporate State, like flowers pushing up through the concrete pavement. Whatever it touches it beautifies and renews. . . . For one almost convinced that it was necessary to accept ugliness and evil, that it was necessary to be a miser of dreams, it is an invitation to cry or laugh. For one who thought the world was irretrievably encased in metal and plastic and sterile stone, it seems a veritable greening of America."[47]

What new world does Reich promise and what is this splendid *Consciousness III?* Reich opens his book with these powerful words: "America is dealing death, not only to people in other lands, but to its own people. So say the most thoughtful and passionate of our youth, from California to Connecticut."[48] He then slashingly describes what he terms "the present American crisis." It is made up of "disorder, corruption and war"; it includes "poverty, distorted priorities, and law-making by private power"; there is "uncontrolled technology and the destruction of the environment"; we see a "decline of democracy and liberty . . . the artificiality of work and culture . . . absence of community . . . powerlessness. . . . all of the forms of impoverishment that can be seen or felt in America, loss of self."[49]

Given a crisis of such magnitude (and Reich is absolutely correct in his description), he sees "the coming American revolution." And this revolution will be made by *Consciousness III*, which has been produced by that very crisis.

Consciousness I was the nineteenth century outlook of the American farmer, the small businessman, and the worker trying to get ahead. *Consciousness II* developed in "an America where organization predominates," where individuality is sacrificed, where "the state, laws, technology, manufactured goods constitute the true reality."[50]

Rejecting Consciousness I and Consciousness II, Consciousness III bases itself upon liberation: "the individual frees himself from automatic acceptance of the imperatives of society and the false consciousness which society imposes."[51] And what are the elements of Consciousness III? First, it postulates "the absolute worth of every human being." It sees the world as a community—"people are brothers." Consciousness III starts with the self. It is "deeply suspicious of logic, rationality, analysis, principles." It believes that thought can be spontaneous and disconnected. It declares experience "to be the most precious of all commodities."

To restore sensitivity and awareness of forgotten sensations, the Consciousness III person "burns incense in his home to restore the sense of smell." He attends "a T-group or sensitivity group" and participates in "touching other people's bodies." Further, "he might cultivate visual sensitivity, and the ability to meditate, by staring for hours at a globe lamp." Reich states: "One of the most important means for restoring dulled consciousness is psychedelic drugs."[52]

Starting with a valid and slashing attack on U.S. society, Reich and his Consciousness III have ended up with the individual self and experience as the true reality. Through a long and rather tortured road, punctuated with flashes of brilliance and perception, Reich has brought us to sensitivity training and encounter groups, sensory awareness, meditation, feeling and touching, and psychedelic drugs. He has assaulted reason and logic. He verges on the mystical in his attribution of intuitive knowledge to the Consciousness III person. Consciousness III ends up to be the sum total of all the forms of altered consciousness which have been examined in this chapter and found wanting.

But Consciousness III cannot be put aside without mentioning its road to revolution. On page 2, Reich proclaims: "There is a revolution coming. It will not be like the revolutions of the past. It will originate with the individual and with culture, and it will change the political structure only as its final act."

On page 327, Reich discloses to us the secret of such a revolution: "Revolution must be cultural. For culture controls the economic and political machine, not vice versa. . . . Consciousness is capable of changing and destroying the Corporate State, without violence, without seizure of political power, without overthrow of any existing group of people. . . . It is only by change of individual lives that we can seize power from the state."

Monopoly may rest easy on its corporate throne—it has nothing to fear from Consciousness III.

The Road to Real Altered Consciousness

The anguish of many young people today is real. It is heartbreaking. Correctly rejecting "The Greed Machine"—The Great Hamburger Grinder, as they call it—they grope for alternative realities which can have meaning, pleasure, purpose, and love. Alienated and feeling powerless, they declare a moratorium on participation in Establishment society and culture.

Some turn to communes as the form of life style for the future. Seeking to escape the Establishment culture and get "back to the earth," they form communes to work together with others who care and who can love one another.

But most communes have a history of failure; the average life is one to two years. Communes generally merge all the negative features of sensitivity training and encounter groups with the altered states of consciousness of psychedelic drugs, transcendental meditation, and mysticism. Further, as Melville points out, "Compared to the ecstatic vision of collective unity, the day-to-day reality of communal life in most groups is marked by such oppressively normal traits as transient affections and apathetic do-your-own-thingism."[53] What starts out as anti-Establishment communes usually ends up in political disengagement, subjectivism, escapism and group sex.

The psychological effects of the various forms of altered consciousness are basically unhealthy. These forms center on either sensory changes of a temporary character or mystical and antirational activities. There is also often a turning to sexuality and homosexuality as a countercultural action. Perhaps most harmful is the turning inward, the turning away from social reality. Abbie Hoffman, the self-proclaimed revolutionary, expresses this most clearly: "One learns reality is a subjective experience. It exists in my head. I am the Revolution."[54]

What changes in social reality have occurred as a result of this turning to altering consciousness in the ways described? None. In fact, these various movements have served the Establishment most effectively in *preventing* social changes—for many of these young people are the very ones who participated splendidly in the civil rights struggles of the sixties and the giant antiwar demonstrations of historic significance.

There are various states of consciousness known to science. Waking, sleeping and hypnosis are three such states of consciousness which are explained by the specific functioning of neurological inhibition in the nervous system. Certain psychotic states also result in serious altering of consciousness. There are also undoubtedly intermediate states such as mere relaxation, as achieved in Transcendental Meditation, or in ordinary states of daydreaming.

But the normal waking state of consciousness is the most basic and important state of consciousness for people. It is this state of consciousness that has enabled us to discover the laws of reality—natural and social—and to utilize them for human benefit. It is precisely reason and knowledge which have resulted in such tremendous technological, human, and social changes. In the "Age of Reason," the great Encyclopedist Denis Diderot fought against the Church's demand that religion must be accepted on faith and that reason must be abandoned; he refused to blow out "my lantern, my sole torch, this feeble candle-end, this poor little reason. . . ."[55]

But it is not reason alone which functions to advance humanity. Reason and knowledge single out tasks to be performed, goals to be achieved, whether political or technological. To perform such tasks and achieve such goals, emotional involvement, commonality of effort, discipline, and organization are necessary. Finally, action and success are necessary in this whole process of thought-into-successful-action.

We must not "empty the mind." We must fill it with knowledge and corresponding feeling. We must not turn away from social reality and into ourselves. We must seek to understand that reality and work collectively with others to change that reality. Expansion of consciousness—the true altering of consciousness—consists of the expansion of knowledge, the enlargement of experience, the working together with others, the experiencing of feelings of companionship, mutual support, and collective activity for common, socially positive goals. Such expansion of consciousness leads to confidence, the development of character and personality, and the setting of goals and purpose to life. It leads to true altered consciousness.

5

Sensitivity Training, Encounter Groups And Est

By now millions of Americans have touched, walked and talked their way through some type of encounter session. Encounter is a loose term for a variety of group techniques, such as T-groups, sensitivity training, sensory awareness, Synanon, psychodrama, gestalt therapy and others that are used as a means of personal growth for ostensibly healthy persons." So writes Robert Reinhold about the Encounter Movement.[1]

A movement of such wide scope, with such a variety of forms and techniques, which promises so desirable a result as "personal growth," and which has involved millions of people, deserves serious consideration and evaluation.

Promised Goals of Encounter

The goals of encounter groups, says Dr. Frederick H. Stoller of the University of Southern California, are "growth and change, new behavioral directions, the realization of potential, heightened self-awareness, and a richer perception of one's circumstances as well as the circumstances of others . . . "[2]

An ad in *The New York Times* announced a conference in New York City under the title "Esalen and N.Y.U." at which participants would "explore the latest dimensions and techniques for redirecting human energies towards greater personal growth."[3]

Aureon, one of the Human Potential centers which mushroomed with the spread of the Encounter Movement, states that its aim is "to maximize man's inherent resources for living life to the fullest." As an added incentive, it promises that "clients may choose from the tasty mental delights of the Aureon 'psychomat.'"[4]

Here, indeed, is offered a most appealing psychological repast, with mental well-being and enriched personal functioning to follow its psychic digestion.

Why did such a promising movement arise and take hold with such vigor and sweep?

Why Encounter?

In an article entitled "Sensitivity Training: Fad, Fraud, or New Frontier?", Ted J. Rakstis writes: "During a time when Americans are torn with conflict and beset by fear, loneliness, and alienation, many are searching for something of meaning."[5] "Loneliness, confusion, and alienation haunt T-groups and therapy groups alike," says researcher Irving Yalom.[6]

The past two decades have witnessed increasingly profound crises in our country. The alienation normally produced by capitalist society has been intensified by mounting uncertainty and social turmoil. Tens of millions of people have been shaken and deeply affected by the Vietnam War, punitive inflation, economic crisis, income-crushing taxation, and Watergate. People have been jolted out of their normal social moorings.

But beyond alienation, and counteracting it, massive struggles have taken place against racism, against poverty and shrinking wages, and against the incredibly immoral Vietnam War. Millions of our people, particularly the young, the Black, and the other minorities, have rejected the Establishment and its values. New searchings have taken place for better ways of communicating, relating, living and behaving. "Who am I? How shall I live? What values should I adopt? How can I grow and fulfill myself?" are among the questions being asked.

Seeking solutions, many joined and continue to participate in movements for social progress. Others, for various psychological and social reasons, turned to ultraleftist groups, to communes, to hallucinogenic drugs. Still others turned to psychotherapy—but, as Dr. Hendrik Ruitenbeek puts it, "the established individual and group therapies simply are not working for a significant number of patients."[7] Psychoanalysis has increasingly been found to be unsatisfactory by patients, while the newer Behavior Therapy is considered to be too cold and mechanical. The Human Potential movement has become the "third force" which many have embraced as an answer to their needs and problems.[8]

In a confused and confusing social-political situation, which wreaked emotional havoc with many people, the Encounter Movement emerged as the modern Nirvana, the therapeutic savior. For, as against the hypocrisy and evil of a lying, genocidal government, it offered honesty, open communication, and love. Instead of death or crippling in Vietnam or a dead-end job with no personal purpose or direction, encounter promised joy, spontaneity, growth of sensitivity, and a new dimension in social living.

Who could resist such a movement? It swept into schools, industry, government, and institutions. Hundreds of thousands partook of its offerings. What were they given? How does encounter work?

Encounter at Work—and Play

The Encounter Movement includes within it sensitivity training groups and various forms of encounter groups. Sensitivity training was developed by the impressively named National Training Laboratories at Bethel, Maine, based partly on the work of psychologist Kurt Lewin.

The T-group (training group) is the heart of sensitivity training. It is usually made up of ten to fifteen members with a "trainer," who usually opens the first session by pointing out "that the T-group's primary task is to create learning opportunities for its members, and that it has no formal leader, preset agenda, or rules by which it must operate."[9] The group is instructed, however, that it must "try to learn from its *own* experienced behavior—the 'here-and-now' situation—rather than to discuss problems outside the group, from the world they left—the 'there-and-then' world."[10]

Encounter groups include many other forms, ranging from sensory awareness, confrontation and Gestalt Therapy to nude encounters, bioenergetics, Rolfing and feeling-and-touching. Sensitivity training and encounter have tended to merge in their approaches. More recently, they have begun to incorporate forms of meditation and altered consciousness.

Describing the Encounter Movement, Robert Rheinhold says: "Encounter methods vary widely, but the group typically consists of eight to 18 persons led by a 'facilitator.' The members are urged to express their emotions toward one another openly, both physically and verbally. Mutual trust, openness, honesty and naturalness are the watchwords, and the assumption is that this stripping away of psychological defenses is healthy and will enhance both interpersonal relationships and self-awareness."[11]

The main center in the development of the Encounter Movement has been Esalen, in Big Sur, California—"Esalen is the rock on which the Church of the Encounter was built," writes Bruce Maliver. At Esalen every variety and form of encounter has been tried by tens of thousands of people, while hundreds of trainers and facilitators have branched out from Esalen to carry "The Word" to the farthest reaches of the United States. What are the major features of encounter and how are they put into practice?

"The Gospel According to Esalen"[12]

"The message given to all seekers (mainly middle class)," writes Hendrik Ruitenbeek, "who attend Esalen, gurus, massage centers, marathons, 'feel' groups, 'movement' groups, truth laboratories, and the like, is that they should live in the now."[13]

The here-and-now is fundamental to the Encounter Movement. Past experiences, personal background, social relationships, work history—all are excluded from encounter groups. Fritz Perls, the father of Gestalt Therapy, and one of the foremost developers of the Encounter Movement, "concentrates on the experience of the moment... the voice, the glance, body sensations."[14] For him, says Rasa Gustaitis, "nothing exists except the now."[15]

Central to experiencing the "now" is to become sensorily aware. As Perls quips, "Lose your mind and come to your senses."[16]

Another encounter leader, Bernard Gunther, states: "Sensory Awakening is de-hypnosis, a way out of rigid rules, feelings, thoughts, constrictions . . . (you must) focus consciousness on direct sensory experience in the here and now."[17]

Every means and method of stimulating the senses is used. In one encounter group it was suggested that the participants "bring with them things that they enjoyed smelling the most, tasting the most, touching the most, and hearing the most . . . as sensory stimulation in a sensory saturation experience, which would induce some kind of peak experience . . . "[18]

For encounter, a "peak experience" is the most sought after experience: it is that height of emotionality approaching ecstasy; it is "blowing your mind!"

For many groups, the body becomes the focal point for experience. Paul Bindrim, the leading exponent of nude marathons, maintains that "these excursions into nudity seem to increase interpersonal transparency, remove inhibitions in the area of physical contact, decrease the sense of personal isolation and estrangement, and culminate in a feeling of freedom and belongingness."[19] Bindrim has proposed the construction of a humanitarium, in which nude people may be seen without distortion, similar to an aquarium where nude fish may be seen.[20]

Bioenergetics is another body-centered encounter theory and practice. Its main propagator is Dr. Alexander Lowen who, building on the work of Wilhelm Reich, maintains that each person's body has an energy field which must "flow in a figure eight if it is to function well."[21] Lowen's basic principle reads: "We have no real existence apart from our bodies. What goes on in our minds is, basically, a reflection of what goes on in our bodies."[22]

Another encounter bodyist is Dr. Ida Rolf, who has developed *Rolfing,* a series of deep and often painful massages of all the major muscle groups, including the face and mouth. These massages, she claims, can cause the return of experiences that were repressed in childhood.[23] Dr. Rolf states that her subjects show "invariable improvement in attitudes, and sometimes quite basic change."[24]

Encounter groups are also based exclusively on feelings and emotions as opposed to intellect and reason. For Fritz Perls, the intellect "is a drag on your life."[25] Following his participation in an all-day workshop at Esalen, Bruce Maliver commented: "Intelligence, rationality and thoughtfulness turn out to be negative values in the encounter culture . . . (you must) get out of your head (and) say what your gut says."[26]

Daniel Casriel, head of the Casriel Institute for Group Dynamics, teaches members of his groups "to grab hold of a feeling—any feeling—and express it in a series of yells, screams, and moans which increase in intensity to almost unbelievable volume."[27]

Complete and total honesty about one's emotions and one's reactions to others is not only expected but rigidly enforced in the encounter group. "Candid leveling" is required of everyone, according to encounterist George Bach, which means that participants must share their here-and-now reactions to one another—"tact is out and brutal frankness is in."[28]

Nonverbal communication and experiences are also vital to encounter practice. William Schutz, another leading encounterist, believes that "words are special culprits in the effort to avoid personal confrontation."[29] Heavy emphasis is placed upon body language (kinesics), "hidden agendas," real" meaning, and physical contact. Maliver reports "a period of touching—shaking hands, placing hand to a face, or one cheek to another, or hugging, or grasping each other's shoulders" at the all-day workshop at Esalen.[30]

The group is king at encounter. The group experience is held to be emotionally cleansing, psychologically inspiring, and therapeutically vital. Resistance to group pressure and to group reaction is assailed and denounced.

Although not proclaimed as an intrinsic part of the Human Potential Movement, sex hovers around encounter groups, is inevitably present in the feeling-touching activities, and is openly advocated as necessary by some encounter leaders such as William Schutz.[31] As Maliver puts it, "Many participants react to the promised 'intimacy' and 'peak experiences' of encounter groups as a sexual promise, remaining alert for sexual cues throughout their group experience, and often attempting to turn the public expression of feelings into personal sexual experience."[32]

Martin Shepard, the psychiatrist who openly calls for sex with patients, has written that, under the encounter banner, he has experienced every one of his sexual fantasies, from performing fellatio, to watching his wife copulate with another man, to group sex.[33]

One encounter leader, Raymond Orsini, puts it bluntly: "Encounter groups are a kind of refined orgy. Where else can a responsible man put his hands on a strange woman's bosom, cavort in the nude, and speak out his most lascivious thoughts? One encounter leader asks members of his groups to pair off and go into a separate room for fifteen minutes, during which time the two are to seek a deeper relationship. Shades of playing 'post office'!"[34]

Emotions and sensory awareness in the here-and-now with group members who touch and feel, use nonverbal communication and sexual activity or overtones, experience spontaneity, honesty, and body awareness, with nudity, body massage, and peak experiences— this is the picture presented by the Encounter Movement. Perhaps Rasa Gustaitis, whose book *Turning On* describes her participation in every variety, form and technique offered at Esalen, best expresses the extremes which encounter has reached: "Madness, promiscuity, all forms of eccentricity are part of the scene . . . Well-heeled weekend seekers from Los Angeles and San Francisco slip and flip, explode— freak out. . . . A mad scene is before me. People are flinging themselves about in time with the music, half-naked and covered from hair to toenails to every inch of their clothing in multicolored paints. They writhe, gyrate, roll around on the paint-covered floor. They're people from Perl's workshop."[35]

The Encounter Movement: A Critique

"I've done marathons. I've hugged and kissed, cried and fought. I've been the whole route, and I still think there's a lot wrong with Encounter."[36] That's how author Bruce Maliver sums up his thorough personal investigation of the Encounter Movement.

Encounter is one-sided and simplistic. In the complex and intricate process of human functioning—which includes sensations, perceptions, ideas, knowledge, experience, emotions, social relations, work, school attendance, problem solving, attitudes, physical activity, love relations, marriage and family, and political and social involvement— encounter selects either this or that feature and treats it in distorted and greatly exaggerated fashion.

Encounter is big on emotions—in fact, the unspoken motto of Esalen is said to be, "I hurt, therefore, I am." That most people are subjected to hurtful and emotionally trying experiences in our society is painfully true. But to center on raw, unanalyzed emotions, mainly of a negative character, as encounter does, and to expect that confrontation of such "pure" emotions will be therapeutic and psychologically cleansing is to pour emotional salt on psychic wounds. There is also an artificiality about the literal extraction of emotions from participants.

Judy Klemesrud reported in a *New York Times* article on an "Encounter Weekend" sponsored by the famous Concord Hotel in up-state New York, that while her group was busily working at "loving," their facilitator rushed up and cried: "Hurry up—you people are supposed to be doing anger now!"[37]

Further, encounter group members are programmed for "peak experiences" completely divorced from their real lives. They are also given the expectation of continually achieving such experiences—a manifestly Utopian and impossible goal.

Encounter, in its emphasis on sensory and body awareness, downgrades the higher forms of human functioning. One extreme proponent of "sensory saturation experience" is Charlotte Selver, who states: "We build upon sensations . . . the constant effort to perceive kills much of perception."[38] In scientific psychology, sensations are the raw materials of perception. Perceptions then lead to thought, reasoning, judgment, and conclusions, the qualitatively higher levels of human psychic functioning. Human behavior is the result of this dynamic complexity of psychological activity. To remain at the levels of sheer sensation or raw perception, as Selver and other encounterists propose, is to push us back towards infantile responses. Certainly, the enjoyment of colors, tastes, sunsets, smells and touch is one pleasurable aspect of human living. It should not be made the be-all and end-all of human responses.

The body encounterists, such as Alexander Lowen, similarly make awareness of the body the apex of human experience. Again, a sense of physical well-being and body vitality is both healthy and mentally valuable. But to bioenergize, to Rolf, and to get body energy flowing in "figure eights" is to mystify ordinary physical activity for the maintenance of physical health. Like most encounter techniques, body awareness unwittingly satirizes itself. At a microlab led by William Schutz, 200 psychologists were instructed to close their eyes and take a mental trip through their own bodies; the reports by the psychologists included "an intriguing array of fantasies: being caught in the blood vessels, being stuck behind the eyeballs; being digested and ground to feces in the lower intestines."[39]

What personal growth or "actualization of potential" can we say occurred for Rasa Gustaitis when she sums up her varied experiences at Esalen as follows: "So I'm home again now, freaked and flipped, zonked and tripped out, rolfed and massaged a little way into the turned on existence."[40] Her psychological survival alone might be termed a minor miracle.

Encounterology, to coin a term, concentrates exclusively on the here-and-now. Philosophically, this is a throwback to David Hume and solipsism (the self alone), that all I can know is the immediate sensations I have at the present moment. Encounter groups are barred from dealing with the most valuable ingredients of real human interaction by such an approach. The dictum of Friz Perls—"The past is no more, the future is not yet."[41]—actually stands human communication on its head: we communicate in the present about the past to cope with the future. In any case, the exclusion of the richness of past relationships, experiences, knowledge, memories, along with a ban on discussion of future activity, trivializes and emaciates true human intercourse.

Perhaps the most glaringly unscientific and harmful feature of encounter is its anti-intellectual, antirational attitude. Psychologist Rollo May chastized the Association for Humanistic Psychology in an open letter, stating that its tendency "has been an anti-intellectual one and we have tended to leave out thinking, reflecting, historical man, and put in only the feeling, touching man in the 'now'."[42]

Human consciousness is dominantly an ideational one—we distinguish ourselves from animals by our thought processes based upon human language. To paraphrase Descartes: "We are, therefore, we think, therefore, we cope." It is rational thought applied to individual and collective problems which is basic to human functioning. In the revulsion at overintellectualizing, at being deceived by ideas in a crass society, at the corruption of science for racism and war, the anti-intellectual backlash throws out the intellectual baby with the polluted bath water. Of course, emotions play a crucial role in psychic activity. But their most important role is not in separation from the intellect but in their mutual functioning for more effective thought and behavior.

Encounter has no coherent theory—or, rather, it is a grab bag of old theories, patches and shreds of theories spun out of the fantasies of encounter leaders. For example, the theory behind the marathon encounter (a 24-hour or 48-hour continuous encounter session) is that fatigue will cause a breakdown or lowering of psychological and emotional defenses so as to reveal the real person. The concept of "the real person" underneath layers of emotional camouflage is unsound.

The real person is the entire person in all his or her consciousness and behavior—fatigue only makes the person behave in a fatigued way, not in a psychologically revealing way.

Many encounterists believe that psychosis is not abnormal—that it might contribute to the process of human growth. The American Psychiatric Association, reporting that most mental health professionals consider psychosis a harmful mental illness, disposed of this unscientific theory in these words: "A psychosis is a manifestation of illness, not a way to health and maturity."[43]

Encounter also incorrectly ascribes therapeutic magic to the group. The group supposedly provides valid analysis of each member, improves communication, creates love and togetherness, offers peak experiences, and is the basis for leaps in personal growth. What the encounter group usually does, as one critic puts it, is to provide "mutual analysis of quick impressions."[44] The unstructured group, with no common tasks or goals in real life, whose members are usually strangers to each other, mainly emitting raw and negative feelings, and dealing solely with immediate happenings, cannot be therapeutically viable.

Since encounter has no scientific theory as its foundation, and since its practice is based upon psychologically distorted or simplistic techniques, any benefit or growth is both limited and accidental. Also, any positive change is usually brief and transient, since it is scientifically utopian to expect basic changes to occur in such emotion-centered, subjective, sensory-oriented, confrontatory, time-limited encounter sessions.

But, for many, encounter is not just ineffective—it is damaging. Very few scientifically acceptable studies have been carried out—this is typical of encounter's hit-or-miss approach. One acceptable study by Lieberman, Yalom and Miles at Stanford University found that, of 210 students who participated in various encounter groups, only one-third benefited, while two-thirds had negative experiences or dropped out. Even more alarming was the 10 percent casualty rate ("a person more psychologically distressed eight months after the group than before.").[45]

The methods used in encounter groups logically explain such psychological casualties. The leader is usually lacking in professional training. Each group member is usually put on the emotional "hot seat" and often subjected to searing criticism ("too rigid . . . can't communicate . . . defensive . . . phony . . . too intellectual . . . a castrator.")

Encounter abuses the basic principles of psychotherapy: the need for a diagnosis, a trained therapist, a case history, a treatment plan specific to the patient, continuation of treatment till no longer needed, and responsibility by the therapist for the results of the therapy.

The principles of healthy social relationships are also violated by encounter, with its infusion of sex, its feely-touchy therapy (also known as "group grope"), its enforced togetherness, its exclusion of the person's entire life except the here-and-now, and its anti-intellectual attitude.

Although many turn to encounter as a form of inexpensive therapy, encounter sessions are costly: the fee for a weekend marathon session is $100-$150. Shorter encounter sessions also cost in the range of other therapy forms, such as psychoanalysis or Behavior Therapy.

It must be concluded that the Encounter Movement violates the major principles of scientific psychology and psychiatry. It offers facile, instant solutions to complex human problems. It offers a "cafeteria of emotional experiences" which supposedly will solve problems, but it fails to provide the means to digest these experiences. Encounter is essentially hedonism—the Quest-for-Zest—run rampant.

Professor Sigmund Koch has characterized encounter as providing a convenient place "for the purchase of a gamut of well-advertised existential 'goodies': authenticity, freedom, wholeness, flexibility, community, love, joy. One enters for such liberating consummation but settles for psychic strip tease."[46] Even a relatively sympathetic professional, Arthur Burton, says: "(Encounter) falls all over itself with the baubles and bangles of meditation, introspection, lowering sensory thresholds, orgiastic response, physical exercise, fantasy experience, touching, nudity, and other manifestations of preciousness."[47]

Encounter's promises have melted away like snow in a New York City heat wave. Instead of personality enrichment, emotional growth, and psychic development, it has provided a psychological catch-as-catch-can, an unhealthy stew of temporary thrills, distorted perceptions, unrealizable goals, and psychic traumas.

The Social Role of Encounter

Encounter has been proclaimed to be revolutionary, a new way to bring about social change through personal change. Encounter leaders speak of "radical therapy," "alternate living styles," and "new value systems." But what encounterists use as slogans and what they achieve in practice are at opposite poles.

Far from rejecting the status quo, sensitivity training has actively wooed and bedded down with Big Business. The National Training Laboratories, chief proponent of sensitivity training, has had lucrative contracts with some of the largest corporations: ITT, General Electric, IBM, Humble Oil, AT & T, Xerox, and Honeywell. The aim of such training of company executives has been "to humanize and democratize industry." There is something lunatic about the concept of humanizing and democratizing ITT, which manipulated the overthrow of the democratically elected government of Chile. How does one "humanize" inflation, speedup, racism, Watergate, and billions in profits—all products of these huge corporations?

Of course, the real reason that Big Business turned to sensitivity training is clearly put by two observers of the encounter scene. Bruce Maliver states simply: "Sensitivity training seems to have been taken up by business largely because it provided executives with a deeper commitment to the profit motive."[48] Psychologist Magda Denes says that half of the interest of industry in sensitivity training "came from what it delivered: the technical adjustment of personnel into more smoothly functioning cogs."[49]

Millions in tax dollars have been spent by the federal government on sensitivity training. One need not be a political genius to conclude that our monopoly-dominated government would scarcely permit federal employees to participate in anything remotely threatening to the Establishment.

Encounter ideology and practices have been an extremely harmful influence on many young peace activists. When Esalen staged three-day exhibitions in New York City in 1970 and 1971, the participants were "almost entirely white, primarily young . . . peace signs and long hair was everywhere."[50] Rasa Gustaitis describes what happened to such young people "who, under other circumstances, might have become political leaders."[51] She writes, "They turned their energies to themselves and their immediate surroundings. Travelers on the turn-on circuit tend to be apolitical but interested in social experiments such as communes, tribal and extended families. They talk a lot about building world peace through the search for personal peace."[52]

The subjectivity, hedonism, hyperemotionality, and social vacuumlike nature of encounter are effective in turning people away from real social action. One encounter critic, Bernard Rosenthal, states that it provides "an escape or diversion from the authentic humanistic challenge of the day-to-day world—the true area of depersonalization and alienation—by allowing its practitioners to get their humanistic fulfillment in those weekends or seminars ... "[53] Fritz Perls works deliberately to create in encounter members an attitude of passive acceptance of social reality because, he says, "a man who knows how to live without expectation will be able to accept whatever the moment brings him without disappointment."[54]

The Black liberation struggles have also been harmed by the encounter thrust. Sensitivity training has been used by city police departments (e.g., Houston) to bring "harmony" between the police and the Black community. The confrontation methods of sensitivity training often increase racism. One example was reported in a *New York Times* article headed "Police Encounter Sessions Here Strive to Achieve Racial Amity." One white police officer was quoted as saying: "This open hostility can only make matters worse." Further, "A white policeman said that the more he attended the sessions the more he disliked the Blacks for what he termed their 'adamant attitudes.'"[55]

Even more crudely racist is the fact that a special form of encounter has been developed for drug addicts. This form is used in Synanon programs: it is a type of psychological karate which aims at humiliating, degrading, and emotionally mashing the addict. Bruce Maliver points out that unlike the usual encounter form, the Synanon-type program "is fitted to his usually lower-class background and the likelihood that he will be black or Puerto Rican."[56]

Encounter, thus, incorporates many harmful political features: escapism, passivity, subjectivism, irrationalism, racism, and sexism. Perhaps climaxing the social role of encounter is the proposal made by William Schutz: an encounter group between American and Soviet political leaders![57]

The penetration of the encounter ideology into wide sections of the youth and the middle class has been harmful. It has also made inroads into the labor movement, the Black liberation movement, and especially in the women's liberation movement. The Encounter Movement runs counter to the needs of these movements and to the social and political struggles of the people.

Marxism and Personal Growth

Marxism is humanism. It has as its goal the fullest development of human potential. Socialism, which is Marxism in actual social practice, seeks the maximum growth of the emotional, intellectual, and physical areas of human functioning. It seeks to develop the most positive and healthiest social relationships through the elimination of racism, sexism, elitism and class distinctions. It expects and allows for diversity in personality, interests, skills, and talents, while striving to limit or nullify negative, antihuman, and egocentric traits.

But Marxists are dialectical materialists. They recognize that revolutionary social change is a complex, long-range, protracted process, with mistakes, problems and difficulties arising in the course of such a massive transformation. Socialism inherits the negative personal features molded under capitalism. These require time, energy, skill, and mass effort to eradicate.

Marxism cannot accept the glib, facile, and simplistic answers offered by encounter to complex problems of personality, emotional life, and social relationships.

William Schutz, in describing a typical week for an encounter group, says that "joy comes about noon Thursday."[58] On May Day, 1973, I saw joy expressed by hundreds of thousands of Cubans in the Plaza de la Revolucion in Havana, Cuba. This was a joy derived from common social achievement, from joint "building of our Revolution," from socialist human relations.

No, not encounter—but real comradely relations, with vital, life-related emotions, with liberating thoughts flowing from the work of economic and political liberation. Such is the path and the essence of fundamental and real personal growth.

Est (Erhard Seminar Training)

Werner Erhard was cruising down a California freeway in the Fall of 1971 when suddenly he GOT IT! "To relate what I experienced at the time," recalls Erhard, "is a true lie. . . . There were no words attached to it. No feelings, no attitudes, no body sensations." What he GOT was "an experience of the world as it is without the intercession of the human understanding." This "life-transforming experience" was so dramatic that Erhard started est "to share the experience with others."[59]

Since that transcendental, semi-mystical flash of "Getting It" in 1971, est (Erhard Seminar Training) attained widespread popularity. By 1977, 83,000 people had gone through the est experience, each paying $250 for the two weekends of training. There had sprung up est centers in a dozen cities. In 1975, est grossed 9.3 million dollars.[60] By April, 1979, there were 21,000 est graduates in New York City alone.[61]

What is est? What are its techniques and does it benefit people?

The aim of est is for the trainees to "Get It," like Werner Erhard did. Toward that end, Erhard has developed a structured, precise, and rigid course of training. After registering and paying the fee—it is now $350—the trainees are put through a total of 60 hours of training, consisting of four 15-hour days over two consecutive weekends. Training takes place in groups of up to 250 trainees with one trainer.

Describing the procedure, New York City est manager, Heidi Sparkes, stated: "There are certain basic rules. The training starts on time. There are no watches permitted in the room. The training goes on until late at night. The assistants don't smile, or they all smile like zombies. One of the things that works about the training is that it is run with very specific guide lines that everybody is clear about."[62] In his article entitled "We're Gonna Tear You Down and Put You Together Again," Mark Brewer wrote that "no one would move, talk, smoke, eat, or take notes, and no one would leave the room at any time . . . Nor, during the nine-day period of training, would anyone partake of alcohol, narcotics or prescription drugs."[63]

Leo Litwak, in his *New York Times* article "Pay Attention, Turkeys!",[64] described the est training session he attended for 250 trainees, conducted by Erhard himself. It was held in a convention meeting room of a San Francisco hotel and began exactly at 8:30 a.m. After an assistant trainer "barked out the ground rules of the training," Erhard read the est statement of purpose—"vague, awkward prose about transforming your ability to experience living." Erhard then spent the next several hours in denouncing and insulting the trainees, calling them "turkeys" and "assholes" whose "life wasn't worth shit."

Erhard, after this relentless and scathing tirade, began to convey one of est's basic messages: That there are no "good" or "bad" experiences—it is the mind that imposes judgment on a neutral world. The experiences we have are our own and individual responsibility. We sacrifice our lives blaming others: THEY caused the war. THEY ruined our childhood. THEY destroyed our chances of happiness. The fact is that there's nothing out there—no one cares. We each make our own lives. Finally, and dramatically, Erhard announces est's major message: "What is, is. And you must accept it!" Erhard emphasizes this point by stating that est in French is the word for "is".

The two weekends include long hours of "directed meditation exercises," lectures, continual confrontation, and constant put-downs of the trainees. Brewer summarizes the training: "It takes nearly 70 hours to get most or all of the trainees converted, and that time is filled with a variety of techniques and processes designed to alternately confuse and enlighten the subjects, to develop the authority of the trainer and build his suggestive power over the hapless 'assholes' . . . the training is a masterful amalgam of conscious-altering techniques."[65]

Getting it, for Erhard, consists of the trainee accepting a number of major principles. First, the trainee must absorb that "I am the cause of my own world."[66] Second, the trainees must abandon reason and discard their whole "belief system and dislodge the old ideas and behavior patterns." Erhard has drawn up "the est chart of thought . . . a table of mental processes delineating all conceivable mental functions, divided into realms of experience and non-experience. Belief, reason, logic and understanding were shown to be non-experiential, and these second-hand mental exercises had to be abandoned to get at the meat of life."[67]

Flowing from this chart is the idea that only experience is real and that the trainees must concentrate on the "here-and-now." Finally, the trainee must "Get IT", which Erhard says "is the awareness that you are and that the only way to be happy is to do what you are doing . . . for you are perfect the way you are."[68]

Articles and books published about est testify to the conversion of the majority of trainees, with up to four-fifths claiming benefit from it. A large number of trainees continue in postgraduate training sessions and many become active proselyters for est. Indeed, many psychiatrists and other therapists have taken est training and recommend it to their patients. Marsh reports on an est course for "an invited group of 250 leaders in psychiatry, education, law, science, aviation and the human potential movement" who, "when the ordeal was over, gave Werner Erhard a standing ovation."[69]

So what is wrong with est?

Criticisms Levelled at Est

Critics of est have leveled a number of sharp barbs. One target is Erhard's abandonment of his wife and four children in 1960 and changing his name from Jack Rosenberg in order to avoid detection. Erhard has also used the aliases of Von Savage and Jack Frost. Another target has been his lack of professional credentials—in fact, Erhard only completed high school. Further, immediately preceding his initiation of est, Erhard spent ten years as a salesman of encyclopedias, Great Books, and a course in Mind Dynamics.

Est is also called a big rip-off aimed at enriching Erhard: his big home, with a chef, chauffeur, and valet, plus a limousine, a Mercedes car, and a rented Cessna plane give credence to this criticism. When it was charged that est is "the ultimate con in consciousness," Erhard proudly admitted the imputation.[70] Campbell found that est was "obsessed with public relations and jargon, with packaging and marketing, even with its leader's clothes and coiffure."[71]

Litwak, after interviewing Erhard and attending the est course, found him to be "taunting, pedantic and loud . . . (and) with his Hollywood handsomeness, charm and nerve, he looks like someone I should keep my eye on. He goes all out for what he wants. My inclination was to close my heart and guard my pockets."[72]

Another biting commentary on est is that it is banal, trivial and overwhelmingly obvious. Vivian Gornick, reviewing several books on est for the *New York Times* wrote: "My favorite Erhard quote is: 'I will now tell you The Truth About Life: What Is Is, What Isn't Isn't.' I tell you: not only is the emperor not wearing any clothes, the emperor himself is invisible."[73]

More substantive is the criticism that the est Establishment is totalitarian: all men trainees dress exactly like Erhard; the assistants give "zombie-like attention to duty and unfailing admiration of Werner."[74] Est has been compared to the Rev. Sun Moon's organization, with its rigid hierarchy and its "moonies." Some critics have called est "psychedelic fascism."[75]

Gornick correctly situates est within the following dynamic: "every two or three years during the past decade and a half we have been inundated by the noisily announced presence of a 'new' system of therapy, a 'new' technique for gaining spiritual and emotional wisdom, a 'new' method that promises to 'put us in touch' with our very own selves and deliver us from the nearly monumental sense of loneliness and isolation from which the American middle-class suffers. Each one of these therapies and spiritual systems comes complete with a prophet-teacher and an amalgamated variant on the psychoanalytic, Eastern-wisdom, self-realization jargon; each one of them—with amazing rapidity—develops an 'institute' or an organizational structure through which the converts and the profits are shuffled with the expert efficiency of the shrewd American businessman who says to himself 'They're buying today, but tomorrow, who knows?'"[76]

Although one's skepticism of est is sharpened by these criticisms, there are fundamental philosophical, scientific, therapeutic, and socio-political grounds for rejecting est.

Marxist Critique of Est

Est is founded on a clearly subjective idealist philosophy, i.e., it denies and rejects the objective real world and accepts only subjective experience. Richard Marsh, a defender of est, stated this openly when he described his conversion to est: "I 'got' that I am the cause of my world and not its effect and am therefore responsible for it. This world I love and hate is my creation and my responsibility."[77] This is open solipsism: only the self exists and creates its own world. In fact, est is the very extreme of subjective idealism, i.e. solipsism of the immediate moment—Erhard calls for "the free and autonomous individual living in the present."[78]

Est is both subjective and individualistic: it exhorts people to take responsibility for their own lives. It eschews collective activity, mutual support and organized struggle. The individual is made asocial, in fact, antisocial, since the individual is alone and psychologically naked. "Many people are seeking the naked self in hotel ballrooms," says Campbell, "and paying money for it."[79]

Not content with stripping the objective world from the individual, est also robs the trainees of their main instruments for coping with problems; reason, belief, logic, and understanding. The entire Age of Reason is repudiated by est, leaving only raw unanalyzed experience. Certainly, without reason and understanding people cannot cope with individual problems, much less with social problems.

Passivity is also the necessary outcome of est. Indeed, Brewer refers to some est graduates who, "consumed by the notion that their mind is not only a machine but a perfect machine, act like robots."[80] How else should one act when told that the world is perfect as it is and you are doing exactly what you should be doing? We are thrown back by est to Leibniz's "best of all possible worlds". This is the perfect excuse for non-action, for passive acceptance of whatever is—because it is.

Est dehumanizes people through its planned ridicule, humiliation, and insults. The tension and anxiety created during est sessions has led to frequent breakdowns. Reports of a number of psychoses following est sessions "prompted three psychiatrists to alert their profession to the possibility that the experience may have devastating effects on some people."[81]

Est is a grab-bag of various other popular "help-yourself" fads. Erhard is, indeed a skilfull salesman of his own brand of consciousness alteration, which he culled from other sources. Litwak reports that, shortly before he developed est, Erhard was avidly studying and practicing "Subud, Scientology, Gestalt, encounter, Rogerian nondirective counseling, Yoga, Zen and Mind Dynamics."[82]

Est has been validly assailed as using classic techniques of indoctrination: long periods of discomfort, monotony and fatigue, assault on belief-systems and behavior patterns, stripping the individual of defences, mockery, authoritarian form and substance, and sobbing, swooning, bawling, writhing on the floor, etc., which "one timid man called 'The Sunday Night Massacre.'"[83]

Even for those who claim to have been greatly benefited by est, we must question such "help." If they have fully accepted Erhard's message, what will it do to their lives? Might it not lead to robot-like behavior or extreme individualism and self-centeredness? Will they not cope less adequately without their beliefs and reason and be left to operate on pure experience? However, est rarely has such serious or permanent effects.

The benefits the trainees claim to have received are of a placebo-like character: they expected to be helped, they paid to be helped, they went through a bizarre experience, they therefore feel they were helped. But the effect is generally transient and impermanent. For how can four days of training undo the consciousness, belief system, behavior, and attitudes of a lifetime? The impermanence of the effects of popular fads like est is attested to unconsciously by Jerry Rubin in his book, *Growing Up at 37.* "In five years, from 1971 to 1975, I directly experienced est, gestalt therapy, bioenergetics, rolfing, massage, jogging, health foods, tai chi, Esalen, hynotism, modern dance, meditation, Silva Mind Control, Arica, acupuncture, sex therapy, Reichian therapy, and More House—a smorgasbord course in New Consciousness."[84] And has Jerry Rubin grown up yet?

The most disturbing effects of est, however, are social and political. While it is true that the overwhelming number of est trainees are middle class and white, its ideas are popularized and seep into the thinking of working people and of young people. The thousands of unpaid est volunteers are in their twenties. Applied to Black people, est is a formula for the acceptance of racism, for the abandonment of social struggles and for the turning inward on the self.

The bottom line of est is that a dedicated capitalist could not improve on Erhard's scenario for producing a docile, non-resisting, contented mass of working people: you are responsible for the world, but it is a perfect world and "the only way to be happy is to do what you're doing."[85] With est, we must abandon theory, class consciousness, struggle and reason. What will you choose?

6

Primal Scream, Transactional Analysis And Behavior Therapy

In an interview with *Vogue* magazine[1], Arthur Janov, founder of Primal Scream Therapy, stated: "We can cure homosexuality, drug addiction, alcoholism, psychosis, as well as endocrine disorders, headaches, stomach ulcers, and asthma." An ad in *The New York Times*[2] for Janov's book *The Primal Revolution* claimed that "Primal Therapy solves neurotic problems faster, more effectively and more permanently than other therapies . . . it gives innovative—even radical—answers to how we can produce an inner revolution in ourselves and in our children that will ultimately create a world that is 'a real and feeling place.'"

Here, indeed appears to be the psychiatric Messiah who will lead the lost neurotics and psychotics to the promised land of normality. What is this remarkable therapy?

Janov claims that neurosis is frozen childhood pain. He states that each time a child is not held when he cries, not fed when he is hungry, ignored when he needs attention, the child suffers a psychic injury. These psychic hurts are called *primal pains* by Janov. These primal pains build up into a pool of hurts which he terms the *primal pool.*

The culmination of such psychic hurting comes in an event, such as giving the child to the baby sitter for the hundredth time, which will render the child neurotic. This event is called the *primal scene*—it is at that point, Janov holds, that the child slips unconsciously into neurosis, with its unreal behavior and continuing pain.[3]

Neurosis, for Janov, thus originates in childhood, is caused by parents' failure to meet the child's need for love and attention, and occurs in *unconscious* fashion. The cure for neurosis asserts Janov, can occur only through direct, dramatic, and extraordinary means: "I believe the only way to eliminate neurosis is with overthrow by force and violence."[4]

Here Janov introduces his Primal Scream Therapy for the cure of neurosis. In his article in *Vogue,* Albert Goldman accurately summarized Primal Scream Therapy as follows:

> Dramatic to the core, Janovian therapy appeals to the patient's imagination and his willingness to suffer present pains for future happiness. Arriving in town the first night clutching a check for the first three-week session, he finds himself cut off from family and friends, work and play; holed up in a cheap hotel ("the sleazier the better"—Janov); forbidden to smoke, drink, watch television; and probably unable to sleep. Next morning he enters The Primal Institute, a heavily padded building situated in an area zoned as well for dog kennels, where bizarre screams go unheeded. Subjected to intense two- and three-hour sessions aimed exclusively at battering down his ego defenses, the patient finally cracks and exposes the core of infantile suffering and dependency buried in every man. Exhorted to express his pain and act out his memories, the patient cries aloud "Mommy!" "Daddy!" screams, weeps, rolls up in the fetal position, enacts birth trauma, vomits, and crawls into a huge crib where he plays with man-sized teddy-bears and dolls. The climax of the whole regressive trip is the Primal Scream, "a piercing, death-like scream," that leaves the patient feeling "cool," "cleaned," and "pure."
>
> Once the patient has "primaled," he's encouraged to repeat the experience over and over again, first in individual, later in group-therapy sessions, until he has opened a broad, direct channel from his deeply impacted emotions to the surface of his mind and body. After less than a year, he is released into life with his tensions resolved, his body temperature lowered, his pulse slowed, his breathing deepened and his brain waves altered.[5]

Whereas Freud had "a talking cure," Javov has "a screaming cure." Janov is basically Freudian in his reliance on the unconscious, in his tracing of neurosis to traumatic childhood experiences and feelings, and in his pinning guilt on the parents for neurosis. Janov acknowledges his debt to Freud in these words:

> In some respects, Primal Therapy has returned full circle to early Freud. It was Freud who stressed the importance of early childhood experience in neurosis and he who understood the relationship of repressed feeling to mental aberration. It was Freud who focused on introspection systematically and who emphasized internal processes as they affect current overt behavior.[6]

However, Janov has introduced changes and modifications in the Freudian model. Unlike Freud, who claimed that "the unconscious" could be reached through dream analysis and free association, Janov believes he can penetrate directly to "the unconscious" with his Primal Scream Therapy. Whereas Freud believed that "ego defenses" are healthy, Janov considers them to be part of the neurosis itself. Freud used psychoanalysis for the gradual uncovering of "unconscious" material until the patient gained "insight" into his neurotic problems. Janov, however, calls for direct and rapid entry into "the unconscious," with the cure resulting from screaming out the pool of pain. Freudian transference—the transfer of neurotic feelings to the person of the therapist—is discarded by Janov in favor of analysis of the parent-child relationship.

Primal Therapy has made some dramatic inroads in the field of psychotherapy. Over 200,000 copies of Janov's *The Primal Scream* were sold in the two years following its publication. At one point, 3,000 to 4,000 people a month were applying to his Primal Institute in Los Angeles. Rock stars John Lennon and Mick Jagger sang the praise of primal therapy and made Janov a psychiatric hero to their many fans. Janov himself has appeared on many TV talk shows—he does not hesitate to use Madison Avenue techniques to "sell" his primal therapy. "Janov's flair for self-advertisement," writes Albert Goldman, "is remarkable."[7] Is Primal Scream Therapy valid or is it like many TV commercials, all words and no substance?

Primal Scream Therapy: Miracle or Fraud?

The appeal of Janov's Primal Scream Therapy is due to his claim to bring about a sure and rapid cure for all who have "emotional pain"—and, of course, their number is legion under capitalism. Janov *guarantees* a cure to every neurotic patient—he claims 100 percent success in such cases.[8]

Janov also maintains that his therapy brings about the most far-reaching and profound personality alterations, including striking shifts in lifelong attitudes, in interests and character traits, in self-concept—and even in body chemistry.[9]

The very simplicity of Janov's theory and therapy has an appeal: you are full of emotional pain from childhood due to your parents' behavior; when you realize this and scream out all the pain, you'll be fine.

Janov is wrong on every count and in every claim. His roots in Freudianism subject his primal therapy to the criticisms leveled at Freudianism: speculative, unscientific, divorced from life and social reality, based dominantly upon "the unconscious," completely subjective, and erroneous in attributing neurosis almost exclusively to childhood trauma due to parents.*

Janov seeks to go beyond Freud by offering a *physiological* explanation for the theory and practice of primal therapy. Here are Janov's actual words as set down in his *The Anatomy of Mental Illness:*

> The motivating need is often diencephalic—perhaps from the hunger center of the hypothalamus. If the need is unfulfilled . . . the pain of the unmet need is stored in the temporal cortex. The frontal cortex acts continuously to prevent the unconscious material from becoming conscious, and the battleground for the conflict is the limbic system.[10]

The limbic system, indeed! Any self-respecting physiologist or neuropsychologist might well be driven to violence or hysterical laughter from reading such scientific drivel. In reviewing Janov's book for *Psychology Today,* Leonore Tiefer writes that the section which deals with the neurophysiological basis for neurosis "provides neither scientific framework nor support for his clinical theory . . . its physiology is incompetent (and consists) of bits of neurophysiology pasted together with clinical metaphor."[11]

Janov offers various statistics to back his claims to the patient's lowered body temperature, slower pulse, altered brain waves, and other positive effects following the "cure" by primal therapy. His reliability in this statistical documentation is shown up by Sam Keen in his article "Janov and Primal Therapy": "At least one research scientist with whom I talked was so incensed with Janov's lack of caution in extrapolating from data to conclusions that he became

*See Chapter 1 on Freudianism.

incoherent."[12] Leonore Tiefer is correct in concluding that Janov's primal therapy "rests on no scientific basis whatsoever."[13]

Janov is equally unscientific in attributing all neurosis to childhood psychic pain caused by parents. Most neuroses are essentially *socially-induced*. They can originate in any of the major areas of activity and may occur at any time in one's life due to current experiences or traumatic events. To select one age period—childhood—and one cause—parents—is to distort grotesquely the nature of psychological reality and of mental abnormality. Neuroses may also have a biological basis.

Neurosis, of course, can have its origins in parents' behavior towards a child. But this explains only a certain number of neuroses. Other neuroses can be due to one or a combination of the many areas of the person's life involvement: school, work, family, distorted ideas, financial problems, unemployment, unhappy marriage or love life, poor and crowded living conditions, alienation and frustration. To ascribe most neuroses to "the enormous impact of the first three years of life,"[14] as Janov does, is to make an "enormous" simplistic error.

Further, to attribute neurosis solely to the failure of parents to give love and attention to the child is to ignore the complexity of child development. Children, of course, need and should be given love and attention by their parents. But children must also develop the necessary mental, emotional, and behavioral capacities to function adaptively in a complex environment. This is a protracted process, in which the parents must play a guiding and directing role as well as a loving role, but a child's development is also greatly affected by school, by friends, by specific social experiences, by opportunity for play and recreation, by brothers and sisters, and by the economic status of his family. Janov blithely ignores these many factors which contribute to mentally and emotionally healthy or unhealthy development.

Janov's whole theoretical and therapeutic edifice rests upon another unsound premise. "Neurosis," he writes, "is a disease of feeling. At its core is the suppression of feeling and its transmutation into a wide range of neurotic behavior."[15] Neurosis is a disease of feeling, cognition, relationship, activity, attitude, behavior—either in combination, or with one area predominant. The mind is far more than feeling, and the disturbed mind is far more than disturbed feeling.

Given the complexity of human functioning and the multi-faceted origin of mental illness, treatment and cure must also be multi-faceted and complex. Janov's "scream cure" takes no account of this complexity. Treatment for mental illness must include in its armamentarium: medication, changed environment, improved social relationships, reeducation, altered attitudes and goals, greater self-control, involvement in group activity, different work activity, and so on.

Janov's claim of a 100 percent cure rate for neurotics must surely rank as the most arrogant claim in the history of psychiatry. Such a claim was based upon about 60 cases, with no long-term follow-up to determine permanence of cure.[16] Janov's arrogance is further illustrated by his claim that his "cured" patients are so mentally and physically healthy that they can be considered to be "evolutionary mutations"[17]—shades of Darwin!

The nature of Janov's therapy must also evoke scientific dismay. It is insulting to patients to utilize screaming as a treatment of neurosis. It is also dehumanizing to reduce all mental problems to pent-up feelings which can only be relieved by screams. It is sometimes psychiatrically repellant. Sam Keen reports: "Primal groups now are organized bedlam. As many as 40 or 50 patients may be on the floor writhing through Primals at the same time."[18]

Janov's theory, although basically Freudian, is an eclectic mishmash. Many of his techniques—isolation, sleep deprivation, fasting—have been used in other forms of therapy, as well as by mystics, gurus, and religious cults.[19]

Albert Goldman describes Janov as "tanned and fit, like an aging beach boy." His disciples call him "The Primal Pope." His extravagant claims—better breathing, "thermal changes," even larger breasts for "moderately flat-chested women,"[20]—arouse suspicion of charlatanry.

Janov's Primal Scream Therapy has no scientific basis. It is speculative and unproved. It runs counter to all the basic laws of physiology, psychology and psychiatry. It borders on the unethical.

But beyond this lack of scientific merit is the harmful social role that primal therapy plays.

The Primal Person: Tensionless and Non-Struggling

All Freudian-based therapy is essentially intrapsychic. It deals almost exclusively with the subjective emotional problems of the individual, while ignoring real social causation, social problems, and social struggle. It extracts the individual from his varied and intricate social milieu and involves him in the narrow, egocentric consideration of his feelings, his dreams, his attitudes towards his parents in childhood, his emotional pain.

Janov's primal therapy certainly fits into this Freudian mold. But Janov also contributes his own psychic twists towards diverting the individual from social reality and social involvement. In a period of world social change, with economic and political problems affecting people in many crucial ways, Janov writes: "The normal has no need to make life what it is not. He has no need for the broad philosophical search. He knows he is just alive and living, no more."[21]

It is precisely today that people most need "the broad philosophical search." It is precisely today that we must "make life what it is not." Working people must not be satisfied to be "just alive and living, no more." They must become more than a "tensionless, nonstruggling person."[22]

Sam Keen describes Janov's "cured" patients as follows: "Hence, primal people have no need or desire to organize or join groups. They are highly individualistic. If the world had been through primal therapy there would be no politics (which is only a sick quest for power). Each person would be content to tend his own emotional garden."[23] Keen makes a keen criticism of Janov's primal therapy:

> To adjust a person so that he does not struggle against the social structures that perpetuate disease is to achieve a "cure" at the price of avoiding reality. In the modern world, any therapy that extinguishes outrage disequips a person to change the world in a manner that may make survival possible.[24]

Janov's primal therapy does indeed extinguish the outrage we should all feel today and does disequip us from changing the world as it needs to be changed.

Life as Strokes and Games: Transactional Analysis

Transactional Analysis burst upon the world in a remarkably popular book by its founder, Eric Berne. This book, *Games People Play,* was read by millions of people because the "games" it described seemed to give insight into *The Psychology of Human Relationships* (the subtitle of the book). "Addressed to the intelligent layman as well as the practicing professional," reads the jacket blurb, "*Games People Play* is written in clear, simple, witty language."

A listing of a few of the 120 psychological "games" dealt with in the book may also explain its popularity: Kick Me; See What You Made Me Do; Look How Hard I've Tried; Rapo; I'm Only Trying To Help You; Schlemiel; Let's You and Him Fight; Frigid Woman; Now I've Got You, You Son of a Bitch. The book became a conversation piece at parties and at work, among friends and between lovers, for the troubled and for the frustrated, since it appeared to describe accurately and to explain many of the ways people behave toward one another.

Transactional Analysis makes a number of sweeping claims. Besides the assertion that the psychology of human relationships is explained by the games people play, Berne says that "transactional analysis is more precise than most other social and psychological theories."[25] Berne further claims that Transactional Analysis is both a theory of personality and social action and a highly effective method of psychotherapy.[26] It also purports to set up a model for examining and changing all forms of social behavior.

What is Transactional Analysis and does it bear out its claims?

The Analysis of "Transactions"

Berne states that every person has three types of *ego states,* which he defines as "coherent systems of thought and feelings manifested by corresponding behavior patterns."[27] These three ego states are: (1) the *Parent* state, in which the individual feels, thinks and acts just as one of his parents did when the individual was a child; (2) the *Child* state, in which the person feels, thinks and acts as though between the ages of two and five; (3) the *Adult* state, in which the person appraises the environment objectively and "functions like a computer."[28]

Berne presents a diagram in which the three states (Parent-Child-Adult) are each shown as circles, with an oval enclosing the three circles. This, according to Berne, represents "the complete personality diagram of any human being whatsoever, encompassing everything he may feel, think, say or do."[29]

Thus, when two people confront each other, six ego states are involved—the Parent-Child-Adult states of each person. Whatever takes place between them is considered by Berne to be a "transaction." These transactions can then be "analyzed" to determine which state of Person A interacted with which state of Person B. Much of Transactional Analysis Therapy—and writings—is devoted to analyzing whether one person was in the Parent state when he responded to another person who was in the Child state, what that means, what was a more appropriate state, etc.

Berne claims that there are many possible transactions between individuals but that only fifteen different transactions commonly occur between two people.

Berne asserts that there are six types of social behavior in transactions between people: strokes, games, ritual, pastimes, withdrawal, and work. Of these, Berne considers "strokes" as the most important. Inventing a physiological need which he calls "stimulus-hunger," Berne defines "strokes" as the urgent need for physical intimacy (the "hunger" for such a "stimulus"), which exists at birth and continues throughout our lives. For Berne, "stroking" is any act which implies recognition of another's presence: greeting, anger, touching, quarreling. "Hence," writes Berne, "a *stroke* may be used as the fundamental unit of social action. An exchange of strokes constitutes a *transaction,* which is the unit of social intercourse."[30]

There is one other major feature of Transactional Analysis: *scripts.* Berne defines scripts as *preconscious life plans* "usually based on childhood illusions, which may persist throughout a whole lifetime."[31] These scripts, which are formed *unconsciously* in childhood, and are usually based upon some myth or fairy tale, predetermine the individual's life and fill it with the unconscious behaviors which Berne calls strokes, games, pastimes, etc. "Berne came to believe," writes Gary Gregg in *Psychology Today,* "that every script is recorded in the world's mythology. 'The life of every human being,' he said, 'is already charted in Bullfinch or Graves.' He called people with winning scripts 'princes' and those stuck with losers, 'frogs.' 'My business,' he said, 'is turning frogs into princes.'"[32]

In summary, Berne's theory is based upon the Parent-Child-Adult ego states of every person, with a script formed in childhood, which determines the transactions carried out with any other person. Every person seeks "strokes" unconsciously and is also unconsciously involved in games, pastimes, etc.

Mental illness, according to Berne, is due to a person being fixated in the wrong ego state. Therapy, he claims, consists of restructuring the ego states through analysis of the transactions of a person. The goal of therapy is to enable the person to be in the right ego state to carry out appropriate transactions with other persons.

Transactional Analysis is fundamentally Freudian. Berne specifically acknowledges his indebtedness to Freud and even claims to be a "better Freudian than the orthodox analysts."[33] With unconscious ego states and unconscious transactions, with scripts which are unconsciously formed in childhood, with parents unconsciously playing the decisive role, Berne may certainly claim membership in the Freudian fraternity.

There are, however, a number of significant features of Transactional Analysis which differ from Freudianism. Berne and his followers eliminate the Freudian categories of *id, ego,* and *superego,* and use everyday language and terms in an effort to be a "therapy of the people."[34] Unlike the silence and "neutrality" of the orthodox Freudian during therapy, the transactional analysts actively and directly intervene in the group process. They make "contracts" with patients for specific changes in ego states to be worked toward, rather than awaiting "insight" by the patient at some indeterminate time, as do the Freudians. Transactional Analysis uses psychodrama and Gestalt techniques at times, and calls for a "here-and-now" awareness, rather than plumbing the depths of the patient's unconscious for childhood Oedipal clues.

These features of Transactional Analysis have given it an immediacy and attractiveness which may well account for its scope and influence.

Scope and Influence of Transactional Analysis

In a review of Berne's *What Do You Say After You Say Hello?,* psychiatrist James S. Gordon wrote:

> Transactional Analysis is practiced throughout the country, its precepts taught in seminars and its applications detailed in professional journals. In short, the system that Eric Berne created has become an important social phenomenon, offering therapy to many thousands and providing advice and counsel to millions more . . . In the 1960s Berne was probably read more widely than any other contemporary psychiatrist.[35]

The International Transactional Analysis Association, with headquarters in Berkeley, California, has a membership of 2400 practicing professionals. The book *I'm O.K.—You're O.K.* by T. A.'er Thomas Harris[36], was at the top of the Best Seller List for many weeks and merited a magazine article in the Sunday *New York Times.*[37]

Berne often referred to himself as "the cowboy therapist" bringing help in direct and earthy language to troubled people. A further attraction of Transactional Analysis is the moderate fees it charges to each person. However, since almost all therapy is conducted in groups of six or more, a moderate fee of $15 or $20 per session, adds up to a whopping fee for the therapist.

With the appeal of simplicity and directness and the promise of rapid cure, with moderate fees and surface plausibility, Transactional Analysis has had a powerful effect on many people.

What can be made of this popular and influential Freudian-based, transaction-analyzing, script-fixated theory and therapy?

Transactional Analysis: A Critique

Transactional Analysis describes the surface behavior of individuals and claims to change abnormal behavior through its therapeutic intervention. Since *descriptions* of behavior can be accurate, Transactional Analysis sometimes is accurate in such description, although it is more often wildly inaccurate. And since abnormal behavior should obviously be changed to normal behavior, Transactional Analysis, with its ego states and transactions, its games and rituals, its psychodrama and its shouts of "Stay in your Adult!," appears to zero in on such abnormal behavior in an effort to make it normal.

But Transactional Analysis has only the glitter of golden therapy; below the golden glitter is only psychiatric dross. There is no scientific merit to Transactional Analysis.

Berne creates a physiological "stimulus-hunger" to explain the need for "strokes." But he offers no proof for its existence nor is there any. Otherwise Berne's theory like that of Freud is pure "mentalism" and "emotionalism," divorced from physiology and nervous system functioning.

Like Freud, Berne and his disciples vent their psychiatric anger at parents, especially mothers, for supposedly acting neurotically and thus creating neuroses in children. The scapegoating of parents for mental illness in their children is both erroneous and psychologically harmful, and unfair to both parents and children.

Berne goes Freud one better by inventing "scripts," which he claims are unconsciously adopted in childhood and thereafter rule the person's life. One may well label this as "psychological pre-determinism": Berne dooms most people to be "frogs" and "losers" with no chance to win, except with Transactional Analysis. In a constantly changing world, with new knowledge, new ideas, new social movements—Berne rejects the influence of science, education and society on people.

Like Freud, Berne invents whatever he needs. One more invention is the Parent-Child-Adult ego states, which split the individual into three different personalities which shift place with dizzying rapidity. Such ego states have no real existence. Each person has only one personality which functions in intricate and dynamic fashion in an intricate, and dynamic social environment.

Berne trivializes human behavior by reducing it to mere transactions between two individuals. These "transactions" are then labeled as "games" and "rackets" and "strokes" in a constant series of role playing, manipulation, and maneuvers between two people. Berne is egregiously simplistic in his theory and his therapy. What kind of game is being played by workers on strike? What were the Parent-Child-Adult ego states of the 10,000 demonstrators against racist and political repression in Raleigh, North Carolina on July 4, 1974? What "strokes" are being sought by the huge numbers of unemployed Black youth when they seek jobs?

Certainly, individuals function differently in different situations and relationships. But it is not because they are playing roles or games; it is because their specific life history and life activity have resulted in the thought, feeling, attitudes, goals, and behavior which they express in their many-sided relationships and activities.

The goal Berne sets for patients is "autonomy," which is the achievement of "spontaneity, awareness, and intimacy."[38] This sounds good, as does so much of the Encounter-Humanistic Psychology movement. But this "awareness" has nothing to do with heightened knowledge of one's self in relation to society and its laws. Nor is Berne's "intimacy" a genuine intimacy based upon shared experiences in the reality of society. The social, in any significant sense, is absent from Berne's thinking.

Transactional Analysis turns people inward into their subjective motives, their game playing, and their unconscious scripts. It turns them away from social consciousness and social struggle. Its "analysis" of society is trivial to the point of absurdity. Harris writes that "the problems of the world are the problems of individuals."[39] The ad for Berne's *What Do You Say After You Say Hello?*" stated: "Everyone while still a young child unconsciously writes the secret script that will govern his decisions and actions for the rest of his life. It is this script that dictates whether you will be a winner or a loser."[40]

Berne and Transactional Analysis are also profoundly male supremacist. Some of the "games" Berne analyzes involve feminine stereotypes of seduction, "bitchiness" and hyperemotionality. The crudest example is the game Berne calls "Rapo," in which the woman leads the man "into compromising physical contact and then claims that he has made a criminal assault on her or has done her irreparable damage."[41] This is the exact example, which the women's liberation movement is fighting, as a sexist way of excusing rape.

Transactional Analysis is, indeed, as James Gordon remarked "a moral and spiritual vacuum.[42] It is speculative, unscientific, trivial, and socially reactionary.

Neurosis Is Just a Bad Habit: Behavior Therapy

FREUDIANS ARE WRONG, THE BEHAVIORISTS SAY—A NEUROSIS IS "JUST" A BAD HABIT: such is the title of a *New York Times Magazine* article on Behavior Therapy[43]. Attacking the Freudian "unconscious" as either nonexistent or irrelevant, the behavior therapists claim that even the most complicated neuroses are nothing but the result of faulty conditioning. Such faulty conditioning or "maladaptive behavior," as they term it, can be changed by training and reconditioning. This has been scientifically demonstrated with lower animals such as rats and cats, they maintain. "Contrary to the popular psychoanalytic conception, a neurosis is 'just' a habit—a persistent habit of unadaptive behavior, acquired by learning," states Joseph Wolpe, one of the founders of Behavior Therapy.[44]

Basing itself on what it calls "experimentally validated findings," Behavior Therapy claims to be scientific. It offers a number of new therapeutic techniques and systems for individual and group treatment of disturbed behavior. It claims cures or marked improvement for up to 90 percent of patients treated, after an average of only thirty therapeutic sessions—some after as few as three or four sessions[45]. In his book *Help Without Psychoanalysis,* behavior therapist Dr. Herbert Fensterheim states: "Behavior Therapy is a revolutionary way of looking at people and their problems."[46]

Behavior Therapy has grown rapidly in the professional community in the past decade and has attained wide popularity both with patients and in mental institutions, schools, etc. With its own organization, the Association for the Advancement of Behavior Therapy, two major journals, dozens of conferences, workshops and symposiums, and the blessing of B.F. Skinner,* Behavior Therapy has won thousands of therapists to its banner. Tens of thousands of nurses, teachers and prison personnel have been trained in its uses with mental patients, disruptive children and prison inmates. Skinner himself claims that his principles of behavioral engineering have had powerful influence in "contingency management in the classroom, behavioral modification in psychotherapy and penology, and many other fields."[47]

Is Behavior Therapy the revolutionary, scientific theory and practice that can cure neuroses and markedly improve psychoses? Is it effective in the schools, the mental institutions, and the prisons?

The Nature of Behavior Therapy

"Behavior therapy," states Joseph Wolpe, "is synonymous with *conditioning therapy.* . . . (It) explicitly denotes the use of experimentally established principles of learning for the purpose of changing unadaptive behavior."[48]

The behavior therapists base their theory and their therapy upon a few simple laws of conditioning and upon "learning theory" in general: since behavior is learned, it can be unlearned and new behavior learned in its place. If behavior has not yet been learned it can be shaped so as to emerge as new behavior.

The "Token economy," which is widely used in mental institutions, prisons, and schools, is based upon the rewarding (positive reinforcement) of desired behaviors and the ignoring (nonreinforcement) or punishing (negative reinforcement) of undesired behaviors. This comprises Skinner's system of behavioral management.

Behavior Therapy is aptly named: it is therapy aimed exclusively at changing behavior. Its theory and techniques deal solely with behavior and how it can be changed. Morton Hunt writes that Wolpe's "therapeutic method assumes that neurosis—in man as well as in the cat—is nothing but a set of maladaptive habits built into the brain in the form of connections between the neurons, or brain cells—connections that can be dismantled by routine training."[49]

With such a theory, it is logical for behavior therapists to conclude that there are no neurotics—only people who have learned unadaptive

*See Chapter 2 on B.F. Skinner.

behavior patterns.[50] If this is so, then such unadaptive patterns or "bad habits" can be changed and new and adaptive ones established. All that is needed are the appropriate techniques for changing behavior.

Therapy, therefore, becomes the use of techniques for changing the behavior of patients, disruptive school children, prison inmates and anyone acting in "undesired" fashion. Fensterheim writes: "B.F. Skinner is responsible for the techniques of modifying behavior by means of rewarding the acquisition of good habits, just as he taught his rats to push levers in order to produce food."[51]

The Techniques of Behavior Therapy

The techniques developed by Behavior Therapy are based upon laws and methods that had some limited success in changing animal behavior.

Systematic desensitization, developed by Wolpe, is one of the main techniques of Behavior Therapy. Utilizing Pavlov's law of reciprocal inhibition—that a stronger stimulus will inhibit a weaker stimulus—the patient is trained to achieve maximum relaxation and then to picture successively more phobic or anxiety-producing situations. Thus, in phobias such as fear of high places or of snakes, the patient would be relaxed and then asked to mentally imagine situations of himself at increasing heights or closer proximity to a snake. Since relaxation is physiologically antagonistic to phobic anxiety, Wolpe claims that it will inhibit the tension of the anxiety-producing situation (high places or snakes) and thus systematically extinguish the phobia in real life as well as in mental imaginings.[52]

Aversive therapy is another major technique in the therapeutic arsenal of Behavior Therapy. This is the pairing of an undesirable habit or behavior pattern with a painful or physically unpleasant stimulus. This is the "Clockwork Orange" technique of reconditioning through shock, nausea or other aversive stimuli.

Fensterheim describes the reconditioning of a woman who had an aversion to penises. She was subjected to continuous painful electric shock which was discontinued only when she looked at a picture of a penis.[53] To overcome male homosexuality, electric shock is administered to the homosexual when he looks at a picture of a nude male and discontinued (and soft music played) when he looks at a picture of a nude female.[54]

In prisons, aversive therapy is regularly used in the form of sensory deprivation, electric shock, respiratory paralysis, and vomit-inducing drugs to control the "undesirable behavior" of prisoners.*

The *token economy* is another major technique of Behavior Therapy. This is a dramatic and even "massive" technique, since it is used in entire wards of hospitals or even in entire prisons. It derives its name from the rewarding of specific "target" behaviors with tokens, which can then be used to purchase articles, better food or sleeping conditions, privileges, etc. The entire institution or ward is converted to such an "economy," with nurses, attendants, guards, or other workers trained to award tokens for specific behaviors. A variation of the token economy is the "tier" or "level" system, in which different tiers or levels are set up in increasing order of desirability and privilege. Thus, the first tier or level would be bare furniture in drab surroundings, with poor food, and no privileges. In some prisons, the first tier consists of sensory deprivation in isolation until the prisoner's behavior changes from its "antisocial" character, at which time, he may move to the second tier. A graded tier system, consisting of four levels is in effect in Patuxent Institution in Jessup, Maryland, "designed to assist the patient in developing behavioral controls, using increased rewards as a motivator."[55]

Sex therapy techniques used by Masters and Johnson have achieved great popularity. The *New York Times* reported that "Clinics for Sex Therapy Proliferate over Nation" following the appearance of the Masters and Johnson book *Human Sexual Inadequacy.*[56] Such techniques are grounded in Behavior Therapy. Some sexual dysfunction is treated by Masters and Johnson with relaxation and "successive approximations": sex activity is carried out gradually in small steps in a relaxed atmosphere. Further, the main emphasis is on the sex activity, not on feelings and relationships.

The technique of *flooding* is used by some behavior therapists. This consists of a massive presentation of the phobic- or anxiety-producing thing or situation, e.g., confronting a patient who has a blood phobia with a film showing huge amounts of blood. Other techniques of Behavior Therapy are role playing of the desired behavior; assertive therapy for the extremely unassertive patient; and "thought-stopping" to overcome obsessions.[57]

The behavior therapists have also developed many kinds of appara-

*See Chapter 3 on Behavior Modification for fuller discussion.

tuses for controlling behavior: electric shock machines, biofeedback devices, Bug-in-the-ear, remote instrumentation systems.

With these techniques and such apparatuses, the behavior therapists claim to have developed a therapy which is effective, rapid, and scientific. They call for an end to psychoanalytic treatment as unscientific, and its replacement by Behavior Therapy. In the more recent period, after the heyday of their "new and revolutionary therapy," the behavior therapists have adopted a somewhat more cautious stance about the effectiveness of their therapy. They also claim now to include more than just behavior in their approach. [58] But the basic principles and techniques of Behavior Therapy remain unchanged and require careful evaluation.

Critique of Behavior Therapy

The most fundamental and most overriding criticism of Behavior Therapy is that it centers on behavior to the exclusion of the many other major areas of human life.

Behavior Therapy deals with human beings as either machines or animals. For Skinner, there is an exact analogy between the computer and "Man Thinking": both receive stimuli which they process and store to be available for decision making when new stimuli are received.[59] Behavior Therapy treats mentally ill people, as well as children and prisoners who show "undesirable" behavior, like machines which need reprogramming.

Approaching humans as *behavioral animals,* Behavior Therapy applies the laws of *animal* learning to the complex and qualitatively different functioning of human beings. Even the laws of animal behavior are not properly understood nor are they applied correctly by behavior therapists to human behavior.

Human beings are neither machines nor animals—they are thinking, feeling, socially involved, problem-solving beings who cannot be manipulated by push buttons.

The sex therapy techniques derived from Skinner's operant conditioning theory also exclude emotion and relationships. While there are cases of physiological sex impairment, sex problems usually have other causes. The relationship of the couple, the existence or nonexistence of love, male supremacy in sexual matters, the past life experiences of the sexually troubled person, receive minimal attention in sex therapy, while physical sex activity is centered upon. Yet it is precisely feeling, ideas, relationship, and mutual experiences which are most relevant to an unhealthy or a healthy sex life.

Behavior Therapy blurs the line between the mentally normal and the mentally abnormal. Neuroses and psychoses, to the extent we understand them today, are not merely "unadaptive habits"—they are mental illnesses which must be treated in a scientific way: with drugs, with work activity, with psychotherapy, with reeducation, with changes of the environment, with changes of relationship, with rest. Treatment must be aimed not only at behavior but at the intellect, the emotions, the relationships, the work activity, the physiology, the social skills, and the entire life activity of the person.

Behavior Therapy is also used on mentally healthy people who present problems to the Establishment. Thus, prisoners are treated as though they were mentally ill and subjected to abuses of the worst sort in the name of Behavior Modification. Black children who are frustrated at their third-rate education are "behavior modified" to conform to the requirements of a racist school system.*

When behavior alone is the focus of attention, as in Behavior Therapy, and when "troublemakers" are the "patients," any means to control behavior is then used. This accounts for the use of electric shock, powerful drugs to stop respiration temporarily, sensory deprivation and other aversive means used in prisons to control socially aware, militant inmates.

Behavior Therapy aims at desirable behavior, at adaptive behavior. Who decides on desirability and adaptiveness? Obviously, it is those in charge of the prison or the school or the mental institution. A punitive warden, a racist school board, and a behavior-fixated psychiatrist may well determine the "target behaviors" for prisoners, Black school children, and patients in mental institutions.

Token economies in mental institutions are graphic examples of the harmful consequences of Behavior Therapy. In a sober and carefully reasoned article entitled *Token and Taboo: Behavior Modification, Token Economies, and the Law,*[60] David B. Wexler points out that token economies in mental institutions infringe upon the constitutional rights of patients to adequate treatment by depriving them of food, clothing and recreational privileges, and then offering these for purchase by tokens which patients can win by "adaptive" behavior. Wexler correctly calls this punishment, rather than reward. Enforced

*See Chapter 3 on Behavior Modification.

labor, with no pay, is often the "target behavior" expected of patients.

Token economies in mental hospitals are clearly violative of the rights of patients, lead to worse treatment and living conditions for the majority of patients, and invade their privacy and dignity.

Although Behavior Therapy is fundamentally onesided and unscientific, it has several features which may have certain validity with a limited group of people. Positive reinforcement when used with autistic children has produced some improvement. Systematic desensitization may be of some value in the treatment of certain phobias. Reconditioning of selected mental patients along Pavlovian lines may have positive results.

The claims of Behavior Therapy to a cure rate of up to 90 percent is unsupported by satisfactory evidence. Follow-up studies have not been carried out, nor have control groups been used as a means of validating the "cures" or "marked improvements." "Cure" is usually based upon the subjective appraisal of the behavior therapist after a period of therapy—the patient may still be mentally ill by other criteria.

Many patients recover without treatment after a period of time. Such patients cannot ascribe their cure to the efficacy of Behavior Therapy. Further, since a change in behavior is all that is aimed at in Behavior Therapy, emotional-cognitive-relational pathology may continue after an "adaptive" behavior change.

In their wider application, Behavior Therapy and Behavior Modification are a means of social and political manipulation and control. They would rob people of their dignity and their freedom by subjecting them to animal-like and machine-like behavior.

Behavior Therapy and Behavior Modification fail to meet the requirements of a scientific, humane and effective therapy. Socially and politically, they are often used as control mechanisms by the Establishment for undemocratic social and political ends.

PART TWO

SCIENCE IN THE SERVICE OF REACTION

The racism prevalent in the United States is due to the dominance of the capitalist class and finds specific expression in the behavioral sciences. The Marxist principle that the ideological superstructure of a society serves the economic foundation is most vividly illustrated by the racist theories and practices in U.S. psychology and psychiatry.

The ideological superstructure of U.S. capitalist society is also permeated by theories of male supremacy and female inferiority. Psychology and psychiatry in our country is shot through with such theories and practices.

Behavior research conducted in the United States provides pseudo-scientific justification for racism, male supremacy and many other reactionary theories. While some of this research pursues scientific aims through genuinely scientific methodology, most behavior research serves to support capitalist ideology.

7

Jensen's "Scientific" Racism

The past decade has seen the emergence of "scientific racism" on a massive scale in our country. With crude, open racism having been rebuffed by science throughout the world, the beneficiaries of racism have had to seek a more subtle, sophisticated, and scientific disguise. Headed by Arthur Jensen, with his theory of Black genetic intellectual inferiority, the Establishment ideologists—James Coleman, Daniel Moynihan, Christopher Jencks, B.F. Skinner, and others—have formulated racist theories which are cloaked with the robe of science. These theories have penetrated every area of our lives—in schools, on the job, in the media.

These theories have had a serious political effect. In 1970, Daniel Moynihan was quoted by *Life* magazine as stating that "the winds of Jensen are gusting through the capital (Washington, D.C.) at gale force."[1]

Confronted by this new "scientific" racist onslaught, the Black liberation movement produced its own scientific and political fightback. Further, leading white scientists and professionals joined progressive people of all colors in seeking to stem this onslaught. The main scientific battleground has been in the area of psychology since most of these racist theories seek to show the inferiority of Black people in intellect or personality.

Racist theories, whatever their nature or disguise, should be outlawed, not debated. But that time has not yet arrived in our country. The Jensens, the Shockleys and the Colemans have the full resources of the media to promote their poison. Jensen himself commented in pleased wonder: "The popular press in the United States picked up and broadcast their interpretation of my *Harvard Educational Review* article with a speed and zeal that seems unprecedented in the publicity given to articles in the academic journals. So swift was the press coverage that I was reading about the article in the newspapers at least two weeks before a copy of the journal had even reached me in California."[2]

Newsweek published its comment on Jensen's article under the heading "Born Dumb," while *Science News* headed its story "Genetics v. Head Start." Jensen's theory proved to be the most sensational of all the pseudoscientific theories. It had the most profound impact both in professional circles and in political life. A full-scale, comprehensive analysis and refutation of Jensen's theory is, therefore, called for.

Jensen's Theory

In February 1969, the prestigious journal *The Harvard Educational Review* published, as its leading feature, a 123-page article entitled "How Much Can We Boost IQ and Scholastic Achievement?" by Arthur R. Jensen, professor of educational psychology and research psychologist of the University of California.[3] In this long, statistic-crammed, highly technical article, Jensen gave to that question a simple racist answer—that the IQ and scholastic achievement of Black children can be boosted very little because Black children are genetically inferior to white children in intelligence.

Although Jensen also includes working-class children* ("lower" class, as he calls them) as genetically inferior in intelligence, his main targets are Black children and all Black people as a race. For, at this point, it should be emphasized that any theory of the intellectual inferiority of children applies equally to adults, i.e., the "intellectually inferior Black child" grows up, barring an intellectual miracle, to be

---

*It should be noted that most Black children are also working-class children, since most Black parents are workers.

"the intellectually inferior Black adult,"—and Jensen bars such miracles. Jensen's theory applies to the entire Black population in our country and to all Black and darker peoples throughout the world. And Jensen throws in the entire working class, for good measure.

Jensen opens his article with the dramatic statement that compensatory education has failed. "Compensatory education" was federally funded on a mass scale beginning in the 1960s as an educational means of "compensating" for the life of poverty, ill health, bad housing, poor nutrition, and overcrowding that millions of poor, Black and other minority children suffer due to economic and political discrimination.

Head Start and other preschool programs for tens of thousands of children were federally financed for eight weeks during the summer, with large scale programs continuing all year round. The theory was that children of lower-income families needed an extra educational "head start" to prepare them for regular elementary school.

Jensen claims, in his article, that such compensatory education programs had failed because they were based upon the theory that all children have equal intellectual potential and that all can learn in essentially similar fashion. He asserts that compensatory education was based upon the "deprivation hypothesis," according to which "academic lag is mainly the result of social, economic, and educational deprivation and discrimination."[4]

Jensen rejects this "deprivation hypothesis." The explanation for the academic lag of Black (and poor) children, he declares, is due to major differences in the *innate* intelligence of white and Black children. Citing the fact that, on the average, white middle-class children score eleven points higher on IQ tests than Black (and poor) children, Jensen concludes that this difference is a genetic (hereditary) difference which cannot be overcome by compensatory education.[5]

Jensen maintains that intelligence is a real human trait which, like height or weight, can be accurately measured. IQ tests, he holds, accurately measure the difference in intelligence between individuals, races, and classes. The average difference of eleven points between white middle-class children and Black and poor children is a real and major difference in intelligence, he states, which is not due to environmental deprivation but to heredity.

Intelligence, Jensen says, is determined predominantly by the genes and is, therefore, basically fixed for life. He proceeds to devote 78 pages to "show" that 80 percent of intelligence is due to heredity and

20 percent is due to environment. He then concludes that Blacks, *as a race,* are inferior in intelligence because they have fewer "intelligence genes."

Intelligence, claims Jensen, has two levels. Level I is associative or rote learning, i.e., memorizing of facts like "2 and 2 are 4." Level II, he says, is cognitive learning and problem-solving ability, a qualitatively higher intelligence which requires more "intelligence genes," as well as certain "inherited neural structures." White middle-class children, according to Jensen, have both Level I and Level II intelligence because they have inherited the right number of intelligence genes and the right neural structures, while Black and working-class children have fewer intelligence genes and have inherited the wrong neural structures, and are thus limited to only Level I intelligence.

Compensatory education, says Jensen, cannot make up for poor heredity, i.e., it cannot provide Level II intelligence. He maintained in his article, and in public appearances, that money was being wasted by being used for compensatory education. What was necessary, he suggested, was the restructuring of the educational system per se, by having a Level I school system for Black and poor children and a Level II school system for white middle-class children.

Jensen then carried his theory to its logical racist extreme. Since intelligence is genetic and thus, hereditary, overbreeding of a less intelligent race and class could pollute the more intelligent race and class. Such "dysgenic" trends must be prevented, he stated. Eugenics must see to it that the inferior are controlled or eliminated while the superior are permitted to breed true to their higher intelligence. Such is how Jensen's theory was bred, a bastard offspring of science and racism.

Jensen's theory found support among a number of psychologists, geneticists, and sociologists. Not content with having published Jensen's article, *The Harvard Educational Review* invited "criticism" of it in its next issue (Spring 1969) and proceeded to publish six articles that praised and approved of Jensen's article, while offering a few mild and mostly inept criticisms. Jensen, of course, was given an opportunity to reply; he utilized it by welcoming their admiration and sweeping away their half-hearted criticisms. One truly critical letter was included in the issue to give the appearance of a real debate.

Professor R.J. Herrnstein of Harvard University supported Jensen's thesis in a long article in *The Atlantic* monthly[6] followed by a book *IQ in the Meritocracy*.[7] British psychologist H.J. Eysenck authored a book which fully supported Jensen.[8] William Shockley, winner of the Nobel Prize in Physics for the invention of the transistor, embarked on a lecture tour to tout the merits of Jensen's theory and to call for sterilization of poor Black women.

But Jensen's article also aroused a storm of protest. Many excellent articles attacked and exposed Jensen's theory as unscientific and as racist. The Eastern Psychology Association voted by a two-to-one margin "to censure the use of inconclusive evidence concerning the heritability of IQ."[9] Leading Black psychologists and educators, such as Dr. Edmund Gordon of Columbia University, Dr. Doxey Wilkerson of Yeshiva University, and Professor Robert L. Williams of Washington University skillfully evaluated and exposed the racist and reactionary nature of Jensen's theory.

A point-by-point refutation of Jensen's theory is necessary.

Jensen and the Nature of Intelligence

Jensen's theory of Black and working-class genetic inferiority in intelligence stands or falls on the nature of intelligence, whether it is measurable, and whether IQ tests measure it.

In 1936, the Soviet Union abolished IQ tests "as categorizing children; in effect, setting limits in advance to their achievement possibilities."[10] IQ tests, it was held, "undermined the basic principle of universal education according to which Soviet educators hold that every child not suffering from severe handicap or brain damage can complete the school course if given proper teaching and help."[11]

Intelligence and its testing has been a central concern of Western psychology since Albert Binet devised a test for mentally retarded children in France in 1905. The idea of quantifying intelligence, of summing it up in a number, became a full-scale industry both for researchers and for the purveyors of IQ tests for profit. Two major IQ tests were developed in the United States, where the testing craze reached its zenith. These were the Stanford-Binet and the Wechsler Intelligence Scale for Children. These IQ tests have built-in assumptions which need closer examination.

The first assumption of IQ tests is that there is a human trait called "intelligence" which is a *unitary* trait, i.e., that intelligence is a single and nondivisible trait. Jensen adopts psychologist Charles Spearman's concept of this trait: that over and apart from special mental abilities, there is a single "general intelligence" that each person possesses as an intellectual trait. Spearman gave this supposed general intelligence the label g. It is this general intelligence or g which Jensen claims exists as a unitary trait and which is accurately measured by IQ tests.

The second assumption of IQ tests is that g can be measured and that the Stanford-Binet and Wechsler IQ tests do measure g.

A third assumption is that intelligence is "normally" distributed, i.e., that intelligence in the population has a distribution according to the bell-shaped "normal probability curve." The normal probability curve locates 2 percent of the population at each of the high and low extremes, 14 percent at each of the fairly high and low extremes, and 34 percent at each side of the mean or average (see Fig. 1). With that assumption, IQ tests are *constructed* so that the population, or a representative sample, will *necessarily and inevitably* score according to the normal probability curve.

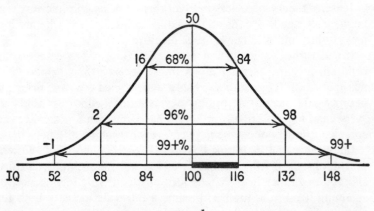

FIG. 1

The Jensen-Spearman concept of intelligence as a unitary trait is unscientific. Psychologist J.P. Guilford correctly points out that many factors, traits, and skills are involved in intelligence, and that IQ tests, such as the Stanford-Binet, test only a small fraction of such factors, traits, and skills.[12] In fact, Guilford believes that there are 120 human abilities in the cognitive domain, rather than a single "general intelligence."[13]

In a refutation of Jensen's theory, which he titled "The Jensen Hypothesis : Social Science Research or Social Science Racism?" [14], Professor Frank Morris, of Massachusetts Institute of Technology, sets forth his own concept of a multi-factored intelligence, as opposed to the unitary *g* concept of Jensen-Spearman. Morris states that "intelligence is clearly more than what intelligence tests measure and the capacity for conceptualization and abstract reasoning." He correctly suggests that the following abilities should be included in any evaluation of human mental ability: learning from experience, cunning and resourcefulness, creativity, ability to successfully adapt to rapidly changing circumstances, ability to understand and act beyond one's own immediate interests, moral appreciation, and sensitivity to other people's cultures and ways of life. [15]

What is "intelligence?" That people differ in their ability to cope with problems, in their "survival" ability, in their knowledge and education, in their social skills, in their moral values, in their attitudes, and in their political understanding is a clear and self-evident fact. But Jensen-Spearman have unwarrantedly and unscientifically divorced human intellectual ability from the full, dynamic complexity of individual development in society. They have reduced this many-faceted intellectual complexity to a single trait which can be measured in two hours in a psychologist's office and summed up in a number.

The individual's intellect is a product of many factors. The child's upbringing in the family, his relationships, his language and emotional development are important factors in his mental development. Academic skills and adequate education make their contribution to intellectual growth. The social relations of the individual greatly affect and influence his mental behavior. Life experience—social, educational, familial, work, political, marital, sexual—helps to mold our ability to function mentally. Reasoning skills—the ability to analyze problems and situations logically and rationally to arrive at correct judgments and actions—is also deeply implicated in mental ability. Imagination and creativity are added dimensions of intellectual life. Further, maturity of emotions, the ability to adapt, moral standards, sensitivity to and consideration of others, objectivity or subjectivity of reaction and viewpoint all enter significantly into one's mental activity. Personality traits, attitudes, philosophic outlook and social consciousness are also vital determinants of mental behavior. And the possession of a healthy and intact brain and nervous system is a prerequisite for normal intelligence.

Hence, the simplistic general intelligence or g of Jensen-Spearman, which is supposedly fixed for life and little affected by environment and life experience, is replaced by an understanding of the dynamic complexity and changeability of human mental development.

In his article, Jensen inveighs against "the belief in the almost infinite plasticity of the intellect."[16] But after decades of experimentally studying higher nervous activity, Pavlov arrived at the conclusion that it is precisely this "plasticity" that is so extraordinary. Pavlov writes::

> The chief, the strongest and the lasting impression gained from the study of the higher nervous activity by our method is the extraordinary plasticity of this activity, its immense potentialities; nothing is immobile, unyielding; everything can always be attained, changed for the better, if only the proper conditions are created. [17]

Pavlov's views regarding plasticity apply not only to the *physiological* basis for mental activity but to the *psychological* reflection which is produced by the brain and the nervous system. Under socialism, the stimulation, growth and enhancement of mental ability are carried out through improved education, collective activity and work, varied and available cultural life, a scientific outlook, and heightened social consciousness. No limits are set for intelligence. Its "immense potentialities" are its crucial feature, not its nonplasticity.

Intelligence, then, is not a simple, single human trait, nor is it static and predetermined. But is intelligence measurable by IQ tests and is it distributed according to the normal probability curve?

The Nature of IQ Tests

All tests measure samples of the subject, trait, skill, or behavior being tested. To be an accurate measure, such tests must be valid, i.e., they must measure what they claim to measure. Thus, IQ tests must actually measure intelligence or they are worthless. Further, what is being measured by the test must be capable of being measured. If a phenomenon cannot be tested because of its intricacy, or unavailability, or idealistic character (How many angels can dance on the head of a pin?), then it is impossible to construct a test of it. Thus, if intelligence is so complex, many-sided, changeable, and plastic, it may not be susceptible to testing.

All tests must be standardized on the population which will be measured by such tests. That is, a representative sample of that population must be used in "trying out" the test for size. A math test for third grade children should not be made up after testing a sample of sixth grade children. If IQ tests are constructed on one population or race or class, they are unsuitable as tests for a different population, race or class.

Tests must be reliable—they must produce consistent results when used. If an IQ test gives one score one day and a greatly different score the next day when used with the same children, it is unreliable and should be discarded.

IQ tests violate all the above accepted principles and procedures of test construction. IQ tests are fundamentally invalid—they do not measure intelligence. Rather, as will be demonstrated, they test the scholastic ahievement and cultural background of white middle-class children.

Further, as indicated in the preceding section, human mental development is so intricate that, at the present stage of testing sophistication, it is impossible to test intelligence. Even if such testing were possible, the tests would have to be of such variety and length, and would have to be used in so many different situations and areas, that they would have no resemblance to the present IQ tests. Indeed, how can emotional maturity, life experience, adaptability, learning rate, creativity, imagination, social skills and personality be adequately tested?

Caution and skepticism should be the watchwords in testing intelligence, as in all testing of human ability and behavior. But arrogance and dogmatism are what characterize Jensen's attitude and use of IQ tests. He accepts them as completely valid and uses their results as a completely accurate measure of intelligence or g. Jensen further defines g as "abstract and problem-solving ability." But IQ tests do not test such ability. Abstract and problem-solving ability is certainly of great importance in human mental behavior. But a careful and detailed analysis of the ten subtests that make up the Wechsler Intelligence Scale for Children shows that it tests only bits and scraps of such ability.

The Wechsler Scale tests the knowledge, skills, and information acquired mainly in school, i.e., scholastic achievement. For example, one subtest ("General Information") consists of 30 questions running from "How many ears have you?" to "What is a lien?," including questions regarding hieroglyphics, a barometer, where is Chile and what the capital of Greece is. Obviously, most of these answers should be taught and learned in school and cannot be produced out of the "problem-solving ability" of the child. Similarly, in the vocabulary subtest, the meaning of words like shilling, belfry, stanza, seclude, spangle, mantis and Hara-kiri (!) are scholastically acquired, not the result of "abstract reasoning ability."

An entire subtest is devoted to arithmetic. Where else, save in school, can the child *systematically* learn addition, multiplication, subtraction and division, or fractions, weight, and time? Is this a test of g or of what the child has been taught in school?

There is one subtest in the Wechsler IQ test that is always pointed to as testing abstract reasoning ability, Jensen's g. In this test, the child is asked, "In what way are a plum and a peach alike?" and similarly for "cat-mouse," "beer-wine," "piano-violin," etc. The best answer (receiving two points) is the general category which includes both things: "fruit" for "plum-peach," "animal" for "cat-mouse," etc. In a small experiment, the present author tested a group of children as prescribed in the manual, and later retested them after explaining in detail what was expected (Give me a word which will include both things, like "fruit" for "plum-peach.") The children did much better on the retest since they understood what the expected answer was. This is only one of many examples that could be cited of the rigidity of the IQ tests and their inability to elicit the true mental ability of children.

In addition to being tests of mainly scholastic achievement, IQ test questions are often outdated (What does C.O.D. mean?), unfair, not included in the school curriculum (Do all schools teach the words spangle, mantis, seclude?) or have little bearing on "intelligence" (Repeat this number backwards: 7-2-9-6).

Another major criticism of IQ tests are that they are culturally biased, that is, they are based upon a white middle- class culture. Thus, the white middle-class child would answer the question "What is the thing to do if a child much smaller than yourself starts to fight with you?" that he would not hit him back, or that he would tell the child's mother—and would receive a two-point score. Black, Puerto Rican, and working-class children most often answer "I'd hit him back," and would receive no credit.

Many serious professionals recognize the culture-biased nature of

IQ tests and their unsuitability for Black, Puerto Rican, Chicano, and working-class children. Desperate efforts have been made in the testing industry to construct either culture-free or culture-fair tests—but with no success. As geneticist Theodosius Dobzhansky, in answering Jensen, put it, "Certainly all existing intelligence tests fall short of being culture-free or culture-fair." [18]

It is not only a fact but a political and social crime that Black children receive qualitatively inferior education. The results of reading and math achievement tests show the educational inadequacy of our school systems in failing to teach these basic skills to Black children. Reading skills are, of course, essential if children are to progress satisfactorily in social studies, science, English, and even in math (for written problems). Since IQ tests basically measure scholastic achievement, Jensen's eleven-point difference between white and Black children on IQ tests, is fully explained: a poorer education will result in lower scholastic achievement, and a lower score on IQ tests.

Add to this the cultural bias of IQ tests in favor of white middle-class children, and the eleven-point difference becomes no difference at all—it is merely a bonus to white middle-class children for being white and middle-class and for receiving a better education.

Both the Stanford-Binet and the Wechsler Intelligence Scale for Children, in the forms relied upon by Jensen in his article before their more recent revision, were standardized on white children, i.e., no Black children were included in the sample of children used when the tests were constructed. [19] This, of course, violates the requirements of correct test construction. By accepted procedure, Blacks should never be tested with such tests. Obviously, the scholastic advantages and the cultural differences of white middle-class children will be built into tests constructed in such fashion. As stated in a current textbook of psychology, "Jensen assumed that the tests' bias in favor of middle-class whites was unimportant, even though many items on the tests obviously depend on familiarity with middle-class white culture." [20]

Several items of these IQ tests are racist or chauvinist. On the Stanford-Binet picture test, a child is marked "right" for picking out as "pretty" a white, prim-looking woman, and "wrong" if he picks a woman with Negro features and unkempt hair. In the 1949 Wechsler IQ test, the only two accepted answers to the question "Who discovered America?" were "Columbus" or "Leif Ericson." The answer "The Indians" was scored wrong! More amazing, in the recent (1974) revision of the same test, the examiner is instructed that, if the child answers "The Indians," he or she should say "Yes, but who else?," and only if the child answers "Columbus, Leif Ericson, the Norsemen, or Amerigo Vespucci" is he to be scored as "correct"—the answer "The Indians" is still wrong! As one Native American Indian leader remarked sarcastically during the takeover of Alcatraz Island, "Columbus was discovered by the Indians—and he was lost!"

IQ tests have been systematically used to test Black children for mental retardation. The result has been the disproportionate placement of Black children in such classes. In California, 62 percent of the students in classes for the mentally retarded are Black, although Blacks constitute only 28 percent of the student population.

In October 1979, U.S. District Judge Robert F. Peckham prohibited California officials from using standardized intelligence tests to place Black children in classes for the mentally retarded. In handing down his ruling, the Judge found that California's use of intelligence tests for such purposes violated Federal and state constitutional guarantees of equal protection, as well as Federal laws on civil rights and education for the handicapped. He also found that standard intelligence tests *were culturally biased against Blacks.*

Judge Peckham also ruled that there was no evidence to support the argument that the reason for the difference in IQ scores of Black and white children was a genetic difference in intelligence. In effect, this court ruling threw out Jensen's conclusions as having no legal or scientific merit.[21]

The "Normal" Distribution of Intelligence

As has been previously indicated, all IQ tests are constructed with the assumption that intelligence is distributed according to the bell-shaped normal probability curve: 4 percent at the extremes, 28 percent at the next extremes and 68 percent clustered around the median of 100 IQ. There is no basis in physiology, genetics or psychology for such an assumption. It is also absurd from the viewpoint of scientific psychology.

Pavlov long since proved in precise experimental fashion that the higher nervous activity of animals develops on the basis of a certain number of unconditioned reflexes existing at birth which, given an intact brain and nervous system, provides the basis for the development of an unlimited number of conditioned reflexes. Thus, animal behavior begins with a limited number of reflex responses which expand to an unlimited number, depending upon the conditions of life of the animal.

In human beings, the same process of development of conditioned reflexes based upon unconditioned reflexes takes place. But Pavlov made the great psychophysiological discovery of the *second signal system,* whereby humans are conditioned to words which become signals for specific stimuli (the first signal system). Here, too, as has been previously expressed in Pavlov's statement regarding the plasticity of mental behavior, Pavlov placed no limit upon the development of human intelligence. He pointed to its "immense potentialities," its mobility, and its expansion if "the proper conditions are created."

Only the undialectical and often racist and elitist psychometricians (constructers of tests) could freeze human intelligence into a fixed mold. There is absolutely no reason why intelligence cannot cluster at the highest levels. Socialist society today is leading the way in showing how the intelligence of the masses can be constantly raised and that the normal can be "abnormally" high.

Jensen's fixed, narrow, and mechanical approach to intelligence as normally distributed, is the foundation of his theory. It is on that basis that he finds the lower IQ scores of Black children to be a deficit in their innate intelligence. The eleven-point difference, he maintains, places them at the lower end of the normal distribution curve, and therefore separates them qualitatively from white children. Placing the eleven-point difference within the framework of scientific psychology, it becomes clear that this difference is due to inferior education, a different culture, and unfair and racist IQ tests. The elimination of this difference then can be achieved through providing quality education to Black children and eliminating racism. Further, the upgrading of education and the improvement of economic conditions will provide the basis for advancing the mental development of *all* children to higher levels.

One other crucial point should be made regarding Jensen's approach to the distribution of intelligence. Jensen concocted two different kinds of intelligence: Level I and Level II. This static and arbitrary division of intelligence into two levels is then converted into a racist theory by Jensen's assertion that the eleven-point difference relegates Black children to Level I intelligence and elevates middle-class white children to Level II intelligence.

If Jensen had any psychological sense, he would recognize that the difference between rote learning intelligence (Level I) and abstract reasoning intelligence (Level II) would not be a mere eleven points—it would be forty or fifty points difference, even on the unscientific IQ tests. Abstract reasoning and problem-solving ability are *fundamental human abilities.* Their absence would reduce human functioning to a quasi-animal level. The very possession and use of language is what permits abstract reasoning and problem solving. All humans, except the severely impaired, can reason abstractly and solve problems. All humans go far beyond mere rote learning.

Further, abstract reasoning and problem solving take place in all areas of life, not merely in school. The Black child, confronted with the additional problems created by poverty and racism, is constantly engaged in problem solving, in abstract reasoning, in so-called Level II intelligence. Jensen's denial of this is both unscientific and racist.

The Changeability of IQ Scores

Jensen fiercely and fixedly maintains that intelligence is a fixed quantity which is inherited through the genes. This inherited intelligence, he holds, remains basically fixed for life. IQ tests accurately measure this fixed "intelligence," he says. From the eleven point average difference in IQ scores between white and Black children, he concludes that Black children (and Black people) have an innate and unchangeable inferior intelligence *as a race.*

Repudiation of these conclusions of Jensen have been forthcoming from truly scientific scholars:

1. "Two psychologists, working independently," reported the *New York Post* on September 4, 1971, "report that any differences in intelligence and achievement test scores between whites and minority groups are due to social and economic factors." Dr. Jane R. Mercer, of the University of California in Riverside, "looked at intelligence tests," while Dr. George W. Mayeske, of the U.S. Office of Education, studied achievement tests. But at the end," the report stated, "they both reached the same conclusions: race and ethnic background have nothing to do with intelligence or scholastic achievement." Commenting on these two studies, Dr. Edward J. Cassavantes, of the U.S.

Commission on Civil Rights, stated at the annual meeting of the American Psychological Association, "These papers refute Shockley and Jensen."[22]

Dr. Mercer found that "Mexican-Americans and blacks, for example, whose families were like middle-class white Americans in Riverside, had IQs that matched the whites. Those who lived in crowded, substandard housing, whose parents didn't speak English and weren't expected to do well in school, fared badly in the IQ tests." Dr. Mayeske reported: "The differences among the racial ethnic groups approach zero as more and more considerations related to differences in their social conditions are taken into account."[23]

2. Dr. Peggy Sanday, professor of anthropology at the University of Pittsburgh, concluded from a research study that "IQ differences between racial groups is exclusively a matter of environment..." "The findings," reports the *New York Times,* "support Dr. Sanday's belief that group differences in IQ test scores are not reflective of genetic differences between racial groups. Thus, the findings oppose the theories of Arthur Jensen, the educational psychologist, and William Shockley, the Nobel Prize-winning physicist, which suggest that genetic factors are determinant.[24]

3. After Arthur Jensen had personally presented his theory at a symposium on "Racial Variations in Man," sponsored by the Institute of Biology in London, Dr. Barbara Tizard, of the Institute of Education at the University of London, said "that she had not been able to find any inborn deficiency of intellect in any ethnic group. Further, she stated that her studies showed IQ was not fixed at birth but could be continually changed by circumstance."[25]

The decisive relationship of IQ scores to environment and life experiences has been fully established. The very point made by Jensen regarding the *unchangeability* of IQ scores gives further confirmation of this relationship. That is, the IQ scores of many people, and even of groups, may remain the same precisely because the environment and the life experiences of these groups and individuals remain the same. Thus, continued inferior education and living conditions of Blacks and poor people will lead to continued lower scores on IQ and achievement tests.

On the other hand, the changeability of IQ scores has also been conclusively demonstrated. Every IQ test has what is called the "standard error of measurement," meaning that it is inaccurate by a certain amount. Thus, the Wechsler IQ test has a five-point error range[26]. This means that a child may score 90, 95 and 100, even on the same day, and the three scores would be considered valid, since an error of five points either way is one of the weaknesses of the test.

John Garcia, in attacking the validity of IQ tests, states: "An estimated 60 percent of persons may change IQ more than 15 points between their sixth and their eighteenth birthdays. In this same period an estimated ten percent of persons may change IQ scores more than 30 points. This is enough to move a child from 'normal' either up to 'genius' or down to 'moron.'"[27] Where, then, is Jensen's fixed IQ?

As long ago as 1935, Dr. Otto Klineberg proved that the longer a Black school age child from the South has resided in the North, the better his performance on intelligence testing.[28] A dramatic example of changeability of IQ scores is given by John Garcia:

> Outside the kibbutz in Israel, Jewish children of European parents have a mean IQ of 105, while a mean IQ of first generation Oriental Jews is only 85. Some would suspect that the difference is genetic. When children of both groups grow up in the kibbutz nursery, after four years, they achieve exactly the same mean IQ scores—115 points.[29]

Jensen might well have attributed the original lower IQ scores of Oriental Jewish children to their darker skins. But how can he explain the higher IQ scores?

Since the IQ is dominantly a test of scholastic achievement, better education would naturally boost IQ scores, as well as boosting scholastic achievement. Obviously, if Black children—or any children—were taught a vocabulary which included words such as those in the Wechsler vocabulary subtest (belfry, stanza, seclude, etc.), their scores on that subtest would go up. Better geography education would teach children that Chile is in South America and that Athens is the capital of Greece—score two more correct answers. Improved math education would enable Black children to answer the arithmetic subtest according to their age level. It would not take much educationally to wipe out the eleven-point difference. Indeed, would not all children shoot up beyond 100 if quality education were provided to all? Where, then is the IQ fixed for life at birth?

The very testing situation in which IQ tests are administered also tends to depress the scores of Black and working-class children. Usually a white male psychologist, a stranger to the child, administers the test in an isolated office in two one-hour sessions. The test itself is made up of a number of unfamiliar questions and tasks and each part is administered until the child makes a certain number of errors. Thus, failure and puzzlement are built into the test.

A study by Dr. Francis Palmer, of the City University of New York, showed that when sufficient time was devoted to orienting the child and placing him at ease *before the test,* the previous low IQ scores of middle- and working-class Black children in Harlem came up to normal.[30] Confirmation of this study is found in the report by Peter Watson, where he finds that both the race of the tester and the expectation of success can significantly affect the IQ scores of Black children, e.g., Black children scored significantly higher when tested by a Black examiner.[31]

It should also be pointed out that a small number of additional correct answers can cause a big jump in an IQ score. Jensen himself points out that *two* additional correct answers at the age of four (Head Start age) can raise the child's IQ by *eight points.*

In addition, IQ scores can be raised by a number of means: coaching, enrichment programs, moves to better schools, tutoring in reading or math.

Jensen is wrong about a fixed and unchangeable IQ. The only thing unchangeable is Jensen's fixed grip on his unscientific theory.

IQ, "Intelligence Genes" and "Inherited Neural Structures"

Jensen is a psychologist by profession. He is neither a geneticist nor a physiologist. However, nothing should prevent a scientist in one field from relying upon and utilizing the scientific knowledge accumulated in other fields. But Jensen violates this right by putting forth statements and conclusions in genetics and physiology that are completely unfounded and unproved.

Jensen must necessarily offer acceptable proof that intelligence is genetic and inherited if he is to validate his theory. Yet, in defending his theory in an article titled "The Differences Are Real," Jensen writes, "The genetic hypothesis, on the other hand, has not yet been put to any direct tests by the standard techniques of genetic research."[32] If genetic research *has not proved* genetic racial differences in intelligence, then Jensen has arrived at conclusions regarding Black people in the United States and in the entire world which are wholly unwarranted.

There is no worse violation of scientific method than to put forth a new and unproved entity or phenomenon as though it exists and has been scientifically proved. Yet, in seeking to show Black genetic intellectual inferiority, Jensen states:

> There are no "Black" genes or "white" genes; there are intelligence genes which are found in populations in different proportions, somewhat like the distribution of blood types. The number of intelligence genes seems to be lower over-all in the black population than in the white.[33]

First, as Shakespeare might put it, this "seems-to-be" would crucify millions of people! Second, there is no such thing as an "intelligence gene." It does not exist. It has never been discovered. It has not been counted nor is there anything known about its alleged distribution. Nobody has found it in any "proportions" in any "population." It is an invention of Jensen.

Two violations of scientific method should be enough for any "scientist." But Jensen proceeds to still more Jensenist fabrications. In the lead article of the *New York Times Magazine* of August 31, 1969, Lee Edson writes, "Jensen contends that for Level 2 abilities to develop requires not merely learning ability but also certain inherited neural structures in the brain. 'Without them, the learning of abstract concepts doesn't develop,' he says."[34]

Jensen, as previously indicated, unwarrantedly and unscientifically invented a Level II intelligence. There is no such intelligence. It has never been proved. To prove his invented Level II intelligence Jensen now invents "inherited neural structures of the brain." There is no proof that intelligence depends upon a specific neural structure, nor that there is a Level I neural structure and a Level II neural structure, nor that such neural structures are inherited, nor that only white children inherit Level II neural structures. These are all inventions of Jensen. In fact, he brings to mind all the absurdities of the discredited field of phrenology—that intelligence depends upon the shape of your skull! One is led to suspect the shape of Jensen's skull and to question *his* "inherited neural structures."

Genetics, Intelligence and Heritability

The brain and the central nervous system are the material bases for thought and consciousness. This is a fundamental physiological and psychological law. A healthy and intact brain provides the basis for normal intelligence. Damage to the brain and nervous system, chromosomal deficiencies, disease, tumors —all can cause subnormal intellectual ability. Such disabilities affect only a small percent of all children and adults.

But these scientific facts have nothing to do with Jensen's theory of racial inherited intelligence. Science has amply rejected Jensen's theory. The National Academy of Sciences has clearly stated that "there is no scientific basis for the statement that there are or are not substantial hereditary differences in intelligence between Negro and white populations."[35] In the official UNESCO publication *Race and Biology,* U.S. geneticist L.C. Dunn stated that, according to modern anthropologists, the species homo sapiens has descended from a common ancestor "and that the similar heredity which the whole species has in common, far outweighs the relative and minor ways in which subgroups differ."[36]

In a scholarly article in *Scientific American,* two leading geneticists, Walter Bodmer and Luigi Cavalli-Sforza, repudiated every major feature of Jensen's theory, including its genetic basis.[37]

History shows that complex civilizations and cultures, denoting high levels of mental ability, have arisen throughout the five continents for all races and populations. It is absurd to explain such civilizations and cultures as due to Jensen's "genetic pools of intelligence" wandering from continent to continent.

Most of Jensen's article seeks to prove that intelligence is 80 percent genetic and 20 percent environmental. He uses various studies (Jensen did no original research) and many tables, charts, and statistics in seeking to make this point.

Jensen admits that there is no "adequate determination of IQ heritability in a sample of the U.S. black population."[38] This means that there is no proof that intelligence is inherited among Black people. Even if there were such proof, Jensen concedes that it would not prove that the difference in intelligence between whites and Blacks is genetic.[39] Yet Jensen comes to that conclusion anyway!

Studies show that higher-income Black people have higher IQ scores than lower -income Black people. How can Jensen explain this difference in scores of different income groups of Black people? Jensen answers that "the average skin color of the black group runs lighter in the higher SES (Socio-Economic Status) groups."[40] In other words, middle-class Blacks are closer to being white and are therefore more intelligent than darker Blacks! Alice could not have surpassed this psychological-genetic Wonderland.

In the very same article, Jensen declares: "Since genetically conditioned physical characteristics differ markedly between racial groups, there is a strong a priori likelihood that genetically conditioned behavioral or mental characteristics will also differ."[41]

In the first place, physical characteristics of racial groups differ, not "markedly," but only slightly (superficial differences in skin color, hair texture, etc.) These superficial differences have no bearing whatsoever on human neurological, mental, or behavioral activity. There is no scientific ground for concluding that such physical differences must, either a priori or a posteriori, also mean behavioral or mental differences between racial groups. It has been conclusively demonstrated that culture, education, life experiences and attitudes play a determining role in thinking and behavior. Finally, Jensen would not dream of concluding that such mental or behavioral differences give *superiority* to Black people—which would be just as likely as otherwise.

Now for the heart of Jensen's proof of qualitatively different intelligences of Blacks and whites inherited through the genes—the identical twin studies.

Sir Cyril Burt and Identical Twin Studies

Jensen's crucial proof of the genetic inheritance of intelligence is derived from the studies of Sir Cyril Burt of identical twins in England. Since identical twins are one-egg (monozygous) twins, they possess the same genes. If the IQ scores of identical twins remain the same regardless of the environment, this would be strong proof of the inheritance of intelligence.

Burt began publishing studies of IQ testing of children in 1912, and continued such studies until shortly before his death in 1971. During that period, Burt rose from research psychologist in the London school system to adviser on education to the British government in the 1930s and 1940s. In the latter capacity, he was mainly responsible for the three-tier system of education based upon his theory that intelligence was basically innate or genetic. This tracking system assigned children permanently to one of three tracks or tiers on the basis of IQ tests given to all school children at the age of eleven. The same rationale is behind the tracking system in the United States, since Burt's influence made deep inroads into educational theory and practice here.[42]

Burt was the first psychologist to be knighted by the Crown. He won the prestigious Thorndike Prize from the American Psychological Association shortly before his death. Indeed, Burt was a giant figure in psychology and had a major impact on both psychology and education in the Western world.

Burt's most important studies, which Jensen used as proof of the inheritance of intelligence, were published in 1955, 1958 and 1966, reporting tests administered to 21 pairs of identical twins, then "over 30" such pairs, and finally 53 pairs. These "classical" studies showed that the IQ correlation of separated twins when reared in different environments was near .80—an almost perfect correlation. For identical twins reared in the same environment, the IQ correlation was over .90—practically perfect.

Burt's conclusions from these and other studies were that intelligence was inherited; that rich children were more intelligent than poor children; that the English were more intelligent than Jewish or Irish people; and that men, across the board, were smarter than women.[43]

The validity of Burt's studies became suspect when Professor Leon Kamin of Princeton University examined the original studies more carefully in 1972. "It didn't take more than ten minutes of reading to begin to suspect that it was fraudulent," Kamin stated. Kamin published his doubts in a book *Science and Politics of IQ* in 1974.[44]

In 1976, a thunderbolt struck the academic world: Burt's major work was shown to have been a complete fraud. *The New York Times* proclaimed this with the heading "Briton's Classic I.Q. Data Now Viewed as Fraudulent." Further investigation of Kamin's suspicions had proven conclusively that Burt faked the data for his studies; that he referred to sources which did not exist; that he gave credit to two mythical assistants; and that he wrote reviews under a pseudonym which highly praised his own work, and which he published in a journal which he edited.[45]

There is an interesting "heritability" of the three major proponents of Black genetic intellectual inferiority—Jensen, Eysenck and Herrnstein—and the charlatan Burt. H.J. Eysenck was Burt's favorite student. Arthur Jensen studied under Eysenck. Richard Herrnstein, of Harvard University, explicitly based his article in *The Atlantic* upholding Jensen's thesis, on Burt's data. The psychological demolition of Burt brings his three disciples crashing down with him.

Jensen's "definitive proof," for which he was hailed by other naive or racist psychologists and transistor inventors (Shockley) has come apart at the seams—or is it, at the genes? His theory has proven worthless. But the pernicious effects of Jensenism, in respect to eugenics and compensatory education, remain to be examined.

Jensen, IQ, and Eugenics

Jensen innocently claims to be a scientist in pursuit of answers to important scientific questions. He charges his critics with blinding themselves to scientific facts because of their social conscience, their concern for democracy and equality.

Science is science—its truth must be accepted, regardless of its political consequences. Jensen's shabbiness as a scholar, his disregard of scientific procedure, his acceptance of unacceptable studies, his invention of nonexistent phenomena have already been demonstrated. What is Jensen's social conscience, his concern for democracy and equality?

Jensen calls for the application of eugenics to official U.S. population policy. What is eugenics? It is the theory and practice of breeding "superior" people and eliminating "inferior" people. Eugenics is based upon the various unscientific theories of the existence of inferior races, classes, nations, and religions. Hitler's "Master Race" theory was, of course, a eugenics theory. It was this theory that led to the massacre of six million Jews, and of countless millions of "inferior" French, Russian, Polish, and Slavic peoples.

The program of the eugenics movement has included the following for "breeding a superior race": sterilization laws to be applied to "the unfit"; inhumane experimentation on the "socially inadequate"; incarceration of "the defective"; exclusion of "the inferior" from certain occupations and educational institutions and, as "The Final Solution" the extermination of the "socially undesirable."[46]

How is Jensen associated with this racist, genocidal, and atrocious movement? In his now notorious article, Jensen asks: "Is there a danger that current welfare policies, unaided by eugenic foresight, could lead to the genetic enslavement of a substantial segment of our population?"[47]

Jensen had just pointed to the fact that Black "lower class" families have more children than middle-class white families. He further points out that such Black families have a shorter "average generation time," i.e., they have children at younger ages so that there is a shorter time between their generations. What does this have to do with eugenics and "eugenic foresight"? Our concerned "scientist" is saying that the "less intelligent" Blacks are breeding faster than the more intelligent whites. He wants welfare policy to show eugenic foresight and prevent such overbreeding by "lower class" Black women. Here is where Shockley got his genocidal idea of sterilizing Black welfare mothers. Without such a policy, Jensen is suggesting, we are in danger of "genetic enslavement" by the "less intelligent race." The U.N. Convention on Genocide, adopted December 9, 1948, specifically condemns as genocide: "Imposing measures intended to prevent births within a group." Is Jensenism not genocide?

William B. Shockley has defined *dysgenics* as "retrogressive evolution through the disproportionate reproduction of the genetically disadvantaged."[48] Jensen's entire theory is aimed at showing that Black people are "genetically disadvantaged" in intelligence. On page 95 of his article, Jensen writes that "a group with a shorter generation length is more likely subject to a possible dysgenic effect." On page 91 of the same article, Jensen heads an entire section "Possible Dysgenic Trends." Jensen is, indeed, one with Shockley in trying to prevent "retrogressive evolution" due to Black "dysgenic behavior."

Jensen is enamored with the concept of breeding people for desirable traits. In this respect, he is similar to Mrs. E. H. Harriman, widow of the railroad tycoon, who founded the first major "scientific" institution devoted to sterilization in the name of eugenics. Mrs. Harriman explained her involvement in eugenics as being due to her interest in horses and their "bloodlines."[49] So, Jensen favors *assortative mating* (like marry like) of the more intelligent. "Thus," he writes, "in the long run, assortative mating may have a eugenic effect in improving the general level of intelligence."[50]

Perhaps the most extreme and elitist eugenics scheme was revealed when Shockley announced that he contributed "more than once" to a sperm bank intended to help produce exceptionally gifted children through artificial insemination of highly intelligent women with sperm from Nobel laureates.[51] Oh, genetics, what crimes are committed in thy name!

Here is the thrust of Jensen-Shockley: Eugenic sterilization of the "less intelligent Blacks," and assortative mating of the "more intelligent whites," will increase the intelligence of the population as a whole. Indeed, a most democratic scheme!

Defining a race as "a breeding population" Jensen offers the following explanation for the "lower intelligence" of Afro-Americans: "It is more likely—though speculative of course—that Negroes brought here as slaves were selected for docility and strength rather than mental ability, and that through selective mating the mental qualities never had a chance to flourish."[52] This obscene statement merits only the comment that Jensen's mental qualities never had a chance to flourish.

Having suggested that the entire Black "breeding population" be eugenically controlled (or eliminated?), Jensen also condemns to inferiority and eugenic control the entire "lower" (working) class. With the same eleven-point difference in IQ scores existing between middle-class white children and "lower class" white children, Jensen states: "If individual differences in intelligence are due largely to genetic factors, then it is virtually impossible that average intelligence differences between social classes . . . do not include a genetic component."[53] Utilizing Jensen's genocidal model for Black people, we can logically conclude that Jensen favors eugenic control (and elimination?) of the working class, as well.

Eugenic sterilization laws presently exist in 26 states in our country. These laws are aimed at "the unfit" and the "socially inadequate." By Jensen's theory, Black people are intellectually "unfit and inadequate."

Tens of thousands of welfare mothers in the United States and Puerto Rico have been sterilized, pursuant to official governmental policy. In the infamous Tuskegee Syphilis Experiment, hundreds of Black men were not treated for syphilis for a period of 40 years. (40 years!) in a federal government experiment (U.S. Public Health Service) conducted by physicians and scientists until 1972.[54] Were those Black men "socially unfit?"

Normal distribution of intelligence, g, heritability, IQ differences, breeding populations, genetic enslavement, eugenic foresight, dysgenics, socially inadequate persons, sterilization, two-track education—this, inevitably, is Jensenism. Only the crematoria are missing.

The "Failure" of Compensatory Education

Jensen began his article with the statement that compensatory education had failed—and ended it with a call for abolishing compensatory education and converting our educational system into a two-track system. The upper track of such a system would provide Level II education for middle-class white children while the lower track would provide rote Level I education for Black and "lower class" children. Has compensatory education failed and do we need a two-track educational system?

Compensatory education legislation was adopted in the mid-sixties by Congress because of mass movements by working people, particularly the vast civil rights movement initiated and carried out by Black people with white allies for decent education for their children. Like most projects that are adopted by our bureaucratic, monopoly-dominated government, compensatory education was hastily organized, poorly planned and bureaucratically administered. The curriculum was modeled on traditional nursery school socialization-and-play curriculum. Untrained teachers, using inappropriate materials, often in inadequate facilities, ran these Head Start classes for tens of thousands of pre-school children.[55]

However, sixteen years later, the Headstart Bureau of the U.S. Department of Health, Education and Welfare issued its report entitled "Lasting Effects of Preschool." The report found that children who participated in Head Start programs "were less likely to be assigned to special education classes and kept back in grade than were peers in control groups." Further, the report stated that Head Start children "scored significantly higher on mathematics achievement tests, had improved IQ scores for at least three years following the program, and had a better self-image."[56]

Another follow-up study of young people now 16 to 21 years old, revealed that 37 percent of those who had attended Head Start programs in the early 1960s were now in college or had acquired steady, skilled jobs, as compared to only 8 percent of those who had not attended Head Start programs.[57]

Compensatory education has not failed. Jensen has failed. Jensen ended his article with a call for converting our public educational system into a two-track system. On the final page, after discussing Level I and II intelligences, Jensen proposes developing "techniques by which school learning can be most effectively achieved in accordance with different patterns of ability . . . If diversity of mental abilities in a basic fact of nature, . . . schools and society must provide a range and diversity of educational methods."[58]

Our public school system, in the main, has already developed a tracking system. This system consists of "ability grouping" by class and within a class, special classes for emotionally disturbed, minimal brain-damaged, and hyperactive children, mentally retarded classes, segregated schools, suspensions and exclusions, etc. All these forms of tracking are used in racist fashion in most school systems. This unofficial tracking system would be made official on a racial basis by Jensen's proposal. It must be rejected.

The Fightback Against Jensenism

In a fine article entitled "Scientific Racism and IQ: The Silent Mugging of the Black Community," Black psychologist Dr. Robert L. Williams, director of Black Studies and professor of psychology at Washington University in St. Louis, wrote:

> Now, blacks suffer another counterforce to survival: scientific racism. It has always been part of the American formula, but recently it has grown more virulent with advances in technology. This cold and inhumane experimentation with, and exclusion of, human beings is insidious because it is housed in universities, nurtured in industry, and cloaked in the language of rational science.[59]

Zeroing in on IQ tests and Jensen, Professor Williams said, "An Ashanti proverb warns, 'It is the calm and silent waters that drown a man.' But the calmness fools no one; scientific racism is part of silent racial war. And the practitioners of it use intelligence tests as their hired guns."

Satirizing in scientific fashion the sacred Jensen IQ tests, Dr. Williams developed the Black Intelligence Test of Cultural Homogeneity (BITCH), which he declared was as fair for Black children as the Wechsler Intelligence Scale for Children (WISC) was for white children. While the WISC measured Blacks' knowledge of the white experience, the BITCH, says Dr. Williams, measures whites' knowledge of Black experience.[60] Of course, white children score significantly lower than Black children on this test.

Dramatically highlighting the Black liberation fight against Jensenism and all racism, the National Black Psychologists Association approved in September 1975 the recommendation of its chairman, Dr. George D. Jackson, "to develop and document a petition to the United Nations charging the United States with genocide against Black Americans."[61] It is doubly significant that Dr. Jackson, in his proposal, pointed out that three great Black leaders, Paul Robeson, William Patterson and Dr. W.E.B. DuBois, had presented a similar petition to the United Nations in 1951.[62]

Eloquently exposing the system of racism in capitalist United States, Dr. Jackson declared:

> This system must be replaced and the land must change hands. Indeed, social change is all around us. And the once powerful reactionary United States has lost its omnipotence. In Africa, in Asia, in South America and in the Caribbean—even in Europe itself—socialism is coming into being... It is clear that socialism is advancing, however you wish to define it. As a matter of fact, our ancestors had socialism long before colonial exploitation. We speak of a new era where man harnesses nature to help himself and his brother, where hunger is unknown and racism is erased by human dignity.[63]

Chicano and Puerto Rican professionals and Hispanic people's organizations have also protested the misuse and abuse of IQ tests with Hispanic children. Thus, John Garcia, in denouncing the use of IQ tests as a measure of the intelligence of Hispanic children, stated: "Jensen, Shockley and Herrnstein confirm that there is a conspiracy to make a narrow, biased collection of items the 'real measure of all persons.'"[64]

Dr. Edward A. De Avila, director of research and planning for Bilingual Children's TV, Inc., makes more specific the nature of this conspiracy. After testing Latin-American children with a battery of developmental tests, Dr. De Avila concluded: "These tests prove that Latin-American children have no built-in inability to learn. Their lack of success in the schools is caused by the unfamiliar language, materials and classroom setting they encounter here. All are keyed to middle-class Anglo-American culture, which they do not happen to share, and they find no bridge between it and the language and culture they know at home."[65]

The fight against Jensenism has also fully involved white professionals and organizations. Population geneticist Richard Lewontin, of the University of Chicago, has charged Jensen with "wilful confusion" of statistics to justify his racist conclusions.[66]

Faculty and staff members of the University of Connecticut issued a statement condemning Jensenism in these words: "The doctrine of racial inferiority is unscientific as well as socially vicious . . . (the new racist) theories, despite their academic garb, do not differ in their scientific character or their social effects from those advanced by American slave-owners, the Nazis, or the advocates of apartheid in South Africa."[67] It might be added here that 2000 years ago, Cicero said, "Do not obtain your slaves from Britain because they are so stupid, and so utterly incapable of being taught."[68] Perhaps Jensen is descended from Cicero and acquired his racism through the genes.

Jensen's theory is, of course, a political theory. One congressman inserted Jensen's entire *Harvard Educational Review* article in the *Congressional Record.* Following Jensen's own testimony before congressional committees that money spent on compensatory education was "lavish and extravagant," the strangulation of Head Start programs began and, by 1974, they had been effectively destroyed by Nixon and the cooperatively-Jensenist Congress.

The fight against Jensenism has even forced Jensen to retreat in certain respects. In his new 786-page book *Bias in Mental Testing,* Jensen maintains his basic position that there is Black genetic inferiority in intelligence. However, he claims that he is "an agnostic" on the question of an environmental explanation of the Black-white difference in IQ performance. Jensen also revised his estimate of genetic influence downward—from 80 percent to 70 percent. He even declares himself against setting up special classes for slow children, and says that he does not think that IQ tests should be used extensively in the elementary schools.[69]

Dr. Robert L. Williams best placed the political nature of Jensenism when he declared:

> The primary issues in the great black-white controversy are not those of cultural test bias, the nature of intelligence, or the heritability of IQ. The issue is admittance to America's mainstream. IQ and achievement tests are nothing but updated versions of the old signs down South that read "For Whites Only."[70]

The fight to defeat Jensenism and all racism is a fight for democracy and equality, just as the banning of Nazi ideology was a democratic necessity following World War II. The words of Frederick Douglass in his appeal for the defeat of the slave-owners during the Civil War have pertinent and inspiring meaning today for all who believe in democracy:

Action! Action! not criticism is the plain duty of this hour. The office of speech now is only to point out when, where and how to strike to best advantage. There is no time to delay. The tide is at its flood that leads on to fortune. From East to West, from North to South, the sky is written all over "NOW OR NEVER."[71]

The struggle against racism, scientific or otherwise, must be led by working people. Perhaps Langston Hughes placed it best in a letter he wrote:

Levee, levee, how high does you have to be
To keep them cold muddy waters from washing over me?
You can take that for a text and say:
"Our levee has to be so high
The exploiters can't get over it,
Neither can they get under it,
Neither can they get through it.
It has to stretch so far,
They can't get by it,
And they can't do nothing about it.
It has to be built
With the sandbags of the working class.
Can't nobody else
Build a levee
That won't break down."
Amen![72]

8

Racism in Psychiatry

Psychiatry is a healing science. In its diagnosis and treatment of mental illness, psychiatry should apply the most scientific, effective and humane principles and techniques, without fear or favor—and without racism. Yet history has witnessed and we witness today in the United States consistent and widespread racism in psychiatry—in its diagnosis and treatment, in its theory and its research, in its facilities and personnel. Rather than becoming a Hippocratic barrier to the institutional and ideological racism which saturates our society, or a healing oasis for the mentally ill and their families, psychiatry has developed its own, specifically racist psychiatric theories and practices—crude and subtle, open and disguised, brutal and sophisticated.

In his foreword to the excellent book *Racism and Psychiatry* by Alexander Thomas and Samuel Sillen, Dr. Kenneth Clark denounces "the pervasive racism of psychiatric assumptions and principles" and states: "Science in the latter third of the 20th Century must be an instrument of truth and justice; if it is not, it is an infernal accessory to dehumanization and death."[1]

Drapetomania

The history of psychiatry in the United States reveals the most savage and vicious uses of psychiatry to uphold the slave system and, following its destruction in the crucible of the liberating Civil War, to maintain an oppressive and exploitative racist system in our country.

Slavery, the system for accumulating massive profits and political power on the blood, sweat and tears of millions of Black people, required ideological rationales. Alienists (as psychiatrists were known at that time) and physicians provided some of them. As a vivid example, what could serve as a satisfactory explanation for the large number of slaves who escaped, besides their hatred of and resistance to their bondage? Why, they must be insane. Since a scientific term for such "insanity" is more readily accepted, Dr. Samuel Cartwright, a well-known physician in Louisiana, coined the term *Drapetomania,* which he defined as "the flight-from-home madness." Further, Dr. Cartwright diagnosed as *Dysaesthesia Aethiopica,* an "insensibility of nerves," another "mental illness" which, in his own words, made many slaves "pay no attention to the rights of property. . . .slight their work . . . raise disturbances with their overseers."[2]

Another potent "scientific" excuse for slavery was that Blacks were physiologically inferior in intelligence. In 1840, Dr. Samuel G. Morton, professor of anatomy at Pennsylvania Medical College, announced his "discovery," based upon his craniometric (measuring of skulls) research, that the brain of different races differed in size, and that the smallest brain belonged to "the Ethiopian."[3] Such "discoveries" have cropped up constantly since then, but Thomas and Sillen report: "In a detailed and careful review of the subject in 1969 in the *American Journal of Physical Anthropology,* anatomist Phillip V. Tobias has effectively demolished the legend that there is a demonstrated correlation between brain-size, gray matter, and race."[4]

The famous European psychiatrist Carl G. Jung developed a twentieth century variant of the "intellectual inferiority" theory. Jung put forth his scientifically ignorant conclusion that there are different layers of the mind and that the Negro has one layer less than the white man, which makes him "childish" and "primitive."[5]

Sharing in the infamy of developing racist theories to uphold racist oppression was the well-known instinct psychologist William McDougall, who attributed the "instinct of submission" to the Negro race.[6] McDougall missed his chance to invent a new scientific term such as "Submissionomania" which could then compete with its opposite, "Drapetomania," the refusal to submit.

Utilization of government agencies has been a favorite method of spreading racist propaganda. The sixth U.S. Census in 1840 reported that "insanity and idiocy" among Negroes was eleven times higher in the North than in the South. The slaveocrats chortled with glee at that statistic, proclaiming that the Black man becomes prey to mental illness when he is given his freedom. Dr. Edward Jarvis, a Massachusetts specialist in mental disorders, who had accepted the census statistic at face value, later investigated the figures himself and concluded that the Census, in that regard, was "a fallacious and self-condemning document."[7]

More recently, A. Deutsch, in an article fittingly entitled "The First U.S. Census of the Insane (1840) and Its Use as Pro-Slavery Propaganda,"[8] concluded that the 1840 census statistics on Negro insanity was "one of the most amazing tissues of statistical falsehood and error ever woven together under government imprint." An example of such "amazing falsehood" in the 1840 census was the listing of "133 Negro lunatics and idiots" in Worcester, Massachusetts. The figure was actually the total number of patients in the Worcester State Hospital for the Insane—*all white!*[9]

The reaction of Blacks to that self-serving lie of slavery is found in the angry but psychologically sound statement made at that time by Dr. James McCune Smith, a leading Black physician, in the New York *Tribune:* "Freedom has not made us mad, it has strengthened our minds by throwing us on our own resources."[10]

The above are just a few of the myriad examples of the racist roles of many in the psychiatric profession in claiming the psychiatric and psychological inferiority of Black people. But even more elaborate and sophisticated theories have become necessary in the more recent period to try to stem the mounting movement for Black liberation.

Pathology or Racism?

"(The Negro mother) tends to be infantilizing and over-protective towards her children who, while receiving maximal gratification at the oral phase of development, are usually subjected to prohibitive, demanding or threatening attitudes at the anal and phallic levels. They are thus obstructed on the road to maturity." So writes A. Sclare in an article with the title "Cultural Determinants in the Neurotic Negro."[11]

Apart from the question of whether such a tortured and convoluted statement is even comprehensible, this quote is typical of the unscientific and objectively racist psychiatric theory applied to Blacks today and in the recent past. Such theory varies from crude, unsupported statements, to elaborate research studies which purport to discover Black personality traits—all negative, pathological and deviant.

In the former category is the statement by Dr. A. Carothers, an official of the World Health Organization: "The African makes very little use of his frontal lobes. All the particularities of African psychiatry can be put down to frontal laziness."[12] Apart from the scientific laziness of Dr. Carothers in failing to provide some basis for such a scientifically illiterate statement, the frontal lobes of the cerebral cortex are essential for any human functioning and are not subject to voluntary control. There can be no question of "laziness"; all humans necessarily utilize their frontal lobes—except possibly Dr. Carothers.

Frantz Fanon, the Black African revolutionary psychiatrist, referred to "the poverty and absurdity" of such theories, remarking scornfully that "Dr. Carothers defined the Mau-Mau revolt as the expression of an unconscious frustration complex whose reoccurrence could be scientifically avoided by spectacular scientific adaptations."[13] As E. Fuller Torrey points out, "(Fanon) saw the real problems of the world as racism and colonialism, not as intrapsychic conflicts related to Oedipus."[14]

Psychiatric racism finds a splendid rationale in the psychodynamic theory of the unconscious, infantile sexual phases, defense mechanisms, and, of course, the Oedipus complex. Examples abound; a few will suffice. R. H. Sharpley believes that slavery caused Blacks to regress to the oral stage, but now they are confronted, like children, by tasks of psychosexual growth.[15] Psychiatrists D.M. Hunter and C.G. Babcock write that Blacks have "failure of ego development" because of regression to or fixation on objects of early childhood.[16] Psychiatrist Helen V. McLean explains "the Negro's hostility against whites" as due to his anxiety and guilt because of his need and dependence on whites.[17]

Thomas and Sillen correctly point out: "The Black man's justified suspicion of white people is mistakenly identified as paranoia pure and simple. His bitter protest against a boss or a slumlord is seen as an expression of 'Oedipal hostility.'"[18]

Not only is Black personality and Black protest seen in Freudian terms but racism itself is given a psychoanalytic twist. So, R. Sterba attributed anti-Black violence by whites during the 1947 race riots in Detroit to sibling jealousy and the Oedipus complex.[19] J.W. Hamilton, in true Freudian fashion, speaks of "the anal components of white hostility and aggression toward the Negro."[20]

Indeed, psychiatric racism, merged with Freudianism, found criminal expression in the staggering statement in the *Journal of the American Psychoanalytic Association* that prejudice can be an ego defense mechanism for dealing with unconscious aggressive impulses and, thus, "is not without a positive measure of value for the individual and in a broad way for society as a whole."[21] The horror of this statement is compounded by the fact, as Thomas and Sillen point out, that it was never refuted in the psychoanalytic literature, and was professionally refuted finally fourteen years later by Dr. H.A. Robinson, a Black psychiatrist.[22]

So pervasive is Freudian theory that two Black psychiatrists were unable to break its stranglehold. In their book *Black Rage*[23] which was based mainly on a study of Black *psychiatric patients,* Drs. William H. Grier and Price M. Cobbs attempted to analyze Black struggles and behavior from the standpoint of psychoanalytic theory. In a review in *The Black Scholar,* Janet Saxe writes: "*Black Rage* is a collection of commonly held assertions about Black people strung on a thin thread of Freudian psychoanalysis and clasped together with interestingly tragic anecdotes about a few unusually unfortunate Black people." In wry fashion, Ms. Saxe comments: "Elsewhere in the book, the authors state that Black people have developed cultural paranoia, cultural depression, cultural masochism and cultural anti-socialism as adaptive devices. Being untutored in the art of psychoanalysis, some of us had thought that Black people survived by perseverance, cunning, skill, guile and some 'tomming.'"[24]

Not only does psychoanalysis lend itself to racist explanations of Black personality, thought and behavior, but in its typically unscientific approach, it arrives at sweeping conclusions on the basis of the flimsiest of studies. A closer examination of one such study can illustrate a major feature of psychiatric racism—racism in research.

Best known, most quoted, and considered a classical work on the Black personality is *The Mark of Oppression* by A. Kardiner and L. Ovesey. Here are the conclusions of this "classic": Blacks have a "wretched internal life"; they suffer from low self-esteem; the basic

Black personality is "a caricature of the corresponding white personality"; Blacks are "vindictive and vituperative"; they have a pathological sense of inferiority; there is a deformity in the Black psyche.[25]

What is the basis for such shocking and all-encompassing psychiatric conclusions concerning the psyche and personality of an entire people? Certainly, massive research of the highest order based upon the strictest scientific criteria must have been carried out by these two "scientists."

In point of fact, Kardiner and Ovesey based their entire book on twenty interviews with each of twenty-five—yes, twenty-five—Black subjects, eleven of whom were paid $1.50 per interview, while twelve other subjects received free psychotherapy. There was neither random selection nor selection of a representative sample of Black people— fundamental requirements of scientific research. All but one of the twenty-five subjects had clear signs of psychological disturbance. No effort was made to include Blacks who were psychologically healthy. There was no control group—Kardiner and Ovesey arrogantly stated that their control group was "the American White Man."

Thus from a paid, unrepresentative sample of twenty-five mostly psychologically disturbed Black people, with no control group, Kardiner and Ovesey arrived at horrendous conclusions about twenty-two million people—conclusions which confirmed every racist stereotype of Black people.

Ignorance usually goes hand-in-hand with racism. Thus, Kardiner and Ovesey observe that one of their patients "insists that she is not Negro, but Afro-American, indicating how deeply vulnerable she is on the subject of color. This means that her predominant trait is self-hatred. . . ."[26] Kardiner and Ovesey are, indeed, "deeply vulnerable" in their cultural ignorance, as well as in their research and psychiatric racism.

The Black Matriarchy: Moynihan v. Blacks

Daniel Patrick Moynihan, Richard Nixon's favorite ideologist, won his spurs for psychiatric racism with the highly publicized Moynihan report.[27] His role as an "infernal accessory to dehumanization" is via the Black family. Here is Moynihan's basic thesis: "In essence, the Negro community has been forced into a matriarchal structure which, because it is so out of line with the rest of American society, seriously retards the progress of the group as a whole, and imposes a crushing burden on the Negro male and, in consequence, on a great many women as well." The result of this "matriarchal structure," according to Moynihan, is that the Black family is "approaching complete breakdown" while "the white family has achieved a high degree of stability and is maintaining that stability." Moynihan's stark conclusion is a psychiatric one: the Black family is "a tangle of pathology."

It is rather difficult to know how to deal with Moynihan's tangle of lies, misstatements, erroneous sociologizing, exorbitantly wrong psychiatric reasoning, and plain racism. First, at the time that Moynihan burst his "Black matriarchy" theory on the political scene (1965), three-fourths of all Black families had both father and mother in the home, according to the Bureau of Labor Statistics (the figure for white families was nine-tenths).[28] This figure alone refutes Moynihan's "Black matriarchy" theory completely, even without taking into account the fact that many "mother-only" Black families have a common-law husband in the house, who must be hidden from public agencies because of their rigid rules.

Second, Moynihan's flat statement regarding the stability of white families is laughable in view of the huge divorce rate, the alienation of many white youth from their families, the harmful effects of unemployment, inflation and impoverishment on many families. Further, there is no convincing psychiatric, psychological, or sociological evidence that pathology results when children are brought up by the mother alone.

Finally, Moynihan's thesis of the "emasculation" of Black men by "the matriarch" has been refuted by the movements of hundreds of thousands of Black men, together with Black women, in struggles for equality and freedom. Some emasculation!

In 1971, the National Urban League issued a report on *The Strength of Black Families* to contradict what it called "widely circulated studies" (are you listening, Daniel Moynihan?) that Black families were "matriarchal, disorganized, pathological and disintegrating." The Urban League's Associate Director of Research, Dr. Robert B. Hill, told newsmen: "Our own lives taught us that these things social scientists were telling us were not true." Dr. Hill listed the five strengths of Black families that were analyzed in the report: " . . . Their adaptability of family roles, strong kinship bonds, strong work orientation, strong religion orientation and strong achievement orientation."[29]

It is significant that the Urban League's report grew out of recommendations made in the book *Black Families in White America* by Dr. Andrew Billingsley, vice-president of Howard University. According to *The New York Times,* "Dr. Billingsley has contended in the book that the studies by white scholars, and especially *The Negro Family: A Call for National Action,* by Daniel Patrick Moynihan, had overlooked the strengths in Black families that allowed them to survive slavery and oppression for centuries in the United States." [30]

It remained only to zero in on Moynihan's *political* goal in putting forth such unscientific and racist ideas. This was aptly done by Robert Staples in an article "The Myth of the Black Matriarchy" in *The Black Scholar,* where he states: "It has been functional for the white ruling class, through its ideological apparatus, to create internal antagonisms in the Black community between men and women to divide them and to ward off effective attacks on the external system or white racism. It is a mere manifestation of the divide-and-conquer strategy, used by most ruling classes, through the annals of man, to continue the exploitation of an oppressed group." [31]

Toward a Scientific Approach to Black Personality

The first element—crucial and indispensable—in the approach to the evaluation of the Black family, their personality, intellect, emotional life and mental health, is the discarding totally and completely of all ideas of Black inferiority, either genetic or acquired. That there are differences, distinctions, uniquenesses and dissimilarities in Black people, as well as in other people, ethnic or national, is clear. A scientific approach, discarding the idea of inferiority, must seek to understand and to delineate such differences and unique features, as well as the fundamental commonalities.

Second, any attempt to discover pathology, deviance, aberrations, or breakdown in the Black people *as a whole* will inevitably land in the swamp of racism. The report of the National Urban League cited above should be a guideline for any evaluation of Black consciousness and Black life: the evaluator must take into account the strengths, skills, knowledge, and coping abilities of Black people in U.S. capitalist society today.

Further, all researchers and behavioral scientists, especially those who are white, must be modest and cautious in their studies and conclusions. Kardiner and Ovesey's *The Mark of Oppression* must stand as a shameful example of *what not to do* in such research. Many racist pitfalls await the arrogant researcher who "samples" the Black community to arrive at conclusions about Black personality, or who approaches ghetto rebellions as expressions of Black family weakness or of Black intrapsychic conflicts. A solid understanding of the sociopolitical character of racism and its effects will prevent egregious blunders. Many tests, beloved of psychologists and social scientists, such as intelligence tests (Wechsler or Stanford-Binet)* or Self-Concept Scales,** become racist as well as unscientific, when applied to Black people.

The attitude of "objectivity and neutrality" so dearly embraced by most researchers usually turns off Black people, sets up a professional wall which separates the researcher from his subjects, and makes most studies worthless. Black suspicion of "objective" white investigators is completely justified since most of those studies end up with wrong and racist conclusions. Finally, all research in Black communities must rest upon the solid foundation that Black people are oppressed by poverty, unemployment, low wages, bad housing, poor health care, inferior education, and institutionalized racism.

Tomorrow's Tomorrow: The Black Woman

A model for research in the Black community is Dr. Joyce A. Ladner's *Tomorrow's Tomorrow: The Black Woman*.[32] Written as her doctoral thesis, this work was undertaken by Dr. Ladner as an effort to understand the lives and personalities of adolescent and preadolescent Black girls in a low-income housing project in St. Louis. In a four-year study, she began with several peer groups of various ages and based her final study on randomly selected girls from these groups.

Dr. Ladner states forcefully that the only reason she was able to conduct her study successfully was by ridding herself of "the deviant perspective," i.e., the perspective that looks for deviance in the Black community, the perspective that academic training builds into the researcher.[33]

Dr. Ladner also soon discarded her "objectivity and neutrality": "As I became more involved with the subjects of this research, I knew that I would not be able to play the role of the dispassionate scientist,

---

*See Chapter 7 for discussion of IQ Tests.
**See Chapter 10 for discussion of instruments used in Behavior Research.

whose major objective was to extract certain data from them that would simply be used to *describe* and *theorize* about their conditions. I began to perceive my role as a Black person, with empathy and attachment, and, to a great extent, their day-to-day lives and future destinies became intricately interwoven with my own."[34]

Rather than looking for pathology, Dr. Ladner sought for and found "a vast amount of strength and adaptability" in Black people: "My primary concern here is with depicting the strength of the Black family and Black girls within the family structure. I will seek to depict the lives of Black people I knew who were utilizing their scant resources for survival purposes, but who on the whole were quite successful in making the necessary adaptive and creative responses to their oppressed circumstances."[35]

Criticizing research in sociology and psychology, Dr. Ladner writes: "The strong resilience and modes of adaptation which Black people developed to combat the forces of poverty and racism, produced by neo-colonialism, were *never* recognized as important areas of intellectual inquiry."[36]

Dr. Ladner remarked that later in her study she realized "that perhaps a very healthy and successful adaptation, given their limited resources, had been made by all these girls to a set of very unhealthy environmental conditions."[37]

Dr. Ladner arrived at a number of specific significant conclusions from her study: poor Black children mature earlier and become *active agents* rather than *passive recipients* in their environment; family life is vital in the Black community; the relationship between parent and child is more open and honest in the Black community because of the need of the parents to communicate with the child on the subject of "external hostile forces" (i.e., institutionalized racism); the extended family, including aunts and grandmothers, often serves to prepare young girls for womanhood; Black girls of low-income families "see their world as one that involves conflict between the rich and the poor";[38] most Black children have a positive self-image; the "black male emasculation" thesis has been developed to "continue systematically to exclude him from equal participation in society."[39]

Dr. Ladner asserts that a scientific approach will find that the Black child is "a more emotionally stable and well-integrated personality than his white middle-class counterparts . . . "[40]

As a real behavioral scientist, who brings knowledge and clarity to her research, she finds that, viewed correctly, *"The society, instead of its members, becomes pathological."*[41]

Dedicating her book, "For my mother, Annie Ruth Perryman, who taught me what it meant to become a Black Woman," Dr. Ladner fittingly sets off the following four lines of the poet Don L. Lee:

> soft: the way her eyes view her children
> hard: her hands; a comment on her will
> warm: just the way she is, jim!
> sure: as yesterday, she's tomorrow's tomorrow.

Black Contact with the Psychiatric World

In her book *Women and Madness,* Phyllis Chesler writes, "(It) is undeniable that Black women and men are discriminated against and misunderstood whenever they make contact with the psychiatric world."[42] Concerning the treatment that Black patients receive when they suffer severe mental illness, Dr. Chesler states: "There is no question that psychiatric hospitalization, with all its attendant cruelties, is both racist in its practices and in its meaning."[43]

Every area of psychiatric diagnosis and treatment is saturated with racism. Here, briefly, is a summary of the facts of such psychiatric racism. Psychiatric facilities are scandalously scant in ghetto communities. Very few psychiatrists and neurologists are available in such areas—Park Avenue pays much better! Besides, huge fees ($50 for the 50-minute psychiatric hour) exclude most Blacks. Blacks who appear to be mentally disturbed are usually taken to jail by the police, while whites are taken to psychiatric emergency rooms. In outpatient clinics, Blacks are treated for shorter periods than are whites.[44]

Blacks rarely see psychiatrists as private patients; 99 percent of the patients in individual therapy are white. When they do, the psychiatrists, only one percent of whom are Black, usually cannot relate to them. Psychiatrists themselves have *preferred* patients: white women, white men, Black women, Black men, in that order.

The poor mentally ill, including many Black patients, receive mainly custodial care and drugs rather than the psychotherapy, activity programs, etc., which are provided for the middle class and the rich.

Dr. Chesler reports a study of 2,279 voluntary patients seen at a Baltimore psychiatric emergency clinic between 1964 and 1966.[45] Among the conclusions of this study were:

1. "Women were diagnosed as 'psychotic' more than men, Black women especially so."

2. Black women were referred for hospitalization more often than white women with the same diagnosis, i.e., Black women are more often seen as needing institutionalization rather than psychotherapy as outpatients, even though they have *the same diagnosis* as white women.

3. Black male alcoholics were hospitalized more often than white male alcoholics—and so received the attendant racist cruelties.

It should also be noted that Black welfare recipients are often required to submit to a psychological and/or psychiatric evaluation, or endure a "rehabilitation program," as a condition for receiving public welfare.[46]

This all-pervasive racist psychiatric treatment results in great distrust by Black people of psychiatrists and psychiatric facilities. Arnold Rogow, in his book *The Psychiatrists,* quotes a young psychiatrist: "I had high hopes of doing something for neglected people who are sick—the Negroes, Mexicans, Puerto Ricans, the poor in general. . . . So when I tried to discuss things with them, they just wouldn't discuss. 'Look, Doc,' they'd say, 'forget the horseshit. Just give me something to get me through the day so I don't lose my temper so much!'"[47]

Specific new—and racist—forms of psychiatric "treatment" have been developed under the heading of Behavior Modification. These forms are specifically discussed in a separate chapter.[48] Here, it should only be noted that these forms—psychosurgery, electric shock, vomit-inducing drugs, electrode implants in the brain, sensory deprivation, electrophysiology, aversive therapy, isolation cells, and remote control of behavior—are being used on prison populations and mentally ill people, large numbers of whom are Black. These are racist instruments for repression and control.

Racism in Psychiatry: The Struggle to End It

In a dramatic speech before the American Psychiatric Association meeting in Cobo Hall, Detroit on May 9, 1974, Coleman Young, the city's Black mayor, stated: "Your profession is being misused, as all professions are misused in a racist society, to justify the continued exploitation not only of Black people but of poor people. Among Black people, psychiatry has been looked upon as another missionary group bent on fitting them to a social and economic status they find unacceptable."

Citing as a particularly frightening tool of psychiatry, the psychosurgery that destroys the portion of the brain said to be the cause of violent behavior, Mayor Young said, "That sounds to me like 1984. We (Black people) are particularly concerned because we are always the experimental subjects, the expendables. I want to tell you right now, I don't want any part of operations on people's brains to change their behavior in a racist society in 1974 with Nixon in the White House . . . Black people are not yet ready to become psychiatrists' guinea pigs and sacrificial lambs. We are not marching docilely off to any ovens. The problem is not what's inside our heads but what's inside the heads of our oppressors."[49]

This statement by Mayor Young emphasizes the urgency of the fight to eradicate racism in psychiatry. Important movements towards this end are taking place in all the behavioral disciplines: psychology, psychiatry, sociology, etc. Radical caucuses and Black caucuses are being formed which are pressing for equality of treatment and facilities.

At the 1969 meeting of the American Psychiatric Association, 100 Black psychiatrists called on that organization to end the traditional "exclusion of Blacks from positions of influence and authority." They also urged the A.P.A. to insure desegregation of all public and private mental health facilities, and to deny or revoke the membership of any psychiatrist who refuses to treat Black patients, maintains a segregated office, or works in a segregated or discriminatory facility. They further demanded that the National Institute of Mental Health "change its whole stance, vis-a-vis the Black community"—in hiring practices, financing mechanisms, use of Black consultants, and program development.[50]

Although Black psychiatrists, psychologists, social workers, and other mental health workers, are leading the fight to end racism in psychiatry, it is the responsibility and duty (Hippocratic, if you will) of white psychiatrists and mental health workers to cleanse the profession of this inhumane, antitherapeutic scourge. The only worthy psychiatry is a nonracist psychiatry.

The A.P.A. Board of Trustees was forced to recognize the justice of the demands of the 100 Black psychiatrists and pledged to act on them. Thomas and Sillen correctly comment: "Implementation of this pledge would indeed have a liberating influence on theory and practice in American psychiatry."[51] Victories *can* be won—the racist walls *can* come tumbling down.

A vital step in purging racism from psychiatry would be the winning of a system of free, comprehensive, available, quality mental health care for all *on an equal basis,* paid for by the rich and controlled by people's organizations—maybe with Coleman Young at its head! This kind of mental health care is precisely what is available to everyone in the Soviet Union, where racism was outlawed when Lenin led the working people to political power, and where psychiatry *is* a healing science.

9

Women and Psychiatry

In his article, "Some Psychological Consequences of the Distinction Between the Sexes," Sigmund Freud wrote:

> I cannot escape the notion . . . that for women the level of what is ethically normal is different from what it is in men . . . that they show less sense of justice, that they are less ready to submit to the great necessities of life, that they are more often influenced in their judgments by feelings of affection or hostility. . . . We must not allow ourselves to be deflected from such conclusions by the denials of the feminists, who are anxious to force us to regard the two sexes as completely equal in position and worth.[1]

The "feminists," in their present-day counterpart in the women's liberation movement, are indeed fighting mightily "to force us to regard the two sexes as completely equal in position and worth." This valiant and valuable struggle for equality of women has attacked Freud and the whole psychiatric establishment as servants of sexism, as ideological and professional upholders of male supremacy and women's oppression. Kate Millet, Shulamith Firestone, Germaine Greer, Dr. Naomi Weisstein, Karen DeCrow and Dr. Phyllis Chesler have launched powerful shots and shells against Freudianism in particular, and against psychiatry in general. Kate Millett, for example, calls Freud "beyond question the strongest individual counter-revolutionary force" against the movement for women's liberation.[2]

The struggle against women's oppression and for full equality is a complex struggle. A Marxist evaluation of the role of psychiatry in women's oppression and of the women's liberation critique of psychiatry is necessary.

Sigmund Freud: Psychiatric Male Supremacist

"Anatomy is destiny." With these three dramatic words, Sigmund Freud pronounced a sentence of psychological and psychiatric inferiority on women. Starting with anatomical sex differences, Freud weaves a psychiatric theory of women's inferiority in every area of life. It is a theory which is male supremacist to the core.

Starting with the obvious anatomical difference between the sexes—penis in the male and vagina in the female—Freud, in speculative and unscientific fashion, arrives at sweeping psychological conclusions. For boys, he asserts, the discovery of this anatomical difference results in male pride in his penis, and in contempt for the "deprived" girl. For girls, to whom, as Freud puts it, "the penis of a brother or a playmate (is) strikingly visible and of large proportions,"[3] such discovery is disastrous. The recognition by girls of the penis as "the superior counterpart of their own small and inconspicuous organ," has dire results according to Freud: "They are then overcome by envy culminating in the wish . . . to be boys themselves."[4]

Pursuing his anatomical theme to its most extreme psychological degree, Freud concludes that the consequences for women are inferiority feelings and self-hatred: "After a woman has become aware of the wound to her narcissism, she develops, like a scar, a sense of inferiority. When she has passed beyond her first attempt at explaining her lack of a penis as being a punishment personal to herself and has realized that the sexual character is a universal one, she begins to share the contempt felt by men for a sex which is lesser in so important a respect."[5]

From anatomy, Freud constructs women's psychological destiny. In hundreds of references throughout his works, Freud characterizes women as strange, secretive and insincere, more envious, less reliable, less self-sufficient, masochistic, passive, childlike, hyperemotional, less rational than men, more prone to neurosis especially hysteria, and filled with inferiority and self-hatred.

Perhaps the most striking sexist feature of Freud's entire theory is his basic assumption and acceptance of the personality and emotional life of men as the norm for human personality. The personality and emotional life of women were measured and judged by Freud against this masculine model, and found to be wanting. As Richard Gilman put it in his article in the *New York Times* entitled "The FemLib Case Against Sigmund Freud,": "In psychoanalysis, maleness is the norm and femaleness an incomplete or, even worse, deficient aspect of it."[6]

Hence, for Freud, women were incomplete and inadequate men; they were *abnormal,* and even *mysteriously* abnormal. As he express-ed it, "the difference of woman from man" is found in "her inexplica-ble, mysterious and strange nature."[7] Scientifically, this is surely an inexplicable, mysterious and strange theory.

Freud invented theories of psychosexual development (different and worse for women), of Oedipus and Electra complexes, of sexual repression and sublimation, of id-ego-super-ego dynamics, which have no relation to psychological or psychiatric reality, and all of which, in intricate and tortured manner, provided his theoretical rationale for his profoundly supremacist conclusions regarding women.

Psychoanalysis: Adjusting the Woman to Her Role

Freud presented both a theory of the psyche and a treatment for the disturbed psyche, for mental illness. His theory is both a psychological theory for explaining the normal personality and a psychiatric theory for explaining the abnormal personality. The treatment for mental illness, which Freud termed psychoanalysis, flowed from his theory in logical, albeit unscientific fashion.

Freud's psychoanalytic treatment of women was based upon his basic theory of women's personality. Since this theory found women to be filled with penis envy, self-hatred and inferiority, to be hyper-emotional, masochistic and passive, to have "wounded narcissism," sex repression and inability to sublimate, it is not surprising that psychoanalysis finds "pathology," "emotional disturbance," and "neurosis" in women as a whole. Thus, we have the Freudian psychi-atric syllogism which flows from his concept that "anatomy is destiny" for women: Any human without a penis is destined for neurosis; women lack penises; women are neurotic.

Obviously, with such a "phallocentric" approach to the female personality, the cure for female neurosis—indeed, the prevention of such neurosis—would be to provide penises to women. Since this is a surgical and anatomical impossibility, Freudian psychoanalysis attempts to adjust women to the acceptance of their inevitably inferior role and personality as "a castrated man." As Dr. Phyllis Chesler phrases it, "The ethic of mental health is masculine in our culture."[8] Hence, women cannot achieve full mental health; but they can, through psychoanalysis, learn to adjust to their inferior role as women, and to accept their "neurotic tendencies" and "defective natures."

Dr. Chesler further points out the double-bind character of psychoanalytic treatment: although it uses the masculine model for normality, traits considered healthy in men, such as assertiveness, independence, and competitiveness, are seen as unhealthy in women.[9]

Psychoanalysis, as developed by Freud, seeks to give women "insight" into their subordinate role as women, to accept this role, and to behave and act in accordance with such a role. As Dr. Freyda Zell, Co-Director of the New York Consultation Center for Women, aptly states, "(T)raditional psychotherapists perpetuate the sexist stereotype in terms of male assertiveness and female nurturing. The effect is to deprive women of their anger, competitiveness and directness and encourage them to have an overabundance of seductiveness, cheerfulness and helplessness. So instead of support for their effort to be a full person, women are getting counseling from traditional therapists that make them feel guilty about trying to be anything beyond what is regarded as feminine."[10]

Freudian psychoanalysis is basically patriarchal. Its theoretical rationale is thoroughly male supremacist. Its treatment, if true to Freud's tenets, obliges women to assume their stereotyped role in society and to adjust to their "deprived and mutilated" condition.

Dr. Natalie Shainess, in the feminist anthology *Sisterhood is Powerful,* points out that Freud's theory maintains that women are defective because they lack penises, with the result that they are naturally passive, masochistic, and have weaker super-egos than men.[11] With this attitude towards female personality, the Freudian analyst must then interpret all assertiveness, independence, anger, and self-reliance as "neurotic rebellion" against the feminine role. Treatment, obviously, must then be geared to eliminate such nonfemininity and to restore passivity, dependence and, if you will, "seductiveness."

"Am I to think of my delicate sweet girl as a competitor?" So wrote Freud to his wife Martha when she expressed interest in a career.[12]

During their engagement, Martha wrote Freud that she found John Stuart Mill's essay *The Subjection of Women* "intriguing." He answered her, as feminist Karen DeCrow puts it, "that she should not trouble her little head with such heavy thoughts, and after the joyous day of their marriage she could concern herself with keeping their home a place of peace and loveliness."[13]

Freud was a male supremacist—personally, as well as in his work. But Freud was also a *conscious* opponent of feminism, a *conscious* defender of the status quo of female inequality. The feminist movement was active, vocal, and an important force in Freud's time. Regardless of his sincerity or his belief in the scientific nature of his theory, Freud played an ideological role in combatting feminism and its demand for full equality. Thus, he attacked "the denials of the feminists" regarding his (and capitalist society's) conclusions of female inferiority and rejected their claim that "the two sexes (should be) completely equal in position and worth."

Freud's major points regarding female personality and the dynamics of female development have, of course, no scientific basis. Dr. Naomi Weisstein is correct in stating that what Freud offered as scientific evidence for his theory "violated the most minimal conditions of scientific rigor."[14]

Freud's "scientific" evidence consisted exclusively of case histories, anecdotes, speculations and arbitrary assumptions. Consider his theory of "penis envy," which is the foundation for his entire theory of female personality, passivity, masochism, neurosis, etc. Freud assumes that the penis is a superior organ and concludes that the discovery of it by the male results in male pride and male contempt for women, but when the female discovers it, the result is female inferiority and self-hatred. Karen Horney put forth the opposite concept: that males had "womb envy." Since this, too, is mere speculation, it has as much or as little merit as the concept of "penis envy."

In another sense, the concept of the little girl feeling envy when she discovers the boy's penis to be "strikingly visible and of large proportions" is absurd. Richard Gilman points out that "the organ of the little boy is much more likely to be tiny and shriveled, ridiculous from some perspectives, than large and imposing."[15] Like Freud, one could equally, and equally incorrectly, derive a theory of "penis shame" from the smallness of the little boy's penis and develop complicated dynamics, a la Freud, for *male* inferiority and *male* self-hatred.

There is no adequate scientific proof to establish the major Freudian theoretical views regarding infantile sexuality, the existence of the id and the super-ego, the Oedipus complex, nor the Freudian mechanisms of repression, sublimation, etc. Indeed the scientific proof is to the contrary.[16]*

The Freudian model of all human personality is both unscientific and socially harmful. This is even more strikingly apparent when his theory of female personality is considered. Freudian theory does more than ignore the objective fact of women's oppression. It provides an ideological rationale for such oppression and for its continuation.

The natural and social sciences, as well as life itself, have proved that women have full potential for intellectual, professional, technical, and scientific achievement. Indeed, in his book *The Natural Superiority of Women,* Dr. Ashley Montagu states that "women are actually better endowed than men. Women, on the whole, have a greater number of biological advantages than men."[17]

Further, the Freudian concept put forth by Freudian analyst Bruno Bettelheim, that women "want first and foremost to be womanly companions of men and to be mothers,"[18] is another false Freudian speculation. People's goals are determined by the character of their society and the opportunities it offers them. In U.S. society, the goals of women are shaped by a social structure which systematically withholds equal opportunities for women, and by tremendous social pressure to function in a "feminine" role.

The social role of women is also wholly distorted by Freud. He asserts that "the difficult development which leads to femininity exhaust(s) all the possibilities of the individual." His conclusion is: "We say also of women that their social interests are weaker than those of men."[19] So much for the social role of women!

Freudian theory and practice regarding women is clearly scientifically incorrect and socially harmful.

Erikson, Reich, Laing, etc.: Supremacists All

Freud's male supremacist theories are not individual, unique products. The major psychological and psychiatric theories regarding

*See chapter 1 for fuller discussion.

women are only variations of the basic themes in our society of female inferiority in personality, intellect, and emotional life.

Freud's disciples (Jung, Otto Rank, Melanie Klein, etc.) have, for the most part, left his views on women unchallenged.[20] Erik Erikson, whose views and practices have wide acceptance today in the psychiatric field, has developed what Germaine Greer correctly terms "the lunatic concept of *inner space* in a woman's *somatic design.*"[21]

In Erikson's words, "(A woman's) somatic design harbors an 'inner space' destined to bear the offspring of chosen men, and with it, a biological, psychological, and ethical commitment to take care of human infancy."[22] Karen DeCrow wittily suggests that Erikson assigns "inner space" to women, leaving "outer space" for men.[23] Erikson, indeed, pronounces a sentence of maternal and household servitude on all women.

The application of Freudian views leads to many other absurd conclusions. Thus, an article in *Psychology Today* entitled "Sexuality and Humor" missed the real humor of the situation when it reported that a newly-married young man "had been stricken impotent when his bride broke into uncontrollable peals of laughter at the sight of her young husband's erection." Rather than granting that "the bride" might well have considered such a sight hilarious, the author gravely concludes in true Freudian fashion: "Her laughter was an anxiety reaction; she may require psychiatric help."[24]

Wilhelm Reich, whose popularity is on the upsurge, developed his unscientific theory of sexual repression and the need for "sexual freedom" in a manner which perpetuates the inferior social and sexual status of women. Reich, like Freud, found sexual repression at the heart of every neurosis and psychosis. Phyllis Chesler points out that "Reich is dangerous or certainly limited when he or his devotees romanticize human sexuality to the exclusion of other activities."[25]

Herbert Marcuse echoes Reich in his call for "free sexuality" to work off the "surplus sexuality" of both men and women. We may be assured that such working off of "surplus sexuality" will victimize women *sexually* en masse, while doing nothing to change their *social* oppression.

As for R. D. Laing, who insanely believes that insanity is normal in our present-day society, Phyllis Chesler properly criticized his book *Sanity, Madness and Family* in this fashion: "Throughout the book, he remains unaware of the universal and objective oppression of women and of its particular relation to madness in women."[26]

Dr. Naomi Weisstein, in an article deftly titled "'Kinder, Kuche, Kirche' As Scientific Law: Psychology Constructs the Female", writes that the causes of failure of clinical psychology are "obvious and appalling": "Freudians and neo-Freudians, Adlerians and neo-Adlerians, classicists and swingers, clinicians and psychiatrists in general have simply refused to look at evidence against their theory and their practice, and have used as evidence for their theory and practice stuff so flimsy and transparently biased as to have absolutely no standing as empirical evidence."[27]

Psychiatric theory is clearly shot through with male supremacist ideology and with rationales for woman's oppression. The newer therapies of the Encounter movement such as Gestalt therapy and so-called Humanistic Psychology make no overt or implied attack on entrenched male supremacist ideas or practices. Conversely, they fortify in both subtle and blatant ways the existing inequality of women.*

Psychiatric Treatment of Women

Psychiatry should treat mental illness with the best methods, techniques, medication, and care. All mentally ill people should receive equal treatment. The goal should be the fullest recovery of mental and emotional functioning of the patient. None of the above is true of the present psychiatric Establishment, and certainly not in its treatment of women.

In 1860, a Mrs. Packard was hospitalized at the Jacksonville State Insane Asylum because of "disagreeing with her minister-husband." She was committed under the Illinois law which stated: "Married women... may be entered or detained in the hospital at the request of the husband of the woman or the guardian... without the evidence of insanity required in other cases."[28] The courageous struggle of Mrs. Packard against this insane law made her case a *cause celebre* at the time. This barbaric law no longer exists but critics of state mental institutions and of psychiatric hospitals generally charge that treatment of women in psychiatric facilities is still cruel and male supremacist to the extreme.

In this regard, Dr. Chesler writes, "The patriarchal nature of

*See chapter 5 on Encounter groups.

psychiatric hospitals has been documented by Michel Foucault, Thomas Szasz, Erving Goffman, and T.J. Scheff.... It is obvious that *state* mental asylums are the 'Indian reservations' for America's non-criminally labeled poor, old, Black, Latin and female populations."[29]

It is a fact that 60 percent of both psychiatric outpatients and inpatients are women. Supremacist practices and psychiatric oppression of women therefore have wider negative consequences since they are used against the female psychiatric majority. The larger female psychiatric population is partly accounted for by the systematic oppression of women in our society. In addition, clinicians adhere to a masuline standard of mental health. Thus, women are often diagnosed as neurotic or psychotic when they are psychiatrically normal. So-called male traits such as cursing, anger, aggressiveness, increased sexuality, and refusal to perform domestic chores (a typical male trait) are diagnosed by many clinicians as neurotic or psychotic behavior by the woman.[30]

Of the 17,000 psychiatrists in the United States, 90 percent are men, while 75 percent of our 30,000 psychologists are male. As Dr. Chesler puts it, "the predominantly female psychiatric population in America has been diagnosed, psychoanalyzed, researched and hospitalized by a predominantly male professional population."[31] Given the male supremacist psychiatric theory and practice which dominates the field, the diagnostic and treatment results for women are often disastrous.

Further, most psychotherapists fail to distinguish clearly between social problems and psychiatric problems. The normal frustration, anger, dissatisfaction, and unhappiness which are evoked by oppressive social conditions are usually diagnosed as neurotic manifestations, whether appearing in men or women. Unhappiness tends to be treated as a disease.

Most therapists behave as though their treatment can cure moral, social and political problems. They fail to understand the social and economic origin of many personal problems. They do not recognize that such problems can be solved only through social struggle and social change. Mental illness must be carefully distinguished from those personal problems which are socially caused, and need social, not psychiatric, solutions.

The reactions of women to their specific oppression in a male supremacist society are also usually dealt with by therapists as mentally ill behavior. Anger and protest against their lives by women patients are viewed psychoanalytically as "sick behavior." In a devastating satirical critique of psychoanalysis in her novel *Fear of Flying,* Erica Jong writes of her analyst: "But Dr. Kolner could only see anything which vaguely smacked of Women's Lib as a neurotic problem. Any protestation against conventional female behavior had to be 'phallic' and 'aggressive.'"[32]

In psychiatric treatment, the norm for behavior of women patients is whether they can perform as expected by society. A study entitled *Women After Treatment* measured the outcome of the hospitalization of women "in terms of the customary roles of women."[33] That is, the "normality" of the woman ex-patient was judged by the normality of her performance of domestic work, and by whether the "significant other"—usually the husband—found her behavior to be normal. Thus, one husband of an ex-patient reported that his wife "always seemed worn out or tired, got grouchy, needed coaxing to do something, acted tense or nervous, misbehaved sexually, got depressed suddenly, neglected household chores, stayed away from people." Such behavior was deemed neurotic and the wife was diagnosed as mentally ill.[34] A careful reading of the above symptoms reveals that such behavior would be considered normal in the male and would rarely lead to a diagnosis of mental illness.

At the same time, we must not abandon a scientific approach to mental illness among women. There is a strong tendency in the women's liberation movement to view women patients only as victims of misdiagnosis by male supremacist clinicians. While such cases, as indicated above, are a common occurrence, neurosis and psychosis, in the scientifically precise sense, do often afflict women. Such mentally ill women must receive adequate and equal psychiatric treatment, rather than for them to be called normal.[35]

Psychiatric treatment of women ranges from paternalistic to barbaric. Dr. Chesler reports that women mental patients are often sexually assaulted, that prostitution, rape, and pregnancy are frequent occurrences. Sexual abuse of private women patients by male therapists is not only common but openly advocated by psychiatrists like Martin Shepherd and some Gestalt therapists.

Women are the more frequent victims of lobotomies and other injurious and unnecessary brain surgery for changing their behavior.

Dr. Peter Breggin has documented the fact that psychosurgery more often victimizes "the old, children, Blacks and women."[36]

Medical indifference and forced labor in many state mental institutions characterize the treatment of women. Dr. Chesler arrives at the following conclusion regarding the treatment of both men and women in mental institutions: "In general psychiatric wards and state hospitals, 'therapy', privacy, and self-determination are either minimal or forbidden. Experimental or traditional medication, surgery, shock, and insulin coma treatment, isolation, physical and sexual violence, medical neglect, and slave labor are routinely enforced."[37] Dr. Chesler points out that these practices are invariably more discriminatory against women.[38]

Such is the picture of the treatment of women mental patients: a false psychiatric theory regarding women's personality and psyche, erroneous diagnoses, unscientific norms, sexual abuse, medical neglect, forced labor, paternalism, and forced conformity to the "feminine role" of sex object, domestic servant, passive behavior, and inferior status.

Psychiatry and Black Women

Psychiatry discriminates against the poor, against Blacks, and against women. Since capitalism impoverishes the vast majority of Black women, there is a triple discrimination against them in psychiatric treatment. Such discrimination and oppression of Black women by psychiatric theory and practice finds its economic source in the extreme economic exploitation of Black women workers who earn 50 percent of what white men workers earn.[39] Of course, this wage differential is pocketed as profit by monopoly.

Racism and male supremacy saturate psychiatric theory. The Daniel Moynihan theory of "the Black matriarchal family" as the cause of massive Black pathology is a racist supremacist theory par excellence. It was officially endorsed by the federal government in the form of the infamous Moynihan report issued under the sponsorship of the U.S. Labor Department.[40] This report describes the Black family as "a tangle of pathology" because the Black woman has become the "matriarch" of the family, resulting in the psychological "emasculation" of the Black male, and causing neurotic and psychotic consequences for Black boys and girls because of confusion in their sexual identity. (More detailed refutation of this theory has been set forth in the previous chapter.) Black sociologist Robert Staples states: "The myth of a black matriarchy is a cruel hoax." He adds, "To label her (the Black mother) a matriarch is a classical example of what Malcolm X called making the victim the criminal."[41]

Dr. Irene Diggs, Black anthropologist, combatted the Moynihan thesis in a paper delivered to a symposium on "Culture and Black Struggle" at Queens College, N.Y., in March 1973: "Sociologists have studied only the most negative examples of black family life in America, perpetuating denigrating myths about 'female domination' and individual instability in the black family."[42]

The entire psychoanalytic theory lends itself to racist and supremacist conclusions when applied to Black women. Dreams that have white objects in them are interpreted by analysts as unconscious wish fulfillment of the Black woman's desire to be white. The exclusive intrapsychic approach of psychoanalysis in seeking causes for the Black woman patient's emotional problems excludes from consideration the harsh social reality of her exploitation as a Black, a woman, and, in most cases, a worker. Oedipal dynamics, as utilized by analysts, place the burden for the patient's emotional difficulties on the Black parents, especially the mother, and on the patient being a woman, with penis envy, etc.

Psychiatric treatment of Black women adds racism to male supremacy, particularly in her treatment as either a sex object or an inferior human being. Dr. Chesler concludes that it is undeniable that Black women are "discriminated against and misunderstood whenever they make contact with the psychiatric world."[43] Dr. Chesler incisively points out: "Many double standards of mental health and treatment exist: one for blacks, another for whites, one for the poor, another for the wealthy, and, of course, one for women and another for men."[44]

Psychiatric theory can be scientific only when it has a scientific understanding of the normal and the abnormal mind. The racist and supremacist bias of most psychiatric theory prevents such a scientific understanding. Private psychiatric treatment can be effective only when the therapist is free from such bias. In hospital treatment, the elimination of both racism and male supremacy is an urgent necessity in order to provide equal and adequate treatment to Black women patients. Racism is intolerable anywhere. It is especially criminal when it prevents the satisfactory and humane treatment of mental patients.

Feminism

The women's liberation movement, which includes groups ranging from the National Organization of Women (NOW) to the "radical feminists," has been a significant and often dramatic force in exposing and fighting the oppression of women in our country. It has exerted a strong influence in changing the attitudes and raising the consciousness of both women and men. As Marxist writer Fern Winston puts it, "Many thousands of women, including working-class women, now realize to a greater degree than before, the roles that sex discrimination and male supremacy play in their oppression."[45]

The beginning of the exposure of Freudianism and the whole psychiatric establishment as male supremacist by feminist groups and writers has been both necessary and politically healthy. It has made women more aware of the perils and the unfair treatment existing in psychiatric treatment. It has resulted in the springing up of feminist psychotherapy centers staffed by feminist therapists. It has also compelled some beginning reforms in the treatment of women in some mental institutions.

However, there are certain weaknesses in the theory and approach of the women's liberation movement. Its basic weakness is that it fails to relate male supremacy and women's oppression to the nature of the capitalist system. It therefore fails to base itself on a working-class viewpoint.

Bourgeois feminism, which has influenced the women's liberation approach, sees the struggle for equality of women as a struggle against men, as a "battle of the sexes." It recognizes that male supremacy exists in all areas of society but it blames this on men in general. It, therefore, makes the struggle for equality one which women alone must wage. It fails to see the interest that men have in ending male supremacist practices and women's oppression. Fern Winston correctly states: "The ideology of male supremacy continues to stunt the growth in the consciousness of women, and also of men. Centuries of ideas that regard women as property, as sex objects, as physically and emotionally weak, have prevented men from seeing their own interests in the struggle for women's equality, and have encouraged the idea that this struggle is one for women to wage, rather than one that is part and parcel of the struggle for the equality of all workers."[46]

Further, there is a strong tendency to place women's struggles on a par with the struggle against racism. Indeed, the "feminist" struggle often seeks priority, claiming that racism has received enough attention! This failure to see the genocidal character of racism, and the massive and qualitatively different oppression of Black people, has weakened the struggle for women's equality.

The women's movement, as it has developed in the past period, has been dominantly white, middle class and young. As such, it highlights those issues, such as sex relations, lesbianism, marriage and family, housework, and "careers," which most concern such a membership. While, of course, every struggle against oppression must analyze every aspect of such oppression, it also must correctly single out its main enemy and its priority issues. It must look for its base in the working class, and, in the case of the struggle for equality, in working-class women. The women's movement has neglected issues of equal pay, working conditions of women, jobs, welfare, racism, day care, and education. It has thus failed to rally the most oppressed around the most oppressive issues.

A working-class approach to winning equality for women sees the capitalist system, led by monopoly, as causing the oppression and exploitation of women for super profits. A working-class approach differentiates between Happy Rockefeller, Jackie Onassis, and their reactionary ilk, on the one hand, and working women, Black women, and welfare mothers, on the other hand. It calls for the unity of working men and women, of Black and white, against monopoly as the common enemy for a struggle which will end inequality and advance working-class interests.

In the area of psychiatry, a working-class approach sees the class nature of Freud's theory, regardless of Freud's sincerity.

Many of the feminist writers, such as Phyllis Chesler, Shulamith Firestone, Elizabeth Janeway, Juliet Mitchell and Kate Millett, while criticizing his male supremacy in psychiatry, give credit to Freud as being fundamentally correct and scientific. But Freud's theory is unscientific both as applied to women and to men. Its major features are ideological: that people are controlled by unconscious sexual forces which cause their problems and require intrapsychic assistance for solution. Its male supremacist features fit snugly into capitalist ideology of women's inferiority.

Feminist theoreticians penetrate the Freudian psychiatric maze at times to show its social role. Thus, Dr. Naomi Weisstein writes: "(C)linicians and psychiatrists . . . have essentially made up myths without any evidence to support these myths; the second reason for psychology's failure is that personality theory has looked for inner traits when it should have been looking at the social context."[47] But what escapes Weisstein et al., is that "the social context" is the existence of monopoly capitalism in its period of general crisis. It is only in *that* social context that male supremacist psychiatric theory can be best understood and fought.

Women earn 40 percent less than men. Male supremacy splits men and women. Profit and power—this is central to capitalist ideology and practice. Dominant psychiatric theory, whether Freudian, neo-Freudian, Eriksonian, Encounter, Gestalt, or Reichian, furthers such power and profit of monopoly capital by stamping "Psychiatric Inferiority" on the brow of women.

A working-class approach, while exposing male supremacist psychiatric theory and treatment, will fight for equal psychiatric treatment for women. A program to achieve such equality of psychiatric treatment for women should include:

1. Full, free, available, comprehensive, nonsupremacist, nonracist mental health care for all women who need it.

2. Exposure of and elimination of male supremacist and racist psychiatric theory and treatment.

3. Support for nonsexist training of thousands of women and Black psychiatrists and psychologists needed for psychiatric treatment of women on a basis of equality.

4. Equality of pay, decent jobs, and decent working conditions for women, plentiful day care centers, adequate welfare allowances and quality education for children to reduce emotional pressure and contribute to mental health of women.

In a statement issued in July 1848 on the occasion of the first Women's Rights Convention, held in Seneca Falls, N.Y., that giant statesman of human rights, Frederick Douglass, wrote:

> Standing as we do upon the watchtower of human freedom, we cannot be deterred from an expression of our approbation of any movement, however humble, to improve and elevate the character of any members of the human family . . . we are free to say that in respect to political rights, we hold woman to be justly entitled to all we claim for man. We go further,

and express our conviction that all political rights which it is expedient for man to exercise, it is equally so for woman. All that distinguishes man as an intelligent and accountable being, is equally true of woman . . . Our doctrine is that "right is of no sex." We therefore bid the women engaged in this movement our humble God-speed.[48]

The struggle for psychiatric equality, against psychiatric oppression of women by word or deed, is fully harmonious with the shining words and profound humanism of Frederick Douglass.

Socialism: Equal Psychiatric Treatment for Women

Women are given equal psychiatric treatment under socialism. Further, such psychiatric treatment is either available or being made more and more available on a basis of comprehensive, free, quality care. Such is my conclusion from my study of and personal visits to psychiatric facilities in the Soviet Union and in Cuba. Such a conclusion can also be derived from an understanding of the humanism which animates Marxism and socialism.

There are no theories of female inferiority in socialist countries. Freudianism, as a whole, including its male supremacist features, has been repudiated as a theory of the normal and abnormal psyche and as a treatment for the mentally ill.

Theories of female psychological or psychiatric inferiority, such as Freud's theory, are incompatible with science and humanism, the bedrocks of socialist life and practices. Comprehensive, free, quality, available psychiatric care is guaranteed by law and provided in practice on an equal basis to women.

Racism and chauvinism have been outlawed in all socialist countries so that Black Cuban women and women of the many nationalities of the Soviet Union receive the fullest of all available psychiatric care. Members of a Black delegation which visited the Soviet Union in 1971 reported that they found no discrimination of any sort in the Soviet Union and that women have attained equality there. Journalist George B. Murphy reported that the "darker peoples" of Uzbekistan and Tadzhikistan, two of the Soviet Republics visited by the delegation, "now have leaped over the era of capitalism with all its brutality, arrogance and exploitation of man by man, directly into socialist society, where exploitation of man by man has been abolished."[49]

Writer-actress-director Alice Childress found "great progress of women in Central Asia . . . Soviet women can work at anything and are also able to study," she reported, "Socialism is acutely needed in the Black community (in the United States)."[50]

Much, though not all, mental illness has its basis in social conditions. Wars, poverty, special oppression, insecurity, and racism—all products of capitalism—provide fertile soil for mental illness. Socialism has eliminated or is eliminating such noxious social products, along with male supremacy. This has resulted in a sharp reduction of pathological factors which affect women. Conditions which are conducive to mental health, and antagonistic to mental illness include equality in productive work; provision of child care facilities; equal opportunity in education, science and the professions; security against old age, disability and unemployment; free health care; collective relations; and a common goal in building socialism.

The one-sided male domination of the psychiatric field is corrected under socialism by equal opportunity. As a matter of fact the majority of doctors in the Soviet Union are women. The many women mental health professionals under socialism are also a healthy antidote to male supremacy in this field.

Karl Marx stated: "Great social changes are impossible without feminine ferment. Social progress can be measured exactly by the social position of the sex."[51] "Feminine ferment" helped mightily to achieve socialism in many countries since 1917, and is found in all areas of social struggle today. It is found in the feminist struggle against male supremacist theory and practice.

The position of women in psychiatric theory and treatment is also an exact measure of social progress. By such measure, capitalism is a failure, while socialism is a success.

10

Behavior Research as A Class Instrument

In an article dramatically entitled "Cheating in Science," Professor Ernest Borek, of the University of Colorado Medical Center, declared: "Increasing numbers of faked data or, less flagrantly, data with 'body English' put on them, make their way into scientific journals."[1] At a meeting of the American Association for the Advancement of Science in February 1975, at least a dozen researchers were reported as stating: "The quality of scientific information being produced by researchers, accepted in scientific journals and disseminated publicly by science reporters is often unacceptably sloppy or misleading."[2]

Cheating, manipulation of data, "fudging" of statistics, unwarranted conclusions, and careless scientific methods have become common in research in both the natural and the social sciences. The director of the National Bureau of Standards, Dr. Richard W. Roberts, states that "fully 50 percent, or even more, of the data reported in the literature are unusable."[3]

The admissions by both the military departments and government agencies of widespread, secret experiments with mind-altering drugs resulting in deaths and psychoses of uninformed subjects, together with tests of gas in the New York City subways, adds to the picture of an alarmingly unscientific, unethical, and inhuman misuse and abuse of behavior research today.

Equally alarming—and unpublicized and unknown to the public—is the unscientific and unreliable character of most behavior research in the social and behavioral sciences, even when such research is carried out with adherence to accepted research procedures. It is, indeed, these "accepted research procedures" which need closest scrutiny and fullest analysis. For it is these procedures which have permitted researchers to produce studies containing racist, anti-human, anti-working-class, and male supremacist "scientific" conclusions. Using a methodology called *Research Design,* the behavioral sciences have systematically, continually, and poisonously "fooled most of the people most of the time."

This chapter will describe and evaluate the cheating, deception, inhuman experimentation, and unethical practices occurring in behavioral research today. A critical evaluation of Research Design and statistical procedures will be made in order to show their limitations, inadequacies, and weaknesses even when they are used strictly and ethically. Further, it will be shown how this methodology and these procedures easily lend themselves to distortion and manipulation by cunning or racist researchers.

Some preliminary comments on the nature of science and its role in society are necessary before embarking on the evaluations indicated.

Marxism and Science

Science is knowledge. It is knowledge of the facts and laws governing nature, society and thought. Knowledge about nature is the province of the natural sciences. Great progress has been made by these sciences and they have contributed enormously to the technological revolution we are witnessing today.

In the area of the social and behavioral sciences, which study individuals, groups and society, a different situation exists. Here, the very nature of capitalism itself prevents real progress in these sciences. A true science of sociology would reveal the obsolescence and senescence of capitalism, and point to the need for socialism. Historical science would reveal capitalism as developing from feudalism and containing within its womb the birth of socialism as the next social stage. A valid science of social psychology would uncover the decisive role of the capitalist social system in determining the behavior of individuals in groups, classes, families, and unions. Real knowledge in psychology would explain the individual personality and intellect in terms of the negative features of individualism, competitiveness, elitism, racism, male supremacy, and anti-working-class ideology, as well as the positive features of struggle, union solidarity. national consciousness, love and companionship, family unity, and political awareness and struggle. Can capitalism, in its monopoly stage, permit such knowledge to reach the people?

The natural sciences are of value to the capitalist class for technological advance for greater profit, as well as for carrying out wars dictated by monopoly interests, such as the Vietnam War. These sciences do not constitute part of the idological superstructure which distorts truth and reality. But the social and behavioral sciences play little role in direct capitalist production. These sciences are heavily pressured by the dominant class to uphold the status quo and to distort the true reality of society and the individual.

It is, therefore, unsurprising to find that the social sciences (political economy, history, sociology) and the behavioral sciences (psychology, social psychology, psychiatry) are shot through with false theories, biased ideology, distorted conclusions, and outright misrepresentations.

It is not sufficient to arrive at such general conclusions regarding the ideological role of the social and behavioral sciences in our country today. The specific methodology used in research to arrive at unscientific and politically harmful conclusions requires careful evaluation.

Research in the Behavioral Sciences

Marxism has tremendous respect for science. It views science as playing a vital role in the evolution and revolution of society, as providing the basis for a new and qualitatively higher society, socialism. Scientific findings, regardless of their nature, must be and are fully accepted by Marxism.

Reality exists objectively. Science is the basic human method for learning about reality. If the findings of science correspond to what exists in reality, they constitute knowledge of such reality. There is only one reality—a changing, developing, complex, many-sided reality. It is by no means a simple task for science to learn about the complex world of nature, of society, and of the human individual. In fact, the scientific enterprise is a difficult, complicated, painstaking process with slow accumulation of facts and sudden leaps in theoretical knowledge. Science requires thought, hypotheses, observation, experiment, reasoning, patience, technology, theory, and objectivity.

In the history of science, various scientific methods have been developed and used by scientists to arrive at new knowledge about our surrounding world. But it has not been scientists alone who have developed scientific methodology. In the period of the Enlightenment, with capitalism and science making rapid progress, philosophers such as Francis Bacon and Denis Diderot made invaluable contributions to scientific methodolgy for the natural sciences. At a later period, philosophers and economists like Karl Marx and Frederick Engels revolutionized—and, in some respects, created—social, economic and historical science.

Behind science, there is philosophy. That is, science, whether natural or social, must be based upon philosophy, must have a philosophy of science.

In his *Dialectics of Nature,* Frederick Engles emphasized the need for a correct philosophy of science for natural scientists. Observation and experimentation must be evaluated and interpreted with philosophical categories and must be fitted into a theoretical framework, he maintained.[4]

What Engels concluded about philosophy and natural science applies equally to social science. Both scientific philosophy and correct methodology are necessary for valid social scientific research.

The development of correct scientific methodologies is consequent upon the contributions of philosophers and scientists. Methodology is, of course, basic to scientific research. If the world of reality were what it appears to the senses, then mere observation and common sense could give anyone scientific knowledge. The sun rises in the east and sets in the west, thus appearing to circle the earth. People believed this for centuries, relying upon observation and common sense. Yet, much later, Copernicus and Galileo proved that the earth rotates on its axis daily and revolves around the sun yearly.

Reality can be understood scientifically only by penetrating beyond appearance. Scientific methodology must enable us to penetrate beyond surface appearance to reality itself, to the underlying laws governing the objective world. Just as in the natural world, reality in the social world is not always what it appears to be.

Karl Marx spent his lifetime penetrating beneath the surface of capitalism to extract the scientific laws of motion of capitalist economic and political reality. Scientific methodology was crucial to Marx's discoveries.

Research methodology in the social and behavioral sciences in the United States has been contaminated by two major features. One such feature is deception and inhuman experimentation. The other is the deifying and misusing of the methodology of Research Design and statistical procedures.

Deception and Inhuman Experimentation

In November 1971, the CIA secretly slipped the hallucinogen LSD into the drink of Frank R. Olson, a biochemist. Under the influence of this powerful drug, this "warm, playful, easy-going man," as Olson has been described, leaped to his death from a tenth-story hotel window in New York. A retired army colonel, who was similarly administered LSD by the CIA without his knowledge, described his own reaction as "the most frightening experience I have had."[5]

In testimony before a U.S. Senate subcommittee, Mary Ray, a young research assistant, stated that she had tried to jump out of a third story window after receiving an injection of LSD in an Air Force-sponsored experiment at the University of Minnesota in 1966. Ms. Ray said that she has been "overwhelmed and flooded with anxiety" since then—a period of nine years.[6]

On January 8, 1953, Harold Blauer, a mental patient at the New York Psychiatric Institute, died 2½ hours after being administered mescaline, a mind-altering drug, as part of an Army-sponsored research study.[7]

The New York Times reported that, from testimony, reports, and other evidence, "there emerges the story of a vast government program ranging over nearly a quarter of a century, a program that, primarily in the name of national security, subjected more than 4,000 persons to such psycho-chemical drugs as LSD, marijuana and a number of other chemical compounds that could produce hallucinations, euphoria and hysteria." The *Times* report lists all the armed services, as well as HEW, the National Institute of Mental Health (!), the Veterans Administration, and the Food and Drug Administration, as participants in this "behavior research," which was conducted at such universities as N.Y.U., Duke, Missouri, Minnesota, and Baylor.[8]

From this evidence, a clear and unmistakable pattern emerges of systematic deception, coercion, and criminal behavior by the armed services, the CIA, and governmental agencies in conducting unethical, inhuman, war-motivated behavior research on thousands of mental patients, prisoners, and unknowing subjects, for sinister political and behavior control purposes, resulting in an unknown number of deaths, psychoses, mental anguishes, and disrupted lives.[9]

Such deceit and inhuman behavior in behavior research is not confined to the armed forces and governmental agencies. Indeed, it is widespread among behavior researchers in all fields. In an article entitled "Deceptive Research: Social Scientists Ought to Stop Lying," Professor Donald P. Warwick states:

> (D)eception is common in social science and, in some areas, virtually the norm . . . Researchers condone deception in the laboratory, on the streets, in our social institutions. They deliberately misrepresent the intent of their experiments, assume false appearances, and use other subterfuges as dubious means to questionable ends. These tactics are unethical and unjustified. They are also dangerous.[10]

Warwick describes various experiments in which there is deliberate deception of the public, including having a subject pretend to collapse in a moving subway train to see if the passengers would come to his aid; staged fights between husbands and wives on the Massachusetts Turnpike; having a nine-year old pretend to be lost; instructing subjects to administer what appear to be painful, even lethal, shocks to subjects; dropping hundreds of letters addressed to "Friends of the Nazi Party" and "Friends of the Communist Party," on city streets to determine the behavior of those who found them.

Another common form of deception is for researchers to infiltrate factories, schools and mental hospitals, under false pretenses in order to covertly gather data on behavior, responses and work attitudes. As Warwick correctly puts it, "When sociologists justify this sort of behavior as necessary for gathering data, it should be no surprise that the FBI condones similar tactics for gathering political intelligence."

Outright lying and misrepresentation abound in social research as is evidenced by the fact that the number of studies using deception in personality and social psychology rose from 18 percent in 1948 to 38 percent in 1963, according to Warwick.

Such a picture of gross, systematic cheating, deceit, human abuse, and any-means-to-research-ends used by both the government and individual researchers, is appalling and abominable. The political and scientific mentality which motivates or condones such deceitful, inhuman, and harmful research and experimentation is, to place it precisely, fascistic.

Such was the mentality which permitted the infamous and horrendous Tuskegee syphilis experiment to be carried out by the United States Goverment in Macon, Alabama, with the full cooperation of leading scientists and medical doctors. In this experiment, medical care was *deliberately* withheld for forty years (40 years!) from over 400 Black men infected with syphilis. Many of these men died or had disabling mental and physical effects from the ravages of this worst of venereal diseases—and this even after the discovery of penicillin as the cure for syphilis! Only the mass outcry of shock and horror when the experiment was publicly exposed in 1972 brought this Nazi-like experiment to an end.

The very same mentality concocted an experiment at the University of Texas in 1956 whereby seventeen infants, twelve of them Black, were deprived of linoleic acid, a fatty substance essential for their development, to observe the effects of such deprivation. These effects include permanent brain damage, severe nervous disorders, respiratory infections, and slow weight gains.[11]

Social and behavioral research is disgraced by such reprehensible conduct by government agencies, universities, scientists, doctors and behavioral researchers.

Beyond the deception and inhuman experimentation in behavioral research, there is another more sophisticated, partly valid, universally used research methodology, which heavily contributes to erroneous, distorted, and pseudoscientific conclusions in the social and behavioral sciences. This methodology is called Research Design.

Research Design, Statistics, and Probability

Research Design is a research methodology, of rather recent origin, which claims to be the sole scientific methodology for arriving at scientific knowledge in the social and behavioral sciences. It is, indeed, the major methodology actually used in these sciences. It is the basis for most research studies in psychology, social psychology, sociology, and education.

It is this Research Design which is the basis for the many studies which arrive at conclusions of Black personality deficits, of Chicano inferiority in intelligence, of "cultural disadvantage" of Puerto Ricans, of hyperemotionality in women, of human masochistic tendencies.

What is the nature of Research Design? Why does it use statistics and probability inference? How does it lend itself to studies which arrive at racist, male supremacist, and antihuman conclusions? An examination of these questions is of importance for the social and behavioral sciences. It is equally of social-political importance.

"It is impossible to do competent research or to read and understand research reports without understanding the probabilistic and statistical thinking of social scientists," writes Professor Fred N. Kerlinger in his book *Foundations of Behavioral Research.*[12] Almost all behavioral research is based upon probability; i.e., upon the probability that a certain idea or hypothesis is correct. The usual probability figure used by researchers (known as the "level of confidence") is 95 percent. That is, a hypothesis will be accepted as true if it can be shown that there is only a 5 percent chance that it is not true. To arrive at such a 95 percent probability, statistical analysis must be made of the data produced by the research study. Thus, in a Research Design study, a hypothesis must be adopted, a method for testing the hypothesis must be set forth, and a means for determining the statistical probability that the hypothesis is 95 percent probable must be utilized.

Research Design in the behavioral sciences usually takes the following form. A hypothesis regarding behavior, personality, or responses is arrived at by the researcher. In technical language, "a hypothesis is a conjectural statement of the relation between two or more variables."[13] In simpler terms, a hypothesis is the idea or belief of the researcher that some behavior, trait, or response is due to certain factors, situations, etc.

An example of a research hypothesis would be: "Elementary school students will learn to read better with Reading Method A than with the present reading methods used in the schools." To test such a hypothesis, a researcher would have to use two or more samples of elementary schoolchildren, all of whom are beginning readers, i.e., starting first grade. One of these samples of first grade children would be taught reading by Reading Method A, while the other samples would be taught reading by the methods used in that school system. At the conclusion of first grade, the different groups would be tested in reading by a standardized reading test. The mean (average) score of each of the groups would then be statistically computed to determine if the group using Reading Method A had a higher score than the groups using the traditional reading methods.

However, even if the group using Reading Method A had a higher mean reading score than the other groups, this still would not be adequate proof of the superiority of Reading Method A. A slight difference in favor of the group using Reading Method A may have been due to chance factors. There has to be a sufficiently large difference in favor of that group so that it can be stated with reasonable certainty that the hypothesis has been upheld. Statistical analysis of the differences in mean scores of the different groups must be used in Research Design studies to show that the difference in favor of the experimental group (learning by Reading Method A) is "significant," that is, that it is 95 percent probable that the difference is due to Method A and not to chance factors.

One further Research Design feature must be explained. The actual hypothesis selected by the researcher is not the one that is tested statistically by Research Design studies. The opposite hypothesis is tested, viz., "Elementary school children will *not* learn to read better with Reading Method A than with the present reading methods used in the schools." This opposite hypothesis is called the Null hypothesis, while the hypothesis which the researcher believes and is testing is called the Positive hypothesis. Testing the Null hypothesis rather than the Positive hypothesis stems from the natural sciences, where skepticism of new hypotheses led to the scientific tradition of requiring the testing of the *opposite* hypothesis to the one put forth by the researcher.

There are a number of variations of Research Designs. The one set forth above is one of the main forms and provides the basis for a point-by-point analysis of the principal features of Research Design: hypotheses, samples, tests, scores, treatment, probability, and conclusions.

The aim is to provide the reader with sufficient understanding and sophistication so that the pseudoscientific conclusions of many research studies can be knowledgeably rejected.

Hypotheses: Null and Otherwise

Hypotheses are the very stuff of which science is made. They are the preliminary ideas, beliefs or conjectures of scientists about natural, social or mental phenomena, which are then subjected to test for proof or disproof of their validity and truth. A hypothesis theorizes that such-and-such may be a feature of reality. The scientist then tests the correspondence of the hypothesis to reality by utilizing experiment, observation, comparison, logical consistency, and coherence with overall theory.

In his *Dialectics of Nature,* Frederick Engels explained the role of the hypothesis in the development of the natural sciences:

> The form of development of natural science, in so far as it thinks, is the *hypothesis.* A new fact is observed which makes impossible the previous mode of explanation of the facts belonging to the same group. From this moment onwards new modes of explanation are required—at first based on only a limited number of facts and observations. Further observational material weeds out these hypotheses, doing away with some and correcting others, until finally the law is established in a pure form. If one should wait until the material for a law was *in a pure form,* it would mean suspending the process of thought until then and, if only for this reason, the law would never come into being.[14]

The hypothesis is just as necessary for scientific development of the social and behavioral sciences as it is in the natural sciences. But hypotheses should not be trivial, unimportant or irrelevant. Hypotheses should seek to arrive at laws governing certain phenomena; they must fit into a theory regarding such phenomena; they should be aimed at adding to the meaningful knowledge we have of reality. But the behavioral sciences have been filled with petty facts parading as proven hypotheses: piddling bits of information are derived from irrelevant studies.

Of even greater concern, however, is the testing of unscientific, reactionary and racist hypotheses to show their "validity" and to arrive at socially harmful conclusions. Thus, we find B.F. Skinner hypothesizing that behavior is the only important feature of human psychological functioning. He arrived at this unscientific and distorted hypothesis from his limited work with animals, where he found that he was able to manipulate animal behavior through reinforcement. Eliminating consciousness, knowledge, emotions, judgment, social relationships and freedom from human psychological functioning, Skinner erroneously hypothesizes that the laws of animal and human behavior are identical. He thus concludes from his animal experiments that humans are no more than animals and can be similarly controlled totally in their behavior.*

Hypotheses may also be derived from psychological theories that are divorced from social reality. Thus, many racist conclusions have been put forth based upon studies using the psychological theory that the poverty and unemployment of Black people is due to Black intellectual or personality traits. Research will be conducted, for example, on the hypothesis that Black unemployment is due to Black "passivity." Such a study will equate passivity with Black discouragement and frustration with a racist system of employment of "last hired, first fired," and thus "confirm" the hypothesis. Or, as Arthur Jensen concludes, Black unemployment is due to Black genetic inferiority in intelligence.** Obviously, such studies are based upon racist hypotheses and inevitably arrive at racist conclusions. Black unemployment and poverty are *socially,* not psychologically, caused; it has its basis in the capitalist system which has deliberately consigned Black people to poverty and unemployment. Failure of behavioral scientists to accept this social truism leads them into a racist research bog.

Studying this kind of research, Caplan and Nelson state:

> The picture clearly emerges that psychologists invest disproportionate amount of time, funds and energy conducting studies that lend themselves, directly or by implication, to interpreting the difficulties of black Americans in terms of personal shortcomings . . . 82% of the research we could classify followed that bias.[15]

Illustrating the distortion and the racist character of such research, they point out:

> Those who believe, for instance, that families headed by a mother alone cause deviancy, non-achievement, and high unemployment among minorities take little interest in the effects of inadequate educational opportunities, discriminatory hiring practices, and other defects of the social system.[16]

Hence, failure to understand social reality and its laws can lead behavioral scientists to adopt hypotheses which distort and falsify the nature of individual or group psychological behavior. Such failure to grasp social and psychological laws leads to hypotheses of "innate"

---

*See Chapter 2 for a fuller analysis of Skinner's theory.
**See chapter 7 on Jensen.

human aggression, fixed "genetic" intelligence, personality distortions due to "Black matriarchy," and the like.

Hypotheses, if they are to advance behavioral science, must be formulated out of the real world of society and the individual, and must be tested in such a real world for their truth. Hypotheses, when tested, must be shown to be in conformity with reality, or be rejected as false. Thus, when social and economic features of society decisively determine the social and economic life of Black people, hypotheses should be formulated regarding the dominant role of capitalist society and its effects on Black life. However, as Caplan and Nelson comment: "They (behavioral scientists) may pay lip service to environmental influences, but when they search for causes, they are more likely to look for what goes on between people's ears."[17]

A hypothesis can be directly tested through observation, experiment, accumulation of facts, and other methods. The testing of the Null hypothesis in Research Design, rather than the testing of the Positive hypothesis, can lead to illogical and unwarranted conclusions. In an article entitled "Statistics: Tool or Master of the Psychologist?" Professor Anthony Signorelli criticizes the conclusions drawn from the testing of the Null hypothesis:

> Bolles pointed out that a significant finding cannot be interpreted as necessarily supporting a hypothesis: " . . . statistical rejection of the null hypothesis tells the scientist only what he was already quite sure of—the subjects are not behaving randomly. The fact that the null hypothesis can be rejected . . . does not give the Experimenter an assurance of his particular hypothesis, but only that some alternative to the null hypothesis is true."[18]

The hypothesis concerning Reading Method A can be used to clarify the meaning of Signorelli's statement. Research Design would test the Null hypothesis that Reading Method A does *not* result in significant differences in reading achievement of first grade children. Following the study, the results may prove significant, i.e., first graders using Reading Method A may be shown by the study to have sufficiently greater reading ability so that the Null hypothesis, which stated there would be no such difference, can be rejected. A difference has been found.

What Signorelli is stating is that the finding of a significant difference between the groups of children does not prove that the difference was due to Reading Method A. Such a difference may have been due to other reasons. Among the alternative hypotheses (explanations) are: the group using Reading Method A had a significantly better teacher; the parents of the children using Reading Method A may have motivated their children more highly; the presence of new materials and new personnel may have stimulated the effort of those children. Hence, the mere rejection of the Null hypothesis does not *prove* the Positive hypothesis—that the difference was due to Reading Method A. Signorelli correctly points out that what is usually considered the concluding point should really be a new starting point for determining which of the alternative hypotheses are valid.

Hypotheses are necessary and basic to scientific research. But their use must be scientific. Research Design frequently violates the requirements of scientific use of hypotheses.

"Selective" Research: Populations and Areas

Behavioral research should be aimed at uncovering the laws governing behavior, personality, attitudes, and relationships of individuals, groups, classes, and society. Social and behavioral science is a young and complex science. Does behavioral research in our country advance this young science by studying the many important areas that require understanding and knowledge?

In behavioral research, groups to be studied are called "populations," and features such as traits, responses, attitudes, income status, and age are called "variables." Behavioral research fails on most counts in the kinds of variables and the populations it studies. When have you read a study of the attitudes and behavior traits of the bank and corporation heads who dominate our country? When have the rich and politically powerful been hypothesized to be manipulative, egocentric, racist and exploitative? How many research studies have sought to prove that working people have greater discipline, concern for others, coping ability, and collectivity than middle- or upper-class people? How many studies by white researchers have proved that the Black experience also produces positive features and traits in Black people?

"Selective" research dominates the behavioral research field. Caplan and Nelson point out that many groups are stigmatized as "problems" because "they are highly visible, easily accessible, and relatively powerless." They perceptively add that the social scientists who select such groups for study usually end up "adding a coating of scientific prestige to the myths that protect political and other vested interests."[19]

The class nature of behavioral research with regard to the populations and variables it studies is implicitly shown in the following passage from Caplan and Nelson's article:

> Behavioral scientists seldom direct their inquiry at those who stigmatize others or who command sufficient power and respect to say, "No, we don't want to be studied!" They avidly study nonachievement among minorities, but not the exaggerated drive for profit among successful businessmen. They fill volumes with data on the deficits of culturally disadvantaged children, but rarely raise their curiosity, let alone their pens, to write about the landlords, bankers, and city officials who permit building-code violations and fail to provide the basic services needed to support a culturally enriched community. They study marijuana as a "drug problem," but not the Federal Government's involvement in drugging "minimal-brain-dysfunction" children in grammar schools or the pharmaceutical industry's multimillion-dollar drives to convince the public that stimulants and tranquilizers provide the shortest path to social adjustment and contentment.
>
> By indulging uncritically in this bias, social science makes legitimate the displacement of blame for political and technological failures from those who have the power to prevent them to those who fall victim to them. In fact, the social sciences are rapidly becoming the institution that "certifies" these politically motivated transfers of blame.[20]

Behavioral research on Black people is soaked in racism, both in its intense concentration on "deviancy," and in its centering on Black personality and intellect as causative of the oppressive conditions under which Black people live. Black psychologist Dr. Robert Williams writes angrily: "The Black community has become the white researcher's hunting ground, the ideal experimental laboratory."[21] Dr. Thomas Gordon, of Temple University, declares, "Black people are used indiscriminately as human guinea pigs to further the 'scholarly' ambitions and success strivings of white social scientists."[22]

Behavioral research carried out by white researchers in the Black community views Black people as deviants from the white middle-class norm, "as biological victims and social anomalies," as Charles W. Thomas, of the University of California at San Diego, phrases it.[23] The highly sensationalized racist studies of James Coleman, Daniel P. Moynihan, and Arthur Jensen are characteristic of the "deviancy perspective" and "biological inferiority" view adopted by most white researchers.

An entire issue of *The Journal of Social Issues* was devoted to the topic "The White Reseacher in Black Society." The editor of that issue, Cedric X (Clark), stated in an introduction:

> It is a historical fact that whatever black thinkers have articulated as relevant, appropriate and good has been used as the basis for defining criteria for what most established systems define as irrelevant, inappropriate and poor. It is for this reason that we have today no established fields in psychology concerned with exploitation, racism, oppression, colonialism, paternalism, capitalism, imperialism, etc. In their stead, we have such specialized areas as deviance, criminality, population, aggression, behavior control, etc.[24]

The selectivity of behavior research along with its racism contaminates and corrupts its findings. Instead of adopting the scientific role of discovering the laws of individual and group behavior and attitudes, behavioral research has essentially become an arm of the Establishment for distorting and falsifying such laws. A struggle must be carried out to make behavioral research truly scientific in the populations and the variables it studies.

Is the Part Equal to the Whole?

Behavioral research must necessarily rely on samples of populations for its studies. It is obviously impossible to conduct a research study on *all* the sixth graders in the United States, or on *all* working people. Samples of such populations must, therefore, be drawn from the population to be studied. It is these samples which are subjected to the testing and treatment of the Research Design. For conclusions regarding the population to be valid, it is, of course, essential that the sample be truly representative of the population.

In accepted Research Design practice, as few as twenty-five subjects are considered an adquate sample for many studies. For example, the "classic" study by Kardiner and Ovesey, which concluded that there is a deformity in the Black psyche was based upon psychoanalytic interviews with a sample of twenty-five Black subjects. Racist conclusions regarding the entire Black population of the United States were drawn by Kardiner and Ovesey from this small sample *and accepted as valid and "classic" in the field.* The size of the sample can thus indict the entire study. Conclusions drawn from small samples must be viewed with great skepticism. When conclusions, that *sound* racist,

---

*See Chapter 8 for discussion of this study.

inhuman or male supremacist, are derived from such small samples, they should be rejected out of hand.

To be representative of a population, the sample must have subjects with the same characteristics as the population from which the sample is drawn. Obviously, if only subjects with unusual or unrepresentative traits are selected, no valid conclusions can be drawn regarding the whole population.

There are two accepted methods used by researchers for achieving representative samples. The first method is to deliberately select subjects so that the sample will have the same characteristics as the population. Thus, in the example of the study using Reading Method A, the first graders must be selected to include an equal number of boys and girls, no specially handicapped children, proportionate in ethnicity, etc. The second, and most utilized method, is to "randomly" select the subjects for the sample, i.e., like picking names out of a hat (although a more technical procedure is used).

Both methods have inherent weaknesses which may distort the study. Where matching of characteristics of the sample with those of the population is used, good matching is difficult to achieve. Further, other characteristics besides those that are matched may have an effect on the results. For instance, it is difficult to draw samples of first graders which will be representative of the level of maturity, personality characteristics and behavioral functioning of the entire first grade population. When the sample is unrepresentative of the population, conclusions regarding the sample will *not* be applicable to the population.

Where "random selection" is used, most such samples will necessarily deviate from the population from which they are drawn, by the very laws of probability used in Research Design. It is a truism in statistics that 100 samples randomly drawn from the same population will be widely dispersed around the mean (average)—few will be identical to the population. Which random sample ended up in the study just reported in your morning newspaper?

A large sample does not necessarily guarantee that it is representative of the population. In the May 1975 *Psychology Today,* it was reported that a survey of 2,164 adults—a large sample—found: "The great majority of Americans are satisfied with their lives; only one percent reports being extremely dissatisfied."[25] This survey was made at a time when our country was in a deep economic crisis, when racism was intensifying, when unemployment and partial employment were rife, and when fear, insecurity, and unhappiness were felt and voiced by the majority of our people. Perhaps the study defined "extremely dissatisfied" as "having a gun against your temple ready to fire." But in the ordinary meaning of "satisfied" and "extremely dissatisfied," can you accept the above conclusion? The sample in this study must have been extremely unrepresentative of our population—there must have been "selective" selection of the 2,164 subjects.

For most Research Design studies, an experimental group (sample) and one or more control groups will be used. The experimental group will be the one which will receive the experimental treatment. Thus, the group which was taught reading by Reading Method A would be considered the experimental group, while the other group, which was taught by the usual reading methods, would be considered the control group. For the study to be considered valid and acceptable, the experimental group and the control group must both be representative of the population being studied. Here, two methods are usually used to achieve such representativeness for each group.

The first method is to match the two groups on the important variables—age, grade, sex, ethnicity, intelligence, academic achievement and socio-economic status. Given the variability of human development and the inadequacy of the tests and scales used to determine those variables, samples that are skewed or distorted inevitably occur in such a matching process. The samples used in many Research Design studies were inevitably so skewed. The results of such studies—and we cannot determine which they are—are, of course, invalid.

The second method of "homogenizing" the two samples is through random assignment of subjects to the two samples. Such randomization, since it is based upon the idea that chance formation of the two samples will equalize the variables, is the most commonly used method. But just as random selection of the larger sample from the population results often in an unrepresentative sample, random assignment will also often result in unequally matched groups.

In both methods, the ease of manipulation of samples is evident. The researcher need only assign a few "favorable" subjects to the experimental group or a few "unfavorable" subjects to the control group and his hypothesis will be proved. As was pointed out previously, deception and cheating in research studies is widespread. Putting "body English" on the samples is one of the simplest—and most common—methods of "proving" a hypothesis. It is also scientifically unethical.

There is another rather simple method of achieving significance of (proving) a hypothesis. The simple increase in the size of a sample will increase the probability that it will turn out significant. Anthony Signorelli points out that "the probability of obtaining significant results increases with sample size, regardless of the validity of the hypothesis under study." "Yet", Signorelli wryly states, "increasing sample size so as to obtain a 'truly representative' sample is a procedure recommended by the majority of statistical textbook authors."[26] Thus, if a study ends up with a nonsignificant finding, i.e., the hypothesis is not proved, the researcher can repeat it with a larger sample and may then "prove" his hypothesis!

Another inadequacy of sampling procedure should be pointed out. Conclusions arrived at, based upon samples of white children or adults, will often be applied to Black children and adults. Thus, both major IQ tests—the Stanford-Binet and the Wechsler—were standardized on samples of white children and adults (until a recent revision) but were used routinely on Black children and adults. This often results in racist findings.

One final point should be made regarding inadequate or weak sampling procedure in Research Design. What is usually being researched is how one variable affects another variable. Variables include: personality traits such as "outgoing or withdrawn"; behavioral features such as "passive or aggressive"; intellectual features such as "bright or slow"; and socioeconomic status such as "low, middle or high income." The complexity and changing character of individual personality, behavior and intellect, as well as the difficulty of "randomizing" or "matching" them into equality, makes Research Design procedures in sampling, a basis for skepticism regarding the validity of research studies.

Samples and sampling methods are clearly implicated in the unreliability, inadequacy, and often racist and antihuman character of research in the behavioral sciences.

Samples are subjected to tests and ratings as an integral feature of Research Design. Such tests and rating scales will now be examined.

Are the Tests and Scales Valid?

Behavioral research, based upon the Research Design model, relies upon quantitative measuring of variables to ultimately arrive at statistical conclusions. Statistics are obtained through testing or rating the subjects and recording their scores. Statistical analysis, which is the very heart of Research Design, is conducted on the scores obtained from testing. Testing, therefore, plays a crucial role in such research.

A test or rating scale must be valid, i.e., it must test what it claims to test. Thus, a spelling test must not include math problems; a personality test must test the specific personality traits it claims to be testing; an IQ test must not be a test of scholastic achievement.

Human intellect, personality, emotions and behavior are not like molecules, blood pressure, height, or geological substances—they cannot be subjected to mathematically exact tests which produce exact results. The testing of human mental and emotional-behavioral functioning is a major problem for behavioral research. Certainty is difficult to achieve. Probable approximation is usually the optimum that can be arrived at. Care, skill, precision, and caution must guide the construction and the utilization of tests. Yet behavioral testing is painfully beset by careless, amateurish, and imprecise construction of tests. Standardization of behavioral tests is woefully inadequate. The administration of such tests is usually beset by factors, such as inadequate choice of answers, lack of comprehensibility and ambiguity of questions, which cast into doubt the scores obtained.

The theoretical basis for some behavioral tests can adversely affect or nullify their validity. Thus, two of the most commonly used instruments for testing personality—the Rohrschach and the Draw-A-Person tests—are based upon the erroneous Freudian thesis that individuals project their *unconscious* feelings, conflicts and attitudes in responding to ink blots or in the kind of drawing they complete. Since this Freudian thesis is faulty and unscientific, these two tests are likewise unscientific, i.e., invalid. It is, indeed, a source of incredulity that, although the lack of validity of the Rohrschach Test has been conclusively demonstrated,[27] it is used by most researchers as a valid instrument for conducting research in personality. Obviously, conclusions based upon the scores or ratings of such invalid tests are worthless.

Intelligence tests are the chief pseudoscientific culprits in the behavioral research field. A detailed documentation of their lack of validity is presented in Chapter 7, in refutation of Jensen's unscientific and racist theory regarding Black genetic inferiority in intelligence. A large number of behavioral research studies use IQ tests either for matching samples or as part of the study itself. Conclusions derived from use of IQ tests are invalid because IQ tests are invalid.

Of more recent vintage are a spate of personality tests which claim validity and are being used as valid instruments. An examination of several of these tests can demonstrate their lack of validity.

The Piers-Harris Children's Self-Concept Scale (The Way I Feel About Myself)[28] consists of eighty statements which the child must mark either "yes" or "no." Here are some of the statements: "I am: shy, unpopular, smart, often sad, a happy person, strong, well-behaved, nervous, lucky, obedient, unhappy, cheerful, dumb, good looking, a good reader." Also, "I: worry a lot, can draw well, have pretty eyes, sleep well, have a good figure, can be trusted."

Answers to these questions are supposed to tell us whether the child has a high or a low "self-concept." The Black child who answers that he is "unhappy, not cheerful, not a good reader, does not sleep well, is not lucky, is often sad" will score low in self-concept. Are there not conditions in the life of many Black children to warrant such realistic answers? The child who gives such answers may well have a high self-concept due to other features of his life such as family love, achievement in other areas, respect of other children—but will receive a low score on the self-concept scale. Since educational theory maintains that low self-concept *causes* low scholastic achievement, the conclusion arrived at from such low self-concept scores is that the cause for low scholastic achievement of Black children is not the school system but the low self-concept of Black children.

The Intellectual Achievement Responsibility Scale (IAR Scale)[29] is based upon the theoretical concept that people have a certain attitude concerning the cause of their achievement or nonachievement in life. This attitude is called "locus of control," i.e., control of their life is in the hands of external events or is due to their own efforts. The IAR Scale claims to measure the child's locus of control regarding his scholastic achievement. This scale is made up of thirty-four items such as: "When you have trouble understanding something in school, is it usually a) because the teacher didn't explain it clearly or b) because you didn't listen carefully?" This is a forced choice: the child must choose either a) or b). The child cannot answer "Sometimes a) and sometimes b)," which is often the appropriate answer. Further, the teacher may well have *not* explained it clearly—but the child who checks that answer will be considered to have external locus of control—and that's bad!

More important, the scale has been used to "explain" the low scholastic achievement of Black children. Statistical studies show that Black children score lower on the IAR Scale than white children, i.e., Black children have more external locus of control than white children. The conclusion arrived at—which is racist to the core—is that the low "intellectual achievement responsibility" of Black children *is the cause* of their low scholastic achievement.[30] Thus the school system, poverty, oppression, and capitalism itself are all let off the hook—the fault lies in the "inadequate personality" of the Black child, on his external "locus of control." Does the Black child, in our racist society, have adequate reason to believe that many things are beyond his internal ability to control, that external factors like poor and segregated schools, poverty, bad housing are responsible for his life and his living conditions? Once more, the Black victim is blamed for his victimization.

So-called objective personality tests have been recently developed which, according to psychologist Paul Kline, have no validity. These tests conceal their true aim but, at the same time, claim to produce accurate scores for personality traits. These tests include the IPAT Humor Test of Personality, which has subjects rate jokes as funny or not funny, and the IPAT Music Preference Test, which has subjects answer whether they liked or disliked brief piano excerpts. These two tests, which are based exclusively on humor and music, claim to yield *twenty-one different personality scores,* ranging from self-composure to eccentricity![31] Studies which use such tests to measure personality traits are, of course, valueless—but they continue to win acceptance.

Give a boy a hammer and he discovers that everything needs hammering. This has wittily been called the Law of the Instrument.[32] Give a behavioral psychologist tests of personality traits and he will use them indiscriminately to arrive at "person-blame" conclusions rather than "system-blame" conclusions. That is, the tests will be used on welfare mothers, Black unemployed, or Puerto Rican children, to "uncover" the personality traits of these subjects which may then be interpreted as the cause for their being on welfare or unemployed or reading poorly. With such testing, the social system is exculpated from responsibility and the victim of the social system is saddled with the blame.

The training and perspective of social scientists, psychologists and behavioral researchers, as well as the pressure on them to consciously or unconsciously defend the status quo, turns them away from seeking social answers and explanations for social problems and leads them to test for "between-the-ears" answers. Black psychologist Robert Williams has aptly stated: "The American testing industry . . . is a multi-million-dollar-a year supermarket of oppression."[33] Dr. Williams is particularly angered by the racist use of IQ and personality tests; because of such invalid tests, he writes, "black children are placed in disproportionate numbers in classes for the mentally retarded, special education classes, or lower educational tracks."[34]

One final criticism of tests and scales used in Research Design studies must be made. Since Research Design is based upon *quantitative* measures, the tests and scales used must come up with numerical scores which can be statistically analyzed. Thus, subjects are given scores like 92 on the Stanford-Binet IQ Test, 62 on the Piers-Harris Children's Self-Concept Scale, 26 on "Intellectual Achievement Responsibility." Numerical scores on such tests and scales give a false appearance of precision. Intellectual functioning and personality traits are basically *qualitative* in their nature. They are either very difficult or impossible to quantify accurately. One can, hence, call into question most studies which use such tests and scales. In any case, the utmost care must be taken to correctly evaluate the validity of any intellectual or personality tests or scales used in behavioral research studies.

Experimental Studies and "The Treatment"

The overwhelming majority of Research Design studies use two or more groups, formed from samples of the population. The experimental group is then given "the treatment," while the other groups serve as control groups. "The treatment" consists of doing something to the experimental group, and not to the control groups. Thus, the new Reading Method A was the treatment used with the experimental group, while the control group used the usual reading method. The hypothesis is, of course, that the treatment (Reading Method A) will result in a significant difference (better reading) of the experimental group as compared to the control group.

What are the weaknesses and limitations of "the treatment" as used in behavioral studies? To begin with, treatment usually occurs over a period of time, e.g., one year of Reading Method A in first grade. It is, of course, impossible to control all the factors in the lives of the children during that year which may affect their reading progress. Reading improvement, if it takes place with the experimental group, may well be due to something besides Reading Method A. It may be due to a particularly skillful teacher who accidentally or deliberately (and unethically) was assigned to the experimental group. Or there may be special attention by the principal or by the parents of the experimental group which will influence the experimental group to try harder, or concentrate better. It may be caused by the famous "self-fulfilling prophecy," whereby the researcher's expectation and desire for success of the experimental group may lead to subtle or open favoring of the experimental group or "disfavoring" of the control group, or both.

Where research is conducted which compares white groups with Black groups, racism often operates in the treatment. Indeed, in many studies, racism really *is* the treatment. Racist attitudes by white researchers during the treatment may well negatively affect the scores of Black subjects. Many Black children and adults feel justifiable anxiety and suspicion about research studies conducted by white researchers, and are reluctant to cooperate, thereby not responding to the treatment.

Beyond all this, is the temptation for the researcher to go beyond the Research Design during the treatment. He may introduce factors which go beyond the treatment called for or he may not control factors that contaminate the treatment. Additional time and attention for the experimental group, special prizes for achievement, neglect of the control group—all may slant the treatment in favor of the experimental group.

The treatment part of behavioral research studies is, thus, heavily suspect. Where the conclusions of such studies are socially reactionary, the cause may well lie in "The Treatment."

The Numbers Game: Statistics and Research Design

The very mention of statistics should alert honest and progressive-minded people that there may be "dirty work at the crossroads." Statistics are misused to slice unemployment in half. This nifty maneuver is accomplished by excluding from the unemployed count new workers, part-time workers, women who are involuntarily back to being housewives, and those who are too discouraged to continue looking for work.

Statistics were used by Fogel and Engerman in their savagely racist book *Time on the Cross* to "show" that there were, as historian Dr. Herbert Aptheker sardonically phrases it, "heavenly days in Dixie" for the slaves under slavery in the United States.[35] Fogel and Engerman used the completely unreliable, distorted and false statistics of the Bureau of Census to computerize their data and document their "findings." Would you believe what a slaveowner told you about the health and conditions of his slaves? Yet this is precisely what was the basis for Bureau of Census statistics on the slaves!

Behavioral research studies use statistical analysis to arrive at conclusions. This means that the scores achieved by the subjects on tests and scales are subjected to the test of significance as to whether there was at least a 95 percent probability of the hypothesis being correct. Complicated formulae (e.g., Analysis of Variance) are used for such statistical analysis. More recently, the use of the computer has become a must for such analysis. While such computer use represents an advance in statistical analysis, only the computer experts are knowledgeable of what statistical manipulations are occurring. The possibility of manipulation favoring the research hypothesis has been increased by computer use.

Research Design studies are probability studies, i.e., such studies can not arrive at 100 percent certainty. This means that there is *always* the possibility that any specific study may be wrong. By the 95 percent probability criterion adopted by Research Design, one out of every twenty studies *must* have an erroneous finding. As Prof. Anthony Signorelli of Union College states: "Statistical procedure leads to the measure of generality and probability. Formulations extracted from their results are stated in terms of probability and are thus imprecise."[36]

Further, as Professor Signorelli points out, *one* exception to a physical law can overthrow the law itself, whereas Research Design is so constructed that at least 5 percent of exceptions are permitted—any of which may be valid and overthrow the law drawn from the 95 percent probability. It must be noted, Signorelli comments, that "intelligence tests and personality and diagnostic scales require the compilation of averages and correlative statistics," and are, therefore similarly imprecise and questionable.[37]

Exact conclusions and precision of results are, thus, not possible in Research Design studies. Indeed, if the results are *too* precise, the study itself becomes suspect. An example of this is cited in Chapter 7: the Cyril Burt studies of identical twins, on which Jensen pegged his theory that intelligence is genetically inherited, contained correlations which were identical to the third decimal place.[38] Such precision of correlations is almost a mathematical impossibility and aroused suspicion. Further investigation led to the exposure of those studies as fraudulent.

Research Design is not based on probability alone. It is based upon the probability that *there is a correlation* between one variable (factor, trait, income) and another variable. Correlation means that two things occur at the same time or that one follows the other. Correlation does not mean causation; as Marvin A. Lavenhar puts it, "Statistical association does not necessarily imply causation. Many variables are statistically correlated but are not causally related."[39]

Thus, correlation does *not* mean that one thing *necessarily* causes the other. Of course, if one thing *does* cause another thing, the two things will be correlated, e.g., when the light switch is flipped, the light will go on, so the switch and the bulb lighting are correlated. But if the rooster crows and the sun rises every morning, it does not mean that the sun rose *because* the rooster crowed, even though the two are statistically correlated. Since Research Design studies arrive only at correlation, causality may or may not be involved—and there is no way, short of other kinds of experimentation or research, to determine if causality is involved in any Research Design study.

Further, the correlation found for a study may be low and yet still be statistically significant. Correlation is expressed in decimals running from .00 (no correlation) to 1.0 (100 percent correlation). Correlations can be very high, such as .97 or quite low, such as .31—and still be statistically significant. The finding of statistical significance is almost always accepted as proof of the hypothesis. But, as Dr. David Gold writes, "A test of significance, under the best of circumstances, provides only an index of reliability. . . .Statistical analysis can be considered only a preliminary screening that any hypothesis must pass to merit further investigation."[40]

The point here is that more than statistical significance is needed for a hypothesis to be accepted as clearly proven. Research Design studies usually provide only a preliminary and tentative basis for accepting hypotheses as true.

Obviously, statistical analysis requires statistics to be analyzed. These statistics usually take the form of scores achieved by subjects on tests or scales. Thus, in the example of the study testing Reading Method A, the scores achieved by the subjects in the experimental and the control groups will be the statistical data which will be analyzed. To compare the two groups, the mean (average) of the scores of each group will be computed.

The fictitious story is told of the nonswimmer inquiring of a student of statistics, who happened to be emerging from the pool, "How deep is the water?" "The average depth is four feet," replied the statistics student. The nonswimmer thereupon jumped into the seven-foot end and almost drowned.

Averages are, of course, computed from all the scores. The mean income of David Rockefeller (who has no mean income!) and the author is very high, although the difference in our individual incomes is astronomical. So it is with mean scores: several very high scores by the experimental subjects may produce a significant finding, even though most of the experimental subjects may have had low scores. In the example of the study of Reading Method A, several of the first grade children in the experimental group may end up reading at fourth grade level, while the rest are just at first grade level. The high scores of the few may result in a mean score of the experimental group which is significant as compared to the control group. The conclusion will be drawn that Reading Method A will lead to improved reading for *most* first grade children—an erroneous conclusion, and a weakness of the statistical analysis of mean scores in Research Design.

Manipulation of scores to achieve significance is a common practice. A Ph.D. student informed the author that the chairman of her dissertation committee casually suggested that she "add a few scores" if she needed them to achieve significance of her hypothesis. The reverse also occurs. In the identical twin studies relied on by Jensen, there was evidence of "the selective exclusion of data," i.e., that scores of certain subjects were kept out of the final computation, thus permitting the conclusion that intelligence is inherited.[41] Some research!

Many Research Design studies rely unscientifically on the normal probability curve of distribution. In this curve various percentages fall into the low, medium and high ranges. However, intellectual, personality, and behavior traits are undoubtedly non-normally distributed in the population. Thus, 90 percent of all people may be kind, cooperative, capable of learning a specific skill, while only 2 percent may be "aggressive" or "hyperactive." Yet, many behavioral studies use the normal curve as applying to such traits. The unscientific conclusion that "intelligence" is normally distributed helped Jensen to relegate the majority of the human race (dark-skinned people) to genetically inferior intelligence.

Research Design studies seek to show the "significance" of hypotheses; if significance is shown, then the hypothesis is accepted as proved. One limitation of this procedure is that all studies which achieve significance are usually treated as equally proven. The study which barely achieved significance (e.g., by a single high score) is ranked equally with the study in which every subject in the experimental group achieved a high score. Yet, it is of crucial scientific importance that we know how *well proven* a hypothesis is.

The achievement of significance in a study is also related both to the tests used to arrive at scores and to the kind of sample which was tested. If the tests used, such as the Self-Concept Scale or the Wechsler IQ Test, are not valid, then the achievement of significance is meaningless. If the sample used was neither matched nor randomly drawn, a significant result based upon such a sample has no value. "Yet casual inspection of almost any issue of the sociological journals," writes David Gold, "will reveal numerous instances of use of tests of significance in cases in which there has been no random sampling at any conceivable level."[42] In addition, as previously pointed out, the increase of the size of the sample is a simple but questionable way of achieving significance.

In sum, Research Design methodology, in addition to the limitations previously discussed, is seriously limited by its probability basis, by its reliance on correlation rather than causality, by the misapplication of mean scores and the normal probability curve, and by its uncritical acceptance of significance as fully adequate proof of hypotheses.

Unwarranted Conclusions from Unreliable Data

Research studies are conducted in order to arrive at conclusions regarding the hypotheses being tested. In many such studies, serious breaches of scientific method occur in the conclusions arrived at by the researchers.

It has already been indicated that it is the Null hypothesis, and not the Positive hypothesis which is tested in Research Design studies. The rejection of the Null hypothesis, i.e., the finding of significance, does not warrant the conclusion that the Positive hypothesis must be accepted as proven. Alternate hypotheses may be true, rather than the Positive hypothesis.

Behavioral research is also rife with conclusions based upon unreliable evidence. Sweeping conclusions, which are statistically unsubstantiated, regarding the intellectual and personality traits of Black children are put forth by Jensen, Moynihan, Coleman and Jencks. The studies on which they relied, or which they carried out, utilized invalid tests, unrepresentative samples, and methodologically inadequate statistics to arrive at huge—and hugely false—conclusions.

In the case of Christopher Jencks, he arrives at racist conclusions regarding the education of Black children *even though he himself admits that his statistics are unreliable.*[43] Arthur Jensen admitted that he had no statistical data to show that Black intelligence was heritable—but he concluded that it was, anyway. [44] Such behavior by putative scholars is totally unacceptable.

Although defenders of Research Design declare that it is aimed at showing correlation and not causality, most researchers assert a *causal* link if they achieve significance in their studies. This is scientifically impermissible—correlation does not necessarily mean causality. Without further evidence, conclusions of causality from mere correlation should not be accepted.

All Research Design studies are probability studies. Yet, when significance is achieved, most researchers draw conclusions that certainty has been achieved and that a proven law can be derived from their studies. This violates scientific methodology because only probable conclusions can be arrived at from a probability study.

Operative in behavioral research is also what the author calls "The

Law of the Grandiose Conclusion." Thirty college sophomores will be subjected to some treatment and the conclusion will be applied to the entire human race. After conducting psychoanalytic interviews with twenty-five Black subjects, most of whom were emotionally disturbed and all of whom were rewarded with money or free therapy, Kardiner and Ovesey arrived at racist personality conclusions regarding *all* Black people in the United States. Compounding their scientific arrogance and racism, when they were criticized for not having a control group, they replied that the entire white population of the United States was the control group. Such a study, which was not even a full Research Design study, has been accepted as scientifically valid and is spread through the media to this very day.[45] One might almost call for the abandonment of behavioral research when such studies are given credence and reliability.

Unwarranted conclusions from unreliable evidence has become the rule and not the exception in behavioral research. Such unwarranted conclusions are inherent in Research Design itself. Modesty, caution, careful reasoning, sober evaluation of data, and warranted conclusions must replace such practices in behavioral research.

Research Design: Summary and Evaluation

Scientific research is necessary for scientific advance. Scientific methodology is the basis for scientific research. Such methodology may differ for different sciences. In some sciences, certainty can be achieved and laws stated with scientific precision. Where certainty can be achieved, we should not rest content with mere probability. Thus, the exact boiling point of water (100°C) could be discovered and science did not have to content itself with a boiling point of "probably 99°C."

In the behavioral sciences, it is more difficult to achieve certainty because of the complexity of human individuals, groups, and society. Instruments to measure human traits and behavior are insufficiently precise, the variables are too numerous to control, sampling methods are inadequate, and treatment is difficult to administer equally and precisely.

Where certainty cannot be achieved, high probability should be accepted. Probability studies *do* tell us more about the world and its phenomena. Probability is a step forward over ignorance, in our difficult and tortuous scientific efforts to wrestle from nature and society their secrets. To the extent that Research Design studies correctly achieve probability in their results, they should be accepted as adding to our knowledge of the individual and society. Thus, Research Design must not be abandoned as a methodology. It should be accepted for what it is—a methodology for arriving at probability about individual and social phenomena.

However, the limitations and weaknesses of Research Design studies have been shown in this chapter in order to correct many excesses and to place Research Design in its proper place in scientific research. It has been shown that, in every feature of Research Design, there are serious shortcomings which may dilute the validity of such studies. It has been further shown that manipulation and fudging of results are not only easy to carry out but are systematically done in many studies, with harmful scientific consequences and reactionary sociopolitical effects.

The detailed analysis of Research Design has had as its aim the alerting of readers against ready and casual acceptance of behavioral research studies as correct because of their scientific veneer and their "statistical respectability." The reader should be especially cautious in accepting any study that sounds antihuman ("All people are aggressive"), antiworking class ("Lower-income people have lower self-concept"), racist ("Black children have deformed personalities"), or male supremacist ("Women are by nature inferior in math and natural science").

Operationalism: Idealist Philosophy

Materialism bases itself upon an objective material world which changes and develops according to definite laws which can be known by human beings. Causality is fundamental to materialism: it is the basis for determining the laws governing nature, society, human thought and personality. Our ability to get to know these laws, to understand cause and effect, to penetrate into reality, is basic to materialism and to science. Appreciation of the dialectical character of reality, its constant change in accordance with natural and social laws, its interrelationships and interdeterminations, its conflicts and contradictions, is also crucial for scientific methodology.

Idealism, of the subjective variety, denies the existence of an objective natural and social world. It also denies the existence of natural and social laws. It rejects causality and certainty and replaces them with probability or indeterminism.

Operationalism is that specific philosophy of science which is rooted in subjective idealism. It denies that we can and do get knowledge of an objective natural and social world. It states that we can only describe the "operations" which are performed on phenomena and the sequential or correlative happenings following such "operations." In place of cause-and-effect, operationalism substitutes probability and correlation. It disclaims science's ability to get to know the laws of reality.

Research Design is the specific scientific methodology which grew out of operationalism. It conforms to its philosophic origin by denying the possibility of certainty and by limiting science to probability. It says that we can only know the operations we perform in making our studies, and not reality itself.

It is, therefore, no accident that Research Design methodology has emerged as dominant in behavioral research. Its limited value in producing some valid studies which give us high probability results must be weighed against the flood of studies which are distorted, biased, unsound, questionable or erroneous.

Further, other scientific methodologies and approaches are available for expanding our knowledge in the social and behavioral sciences.

Alternatives

Research Design with its statistical approach has dominated recent behavioral research. Preoccupation with statistical procedure "has invaded experimental psychology more pervasively than any other division of psychology, although no division is uncontaminated," writes Anthony Signorelli.[46]

However, the statistical approach is not the only, nor necessarily the best, approach in behavioral research. In a brilliant article on *Aims and Methods of Scientific Research,* Dr. Robert Hodes writes:

> I might point out that the statistical approach, far from being a fundamental one, is rather a makeshift. It should be utilized only when there exists no better way of handling the data. And I suspect that frequently there is no better way of handling the data because we have not searched diligently for other directions. For once the fundamental relationship between process A and process B is established, statistics become unnecessary.[47]

Science must base itself upon the fundamental principle that all phenomena and processes are governed by law. It follows from this principle that the unique event or process, as well as the statistically frequent events or processes, is amenable to lawful explanation. Thus, the statistically *infrequent* must also be explained by law.

Hodes cites as an example his own experiment which sought to study the results of stimulation of subcortical structures on the electrical activity of the cerebral cortex. Of fourteen such stimulations, twelve were the same but two were different. Hodes comments that, if he had used the statistical approach and had found that the twelve responses were "statistically significant," he would not have investigated the two unique responses further. But such further investigation revealed that the occurrence of those two responses was due to a change in the state of the cerebral cortex which took place during the stimulations. Thus, a new law was uncovered, despite the fact that there was no "statistical significance" of the two unique responses.[48]

Experiment and statistics are, of course, necessary tools of science. But they are not the only tools. Indeed, as Hodes points out, other methods frequently result in major scientific discoveries:

> Experiment yields information, but experiment alone does not produce science. Nor is experiment the only means of obtaining scientific information. Careful observation of natural phenomena is another way of securing serviceable facts of science . . . one of the truly great scientific theories of all time was elaborated without recourse to a single experiment. I refer here to Darwin's theory of evolution. [49]

Observation, comparison and reasoning are basic to geology and astronomy, two major natural sciences that have produced many scientific laws.

Observation is also capable of achieving major discoveries in the social and behavioral sciences, as well. Piaget's major findings regarding children were based upon careful observation and reasoning, without recourse to Research Design. Soviet researcher professor Alexander Luria discovered important laws regarding the role of language in mental development without utilizing samples, control groups, or statistics. Working with six-year old twins who had no comprehensible language, Luria exposed them to two different language development programs, both of which resulted in tremendous progress in thought processes, communication, behavior and social maturity. The twin who was exposed to the more intensive program made greater progress in these areas.[50]

Experiment *and* observation are, thus, necessary for scientific research. But research has other requirements. A sound theoretical framework for experiment and observation is also requisite. As Hodes puts it, "Research must be based on sound theoretical foundations, if it is to be consistently profitable; casual, undirected research, instituted without adequate emphasis on basic theory, leads to progress in the field by accident only, if it leads to progress at all."[51]

In addition to "a sound theoretical foundation," scientific research also requires that the facts derived from experiment or observation be subjected to sound reasoning, to what Engels called "thought determinations."[52] Merely to discover certain facts does not give us the laws governing such facts. The noted Dr. Hughlings Jackson wisely stated: "A collection of numberless facts, however accurately gathered, is not a real experience. Unless a man can put a particular phenomenon he himself sees under more general laws, or unless he tried to do so, he scarcely can be said to know or to be studying a thing in any very valuable sense."[53]

Facts must be reasoned about within a framework of sound theory in order to arrive at specific laws. Dr. Hodes writes:

> Stated simply, the logical components of scientific methods involve reasoning about the facts in order to understand them better and to devise an orderly array between apparently disconnected facts. One thus attempts to place as many different kinds of specific facts into more general terms or laws.[54]

Marx and Engels, and later Lenin, were scientists in the fullest sense in their utilization of observation, in their formulation of more general theories regarding nature, society and thought, in their "devising of an orderly array between apparently disconnected facts." They were thus able to advance qualitatively the sciences of political economy, of historical development, and of class struggle. The nonexistence of Research Design did not prevent such discoveries. Indeed, the claim of Research Design to be a new and more scientific method of research is refuted by the rapid advance of science in both the natural and the social spheres long before Research Design was born.

It must be concluded that Research Design, when properly used, can make modest contributions to social science. But other methods and approaches have validity and importance in scientific research.

Research Design, Behavioral Research and Capitalism

Behavioral research does not take place in a social vacuum, nor is it necessarily conducted by objective, impartial social scientists. Behavioral research has social and political implications. It deals with people and their attitudes, their feelings, their intellect, their relationships, their motivations, and their behavior.

Behavioral research takes place in a capitalist-permeated atmosphere. The link of the capitalist class to behavior research and researchers is unquestionable. Evidence of this slips through, even in the capitalist media. In reporting the quality of scientific research today as often "unacceptably sloppy or misleading," *The New York Times* added, "The scientists largely agreed that the most serious consequences of this carelessness, sometimes committed to further a partisan or commercial interest, was to frighten or soothe the public unjustifiably and to force governments into policy decisions that may turn out to be unwise or counterproductive."[55]

The prestigious and supposedly nonpolitical universities, where most behavioral research takes place, are also heavily implicated in such "partisan or commercial interest." The very same *New York Times* article reports: "Dr. George Bugiarello, president of the Polytechnic Institute of New York, warned that the popular view of the university as neutral ground was often wrong. Many academic institutions, he said, must form political alliances to insure their survival. He said it was not unusual for academic scientists to have financial interests in commercial concerns related to their area of expertise."[56]

What about the social and behavioral scientists themselves? It must be stated that the majority of them believe in their research, and do not consciously aim at unscientific or antisocial conclusions. In fact, a number of them have broken with the Establishment and have subjected behavioral research to serious and valid criticism. A significant minority, especially Black professionals, have adopted progressive views and have made worthy efforts to relate their research to social reality.

However, behavioral research is sponsored and financed largely by government and big business. Caplan and Nelson perceptively reveal how this affects psychologists in their research efforts:

> When governments, foundations or business provide funds to conduct person-centered research on disadvantaged groups, the psychologist's disciplinary outlook, career goals, and patriotic duty suddenly converge.

By investigating a social problem in the terms given him, he establishes a mutually beneficial exchange relationship: the researcher gets both material and prestige rewards for applying the tools of his trade, and officialdom gets its preferred interpretation, buttressed by the respectability of scientific data.[57]

Here we have part of the explanation for much of behavioral research becoming a form of ideology. Such ideology generally serves to maintain and perpetuate capitalism and its profit system. But certain specific features of capitalist ideology saturate all areas. Most prominent of these is racism. It is no accident that behavioral research is one of the most important producers of racist conclusions and theories. What better tool exists than "scientific" studies of Black intellect, personality, and behavior to reinforce racism?

After pointing out that a "race-caste cognitive system" exists in the field of psychology to uphold the dominant racist views in our country, Black psychologist Dr. Charles W. Thomas, of the University of California, declares:

> The theory and data flowing from the race-caste cognitive system cannot help but support a ruling class perspective. Psychologists have yet to recognize that their social positions have historically linked them with injustice and oppression.[58]

Noting that "there are tremendous pressures on the white investigator," which makes him "part of the problem," Professor William F. Brazziel, of the University of Connecticut, keenly adds:

> And there are those researchers who know how racism operates in society but who harbor deep fears about incorporating this in their reports. To do so would guarantee editorial rejection. What would happen to a good researcher if he forthrightly interpreted his research findings linking deprivation to centuries of bigotry? What would happen to the researcher who stated that the implications of his research call for an immediate end to the very journal publishing his reports?[59]

Similar documentation could be provided to show how other main ideological features of the capitalist superstructure permeate behavioral research: male supremacist findings, conclusions of innate aggression and sadism of people, the deviancy of the poor.

At the Bulgarian-American Symposium, held in Varna, Bulgaria in August 1975, Professor Dale Riepe, of the New York State University at Buffalo, submitted a paper on the social sciences. The *Daily World* reported:

Professor Riepe's paper on "Social Progress" offered a critique of the social sciences under capitalism. He noted that the general trend in the social sciences under capitalism emphasized methodology rather than content, and that its emphasis on individualistic rather than social life tended towards isolation and "hyper-specialization," and avoided sociopolitical issues. Underlying these general currents is the belief that capitalism will last forever, Riepe said. Thus, the social sciences often abrogate science, act as if science has no social purpose and, generally, defend various forms of philosophical idealism, he said.[60]

A struggle is needed in the social sciences to counteract this dominant orientation. Black professionals are already strongly involved in such a struggle. Many of their white colleagues have moved, either strongly or timidly, to join in this "good fight." To make social science truly scientific, a number of guidelines are necessary.

Cheating and fudging of research must be subjected to severe penalties with appropriate boards set up to monitor all research. Deception in research must be banned. Racist research must be outlawed. Here, the suggestions of Professor Brazziel should be followed: suspend racial comparisons in tests; end research on "the pathology of black behavior"; set up Black parent panels to review and monitor all research involving Black children; desegregation of editorial boards of journals and of the research staffs of HEW and other governmental agencies; hearings by the House Education and Labor Committee to expose the racist character of government-sponsored research.[61]

Truth-in-Research laws have also been recommended by Professor Donald P. Warwick.[62] All the social and behavioral sciences must adopt *codes of ethics* to prohibit all research which would be physically or psychologically harmful to the subjects. Written, informed, uncoerced consent to participate in any study must be obtained from the subjects.

Honest, democratic-minded professionals should join in the struggle against unscientific ideas, practices and methodologies. People's movements must also increasingly bring to bear their activity and strength to this important struggle.

PART THREE

A SCIENTIFIC AND HUMANIST PSYCHIATRY

The weaknesses, racism, sexism, and inhumanism in psychiatric theory and practice in the United States have been demonstrated throughout this book. The causative agent for such ideological perversion and psychiatric malpractice in what should be a caring and healing science has been shown to be the nature of capitalist society and its dominant class.

The emergence of socialism on a world scale brought with it the challenge to eliminate these evils and injustices, and to make psychiatry humane and fully scientific. Such a process is under way in socialist countries. The contributions of socialist psychiatry to theory and to mental health practice have been largely ignored in our country, while slanderous accusations have been widely publicized. A clear picture of the theory and practice of socialist psychiatry is needed.

11

Psychiatry and Socialism

The nature and quality of a society can be gauged by the treatment of children, the aged and the ill. The treatment of the mentally ill is a particularly accurate criterion of the humaneness and concern for people by a society. By such a criterion, capitalist society in the United States must be ranked near the bottom of the scale, while socialist societies must be scored high.

Alabama's Bryce State Mental Hospital has been called "a second-rate concentration camp for its several thousand patients" by Dr. James C. Folsom, the Deputy Mental Health Commissioner of Alabama. "I'm delighted when patients run away," he said, "For many, it's the best decision they've made in years."[1] Dozens of such "snake pits" exist in the United States.

The Havana Psychiatric Hospital, which I visited with a U.S. Health Workers delegation in 1973, has been transformed from the monstrous snake pit it was under the brutal Batista regime, to a humane, fully staffed, well-equipped psychiatric treatment center for its several thousand chronic mental patients.

The Kaschenko Mental Hospital in Moscow, which I visited in 1971, has one doctor for every fourteen patients and one trained nurse for every ten patients.[2] It has fully equipped workshops for its 3,000 patients, who are paid regular wage scale for their work, with comprehensive treatment for their mental illness.

In a period when funds for mental health facilities are being drastically reduced and the program for establishing community mental health centers has been virtually abandoned in our country, it is both instructive and valuable to look more closely at the psychiatric theory and practice in socialist countries.

Psychiatric Theory in Socialist Countries

Psychiatry is one of the most difficult of sciences. It deals with mental illness, i.e., with abnormal mental, emotional and behavioral functioning due to a variety of causes. Many areas may be contributory to mental illness. Genetic, somatic, chemical or neurological factors may be implicated. Medical problems may trigger mental breakdown. Social factors of family, work, school, marriage or love life may be causative, as may pressure, frustration, fatigue or conflict.

It has been said that nature is in no hurry to reveal her secrets to us—they must be wrested from her. In a science where brain activity and neurological functioning are still largely a mystery, it must be said that psychiatry is not yet an exact science. However, despite its youth and incompleteness, there are certain principles and approaches which are commonly accepted by psychiatrists in socialist countries.

First, as in all sciences under socialism, a dialectical materialist approach is the basis for theoretical research and conclusions, and for practical application of scientific discoveries. Second, the brain and central nervous system are viewed as the basis for mental and emotional behavior. Thus, the findings of the science of higher nervous activity play a significant part in psychiatric orientation. Further, the vital role of consciousness, language and cognition are highlighted in socialist psychiatric theory.

However, socialist psychiatric theory is by no means monolithic— other theories and approaches also exist. In a science as complex and difficult as psychiatry, no single scientist or scientific discovery can provide the definitive and comprehensive theory required. Much work in brain research in the United States is valued and accepted by Soviet researchers. The views and methods of V.M. Bekhterev, the Russian neurologist, are applied at the Leningrad Psychoneurological Institute both in research and in treatment of the mental patients.

Psychiatrists from socialist countries participate in international congresses and conferences to exchange information and to mutually advance psychiatry in its various areas. Scientific exchange, openness to new approaches and theories, research along new and unorthodox lines, and divergences among psychiatrists themselves are characteristics of psychiatry in socialist countries.

Common to both psychiatry under socialism and in capitalist countries is the use of psychopharmaceutical agents in the treatment of mental illness. In his book *Psychiatry in the Communist World*, Dr. Ari Kiev of Cornell Medical College writes:

> The introduction of chlorpromazine and reserpine in the early 1950's, of numerous major and minor tranquilizing drugs, and, more recently, of antidepressants or psychic energizers has had as significant an effect in the Communist countries as in other parts of the world. Hospital practice has been immeasurably affected. The drugs have reduced the incidence of psychomotor agitation and aggressiveness, have made possible the elimination of mechanical restraints, and have facilitated the development of many of the open-door and community-oriented programs which characterize psychiatry today.[3]

Since the brain and central nervous system are the organic foundation for normal mental and emotional behavior, chemical agents, through stimulation, tranquilization or other effects, can and do play a positive role in the treatment of mental illness.

As indicated by Dr. Kiev, there is a major orientation in psychiatry in both capitalist and socialist countries towards open-door and community-oriented programs.[4] This approach is based upon the theory that mental patients will improve more rapidly in normal conditions of life—without bars, locked doors and restraints—and in the everyday life activity in their community. In socialist countries, psychiatry carries out this theory in another area that it views as crucial in the patient's life: work activity. Unlike the approach in capitalist countries, patients in socialist mental hospitals work in workshops producing a variety of products for which they are paid regular wages.[5]

Great emphasis is placed upon biological factors in socialist psychiatric theory; Kiev writes that "constitutional, genetic and physical factors are all stressed."[6] A medical approach is taken to severe psychiatric disorders, with orientation towards discovering the organic basis for such disorders.

A much sharper distinction is made between neurosis and psychosis in socialist psychiatric theory and treatment than in our country, where the two are generally viewed as a continuum. Psychosis is considered far more severe and disabling and is viewed as an organic illness. Thus, schizophrenia, which is the most common of all psychoses in both worlds, is considered to have a biological origin. The book *Research on the Etiology of Schizophrenia,* by Soviet Professor G. Yu. Malis,[7] sets forth the view that toxic factors lie at the basis of the schizophrenic process and that the toxin causing schizophrenia may be produced by a virus.

Most neuroses, on the other hand, are viewed as having a socio-psychological origin. Treatment of neuroses is, therefore, aimed mainly at relieving environmental and psychological stresses and at strengthening the coping ability of the patient.

Socialist psychiatric theory views mental illness as illness which affects the physiology, the work ability, the family life, the ideational, the emotional and the behavioral components of the individual's psychology. Therefore, no single treatment is viewed as being curative; a wide range of techniques including therapy, drugs, and hypnosis, are used. Indeed, a veritable armamentarium of therapeutic techniques is utilized in treatment, as will later be discussed.

Freudian theory and practice are repudiated by socialist psychiatry. Psychoanalysis is rejected on the grounds that it unscientifically attributes abnormal human behavior to unconscious forces over which the individual has no control; as exaggerating the role of sexual instincts; as arbitrary; and as unsubstantiated by acceptable scientific data.

It should be pointed out that, within the general framework of theory outlined above, there are great variations in research, treatment techniques, therapeutic emphasis, and scientific hypotheses from one socialist country to another, as well as within each socialist country. One example of this was the different overall approach of the Kaschenko Psychiatric Hospital in Moscow and the Bekhterev Psychoneurological Institute in Leningrad.[8] This difference reflected the historical origin of each hospital, the theoretical orientation of the two staffs, and the different research being conducted. However, both included in their theory and treatment the major views and approaches outlined above.

Science advances through conflict, novel approaches, original research, new theories, rejection of unsubstantiated theory, and an overall conscious or implicit dialectical materialist view of human thought and behavior. Socialist psychiatry corresponds to this model of scientific theory and research.

Organization and Facilities

Socialist psychiatry is based upon the socialist organization of society. Rather than the confusing, irrational, fee-oriented, public and private psychiatric care found in our country, socialist psychiatry is planned, rationally distributed, community or enterprise-based, and readily available at no fee to those in need.

Kiev writes:

> The range of psychiatric treatment facilities that has been developed throughout Eastern Europe is extensive. Besides traditional mental hospitals and outpatient clinics, there are special institutions for the treatment of oligophrenics (mentally retarded—J.N.), epileptics, and alcoholics. In recent years units of 25 to 100 beds for treatment of milder psychiatric disorders have been opened in general hospitals, and attempts are being made to end the separation of somatic from mental cases. Child-guidance clinic, municipal child-welfare committees, and schools, as well as special institutions for antisocial personalities, have been established.[9]

Mike Gorman, Executive Director of the National Committee Against Mental Illness, stated, after a visit to Soviet psychiatric facilities, that overall statistics "do not convey the astounding richness of personnel resources characteristic of a score or more hospitals and clinics which we visited during our three weeks in the USSR."[10] Compared to the disgraceful and inhumane Willowbrook State School in Staten Island, N.Y., which in 1973 had one staff member for every twenty to thirty patients, Soviet staff-patient ratio varies from two staff members for every 3 patients in an inpatient hospital like Kaschenko to one staff member for every three and half in an outpatient clinic such as Moscow's #8 which serves the Kubishev and Sokolniki districts.[11]

Outpatient services are the very heart of the organization of psychiatric care under socialism. For example, the neuropsychiatric dispensary is the most important treatment facility in Soviet psychiatry. These clinics provide comprehensive psychiatric treatment for all kinds of patients, except those in need of hospitalization. They also provide vocational, financial, legal and educational support when indicated.[12]

At clinic #8, the chief doctor, Dr. Elena Abratsova, explained the aim of her clinic as follows: "The task of our clinic is to *prevent* complications, to treat in time, to follow carefully and conscientiously every case so that everything possible is done to make useful Soviet citizens of all our people—to make them part of Soviet society." Dr. Abratsova added that full psychiatric histories are kept of the people in the district, with consultation and care starting immediately when a problem appears. "We know the families like our own and so we often know what may complicate the problem." she said. "Each doctor has assigned to her a group of families." Home visits are part of psychiatric care and all treatment is free.[13]

Few paraprofessionals are used for psychiatric care in socialist countries. The simple and medically logical answer to why paraprofessionals are not used was given by the psychiatrist who met with our group in Kaschenko hospital: "We use fully trained doctors and nurses to treat patients."

Facilities at the two hospitals visited could be rated from good to excellent. Apart from statistics, there appeared to be an abundance of staff, with extensive facilities for recreation, exercise, and art therapy, along with fully equipped workshops, and grounds for walks, fresh air and sunshine.

Treatment of Mental Patients

Mental illness results in disorganization and dysfunction in one or more areas of human activity. Irrational thinking, hyperemotionality, incapacity to work, inability to relate to others, phobic or paranoiac reactions, bizarre behavior, body pains, and deep depression are some of the injurious results of mental illness. With such manifold and serious effects, mental illness must be treated in both a humane and a scientific fashion.

Humane treatment of patients, mental or medical, is dictated by the very nature of socialist society—a society whose aim and essence are to serve the needs of the people in every way. One of the more humane approaches to treatment of mental patients is known as "social psychiatry" or "community psychiatry" in our country and it takes the form of community mental health centers. In their report to the American Psychiatric Association in May 1971, Mike Gorman and Dr. Isidore Ziferstein told of inquiring about social and community psychiatry during their visit to the Soviet Union and being answered by a Soviet psychiatrist, "But isn't all psychiatry community psychiatry?" Gorman and Ziferstein go on to state:

> Russian psychiatrists don't talk or write about social and community psychiatry because they practice it day in and day out. The Soviet psychiatrist does not think of himself as a private entrepreneur in a business relationship with an individual patient. While many American psychiatrists contend that payment by the patient for his treatment is an important part of the therapeutic relationship, Soviet psychiatrists express the view that such an arrangement would be anti-therapeutic, if not downright immoral, antisocial and beneath the dignity of a health professional.
>
> The Soviet psychiatrist considers the whole society to be a therapeutic community, available for the benefit of his patients. He considers himself and his work an integral part of the overall social effort. Every dispensary psychiatrist in Russia functions as the public health officer, early case finder and mental health educator of the "micro-district" in which he works. Soviet psychiatrists emphasize that all their therapeutic, psycho-prophylactic, and mental-health educational measures would not be so effective if they were not supported by the general health-promoting measures of what they call their "therapeutic society." They refer to such factors of primary prevention as the absence of unemployment; material security in case of illness and old age; free medical care for all; free higher education with stipends for students, etc. The primary-preventive, mental-health factor common to all these measures is the elimination or reduction of social sources of anxiety in the individual. The hallmarks of social psychiatry in the Soviet Union are: the availability of psychiatric treatment to all who need it; the easy accessibility of the therapist to his patient; the active participation of the psychiatrist in the life of his patient and in the community; and the use of the collective for therapy and prophylaxis.[14]

Mental illness is a catastrophe for the patient, his family and his friends. Adequate, scientific treatment of mental illness is necessary. But neither socialist nor capitalist psychiatry have all the cures for mental illness. The difference in treatment may often revolve around the kindness and concern with which a patient is treated. Mike Davidow, reporter for the *Daily World,* wrote from Moscow that the treatment of his mentally retarded son Robert at Kaschenko hospital for three years made a great human difference as compared to previous institutionalization in the United States, despite the fact that there was no substantial change in his son's condition from a medical point of view. "Gone is that fear we used to see in his face," writes Davidow, "that rigid bearing that made every visit to him in Wassaic (a New York State institution for the retarded—J.N.) a haunting and painful experience. His entire appearance has changed; he is incomparably more relaxed. The basic reason is in the warmth of the nurses (mostly women), who can also be quite firm when necessary, in the consistent attentiveness of the doctors and psychiatrists, in the pleasant, relaxed atmosphere."[15]

Beyond the directly human is the *material* humaneness of socialist society. Chief Judge David L. Bazelon of the U.S. Court of Appeals, a member of a prestigious delegation which visited Soviet psychiatric facilities, reported that the effectiveness of the Soviet psychiatric program "depends in large part on the fact that the all-pervasive government can commandeer jobs, apartments, etc., for the patient."[16] Perhaps we need such governmental "all-pervasiveness" for mental patients in our country.

In a more specific manner, Dr. Abratsova states that her clinic #8 can arrange a job change or better living quarters for mental patients. "What our doctors recommend has to be done," she says, "and the plant or office management and executive committee of the local Soviets understand this and cooperate with us. We have a special committee attached to the executive committee of the local Soviets which help find the proper job. Annually a number of apartments with more comfortable quarters are set aside for those with special needs and those we recommend receive them without taking their place on the waiting list. Our patients pay less rent for the added space. We have a special sanitorium to which we can also send those in need of such care."[17]

Equal and nondiscriminatory care also lies at the heart of proper psychiatric treatment. The racism that saturates psychiatric treatment of Black and other ethnic minorities in our country and which existed in Batista's Cuba has been eliminated in socialist countries. Male supremacist and discriminatory treatment of women is also being done away with in socialist psychiatry. The nonavailability of psychiatric care for rural masses is also being overcome, e.g., in Cuba, the building of clinics and hospitals in rural areas has received top priority.

Unlike the increase in psychosurgery in our country, lobotomy is illegal in socialist psychiatry,[18] which maintains that surgical tampering with the brain to alter behavior is both unscientific and inhumane.

Incidence of Psychiatric Disorders

The incidence of mental disorder in socialist countries, as compared to capitalist countries, is a rather complex question. There is fairly common agreement that "rates of incidence of the major psychoses, such as schizophrenia, are approximately the same in capitalist and Communist countries."[19] The prevailing view in socialist psychiatry that major psychoses are biologically caused would place such psychoses in the category of a medical illness for which a medical cure must be sought.

On the other hand, less severe psychiatric disorders such as neuroses, are believed to be, in the main, socially induced. Rates of incidence of such disorders are found to be lower than in capitalist countries.

"This lower incidence," Kiev writes, "is attributed to the people's unity in the common purpose of building up Communist societies, to the slower tempo of life, to the fact that individuals have fewer decisions to make, and to a group life that involves the mental and emotional therapy of sharing one another's problems and affairs."[20]

However, a direct comparison of the number of cases of mental illness under capitalism and under socialism is complicated by the fact that many mentally ill people do not receive treatment under capitalism. This is due to the unavailability of facilities or therapists; lack of money to pay the required fees; racism; or sheer indifference to human suffering, as in the case of the shocking neglect of the aged, many of whom are mentally ill, in nursing homes in the United States.

The availability of free psychiatric care under socialism, on the other hand, leads to the full utilization of psychiatric facilities. In a country like Cuba, which is in an early statge of building socialism, new and different psychiatric problems arise. As explained by Dr. Claudio A. Palacios Mesa, professor of psychiatry at the Havana Medical School, "Now our problems are more human ones—conflicts of family life, 'machismo,' separation of families due to work requirements, tensions associated with achievement, problems of love life, child development, boarding schools, sexual problems, work problems, etc."[21]

There is no question, however, but that socialist psychiatry, due to its humane treatment, its availability of facilities, and its varied methods of treatment, is providing the basis for a decline in the amount of mental illness, for reducing the severity of psychiatric disorder through prevention and early treatment, and for improvement or cure of mental patients.

Forms of Treatment

The scientific treatment of mental illness is still at an early stage of development. However, many approaches and techniques have been successfully applied in the amelioration as well as in the cure of mental illness in socialist countries.

As has been previously pointed out, the use of psychotropic drugs to relieve anxiety, depression, psychomotor agitation, and violent behavior has proved a boon to psychiatry throughout the world, including in socialist countries. A distinction should be made, however, between our "pill-happy" society, with pressure from monopoly drug companies resulting in overuse of tranquilizers, antidepressants, etc., and the careful prescription and monitoring of drugs by psychiatrists in socialist countries.

Rational psychotherapy is used in treatment of neuroses in many socialist psychiatric facilities such as the Bekhterev Psychoneurological Institute in Leningrad. This type of group psychotherapy is called "collective psychotherapy" in the Soviet Union. A major aspect of collective psychotherapy "is education and reeducation—employing the powerful influence of the peer-group collective under the guidance of the therapist, who is the 'teacher of life.'"[22] A clear distinction is made by Soviet psychiatrists between Western group psychotherapy and Soviet collective psychotherapy. As Professor N.V. Ivanov puts it:

> In place of the retrospective emphasis of group psychotherapy abroad, the Soviet psychotherapist is concerned with the active mobilization of the personality and its compensatory powers on the basis of the elaboration of new connections, the conditioning of nervous processes and the objective of creating new, powerful dynamic structures which, insofar as they are the more powerful, are capable, in accordance with the law of induction, of extinguishing and destroying the pathologically dynamic structures that have given rise to the illness.[23]

Unlike the passive role played by most therapists in the United States, the therapist in collective psychotherapy plays an active role: he gives emotional support and guidance in solving daily problems; he helps the patient reorder priorities and values. Further, the therapist "intervenes directly in the patient's reality situation, helping the patient change those circumstances in his life which the doctor considers to be causative factors in his illness. He may help the patient obtain a change in residence, a change of job, and even a change in profession."[24]

Sleep therapy is also used fairly extensively in socialist psycho-therapy. Based upon Pavlov's theory that sleep is protective inhibition which restores the nervous system to normal functioning, the inducing of sleep for long periods of time permits the nervous system to recover from exhaustion induced by stress, anxiety, or conflict. Good results are reported from the use of sleep therapy in the treatment of neuroses.[25]

Hypnosis is also used in the treatment of mental illness in socialist countries. Hypnosis, as a state of partial inhibition, increases the response of the patient to therapeutic suggestion. Successful results are reported also for hypnotherapy.[26]

Many forms of physical therapy are used in psychiatric treatment. Kiev lists such techniques as massage, remedial exercises, phys-iotherapy, inhalation therapy, and balneology (therapeutic bathing).[27]

A novel form of treatment, using nature as the therapeutic agent, is reported by Bulgarian psychiatrists. Staff members of the Center of Neurology, Psychiatry and Neurosurgery of the Academy of Medi-cine in Sofia organized mobile neurological wards where patients suffering from different forms of neuroses spend twenty days every year in the mountains, in centers on the Black Sea coast, or on cooperative farms in hilly areas. Since 1968, 300 patients have been treated in ten such mobile wards, with good results in all ten wards: for example, in a group of 87 patients with neurasthenic neurosis, 30 percent were fully cured, while there was marked improvement in another 68 percent. The Bulgarian therapists conclude that hiking, physical exercise, and work in the mountains and on the seashore take the patients away from the harmful psychological irritants of work or home and "create new psychological dominants which play a decisive role in the cure."[28]

Art therapy is also a modality of treatment in socialist mental hospitals.

A prolonged fasting treatment is reported to be used by Professor Uri Nikolayev of the Moscow Psychiatric Institute. Patients, includ-ing schizophrenics and catatonics, are placed on a hospital-supervised program of fasting for up to thirty days, followed by the reintroduc-tion of foods gradually and the tailoring of a specific diet for the specific patient. Dr. Nikolayev reported an improvement in 65 percent of 7000 cases treated, with virtually no relapse among those who maintained their new diets.[29]

Perhaps the most important form of therapy used in socialist psychiatric treatment is work therapy. This is actual work performed by the patient in a workshop producing products for sale on the socialist market. Gorman writes: "Regulated pay for work performed is viewed as a powerful therapeutic and motivational force in the treatment of the disabled worker. The dignity of work is enshrined in the Soviet culture; Russian psychiatrists feel very strongly that the continuation of work habits while under treatment keeps the patient from regressing into dependency and losing his self-esteem."[30]

Patients at day hospitals are paid full price for their work, while inpatients have the cost of their food and drugs deducted from their pay. Even homebound patients are given work to do at home and are paid full market value. The workshops at the Bekhterev Institute in Leningrad are engaged in the production of shirts, pillow cases, cord articles and electronic equipment. The patients are divided into three groups, according to the severity of their illness, with simple tasks being given to the most seriously ill and more complex work to the less disturbed patients. Hours also vary according to severity of illness.

New Features

Besides the various forms of treatment discussed above, it is important to direct attention to certain features of socialist psychiatry which are either nonexistent in our country or which differ in degree or substance. These features include the psychiatric treatment of children and of workers, the specific treatment for alcoholism, the openness of staff to new ideas, special staff incentives, and emergency psychiatric care.

After describing the wide variety of facilities available for treatment of children, the continuity of care, the careful attention to proper diagnosis, Gorman states:

> There is no doubt that the Russian children's polyclinic—strongly backed up by the children's department of the outpatient neuropsychiatric dispensary—is far superior to the American child guidance clinic. In America, continuity of service is almost totally absent, the child may be buffeted between a pediatrician, a child psychiatrist, a clinic welfare agency or what-have-you, with very little in the way of mutual consultation and medical follow-up. The Russian system is impressive because it is based upon *joint* pediatric and psychiatric responsibility for the child. He is not lost in a welter of agencies—the district polyclinic is home base for him and it has all his records, medical and psychiatric, from infancy. Furthermore, the polyclinic takes care of the total child—the doctors see

him in the home, or in the kindergarten, or at grade school. They don't have to break down any jurisdictional walls to do this. The dispensary child psychiatrist, for example, must spend an assigned number of hours each week in home visiting or in consultations.[31]

Although the district neuropsychiatric clinic is available to all residents, psychiatric care is made available at the worker's place of work. Thus, at the Likhatchov Motor Plant in Moscow, which employs 70,000 workers in the production of cars and trucks, there are two psychiatrists and nine neurologists on the staff. There is little stigma attached to mental illness and fellow workers try to help a worker with an emotional problem.[32]

Alcoholism remains a real psychiatric problem in some socialist countries, such as the Soviet Union. Treatment for alcoholism is vigorously pressed at the dispensaries and in the mental hospitals. Environmental influences are carefully investigated and efforts to change their effects are made. Group therapy is used with alcoholics. Pharmacological therapy is also employed, as is hypnosis.

The importance of work in the mental health field is indicated by the fact that bonuses of 15 percent are paid to mental health workers with adult patients, while 30 percent bonuses are paid to those who work with children. In addition, mental health workers who are in constant contact with psychiatric patients, especially psychotics, are granted double vacations, in recognition of the strain of such work.[33]

Emergency psychiatric care in the Soviet Union also merits comment. In 1965, reports Dr. E. Fuller Torrey, an experiment was begun of using an ambulance staffed with a psychiatrist and two assistants to provide immediate treatment of the psychiatric crisis at the scene. Dr. Torrey says that Soviet psychiatrists maintain that this system reduces the length of patient hospitalization, is more rational, humane, and therapeutic, and that more information regarding the crisis can be obtained right at the scene than at some later time.[34]

Openness to new ideas is also characteristic of socialist psychiatry. Open wards and the discarding of uniforms has been adopted in most socialist countries. There is a lively interest shown by socialist psychiatrists in community mental health centers in the United States. Although theoretical differences may exist, and although socialist society differs markedly from capitalist society, psychiatric science can be advanced anywhere in the world and exchange of ideas and methods can benefit patients in both societies.

Scientific interchange requires the dropping of "Cold War" attitudes, such as the capitalist charge that dissidents are committed to mental hospitals in the Soviet Union. This charge has been emphatically denied.[35] Only mentally ill people are in mental hospitals in the Soviet Union; political dissidence is counteracted through ideological not psychiatric means.

Socialist psychiatry has shown itself to be both a humane and a scientific system of treatment for the mentally ill. It can provide much for us to emulate in a world of peaceful coexistence. Perhaps psychiatry world wide should adopt as its slogan what Dr. Sidney Orret, vice-director of the Havana Psychiatric Hospital told a visiting U.S. Health Workers Delegation: "Treat a patient like a human being and he or she will act like a human being."[36]

Conclusion

I've brought the care at Manhattan State Psychiatric Center to what would be proper for the 18th century." This statement was made on March 5, 1980 by Dr. Gabriel Koz, director of the large state psychiatric hospital, which is in the heart of New York City.

Dr. Koz spoke of crowded wards ("40 psychotic patients in a ward which should be holding 25"), understaffing (a one-third cut in staff in the past two years), underfunding ($60 per day per patient compared to $170 per day for other similar institutions), and the fact that "many physicians on his staff are demoralized by what they consider a lack of concern by the state for a hospital that should be a showcase of care rather than uncontrolled chaos."*

This single example graphically depicts the quality of psychiatric care for patients in our largest city at the beginning of the ninth decade of the twentieth century. The state of psychology and psychiatry in our country today is indeed of a crisis character. It demands a strong and vigorous response from professionals in these fields and from people's organizations.

A critique of a number of areas of psychology and psychiatry has been offered in this book to provide a ground for progressive change in theory and practice in these fields. Emphasis has been placed on the unscientific character and the regressive ideological role of much of the theory in these sciences. The racism, sexism, inhumanism, and

*New York Daily News, March 6, 1980.

anti-working-class features of various psychological and psychiatric theories and practices has also been dealt with at length. But each chapter has sought to offer scientific alternatives, along with voices of reason and struggle in these fields. For a Skinner, there is the science of higher nervous activity of Pavlov and his followers to redress the scientific balance. The racist theory of Jensen is shown to be confronted by the massed anger of Black and white professionals and people's organizations. The psychosurgeons find a Mayor Coleman Young of Detroit blocking their path. Freudian sexism is given a stunning riposte by the women's liberation movement writers. Behavior Modification finds its foes everywhere.

A central theme of this book has been that capitalism is the soil which nourishes poisonous weeds in psychology and psychiatry. Social evils like the Vietnam War, Watergate, mass unemployment, unceasing inflation and racism create mass unhappiness, despair, anxiety and insecurity. People hunger for security in home and job, decent medical care, adequate wages and a feeling of self-worth. Such hunger and searching for solutions may turn people toward radical solutions such as mass struggles against the establishment, and even toward a socialist solution. To fend off such strivings, the ideological superstructure furnishes escapist, subjectivist, individualist solutions in the guise of self-fulfillment of human potential. These serve to pacify and to paralyze social action.

However, psychology and psychiatry are not mere wastelands. They are sciences in which battles are raging. The outcome of these battles is of great and serious significance for the sciences and for the mental health of the people of our country. For those who wish to join in the "good fight", the following guidelines are suggested:

1. All theories and practices which express or support inequality should be exposed and repudiated. Racism and national chauvinism must be consistenly and relentlessly fought because of their deeply harmful effects of oppression and division.

2. Humanism and humane treatment must replace inhumanism and inhumane practices in psychology and psychiatry. These healing sciences should not be permitted to deceive, to oppress, or to mistreat people.

3. Psychology and psychiatry should be treated as sciences, not as havens for every frippery or fad concocted by psychological fast-buck operators. There should be no place for them in sciences which require

a sober, scholarly approach, and in treatment areas which require concern, care and cure

4. Mental health care should be free, available, comprehensive, and of a high quality. This can only be achieved by a National Health Service (including Mental Health) paid for from general tax money and administered by consumers and professionals. Mass action by professional organizations and people's organizations must correct a situation where the United States is the only major capitalist country without such a system.

5. Science is international. Concern for people's mental health and welfare should also be international. International cooperation and exchange in the fields of psychology and psychiatry can be of great benefit to these sciences and to the welfare of peoples in both capitalist and socialist countries.

When asked for the single word he would use to characterize life, Karl Marx replied: "Struggle." Struggle can achieve scientific advance in psychology and psychiatry. It can result in proper mental health care for all in our country. It can benefit all people through achieving international cooperation in science, and peaceful coexistence in the world.

Notes

Introduction

1. *Dialectics of Nature,* International Publishers, New York, 1940, pp. 183–184.
2. Pavlov. I.P., *Selected Works,* Foreign Languages Publishing House, Moscow, 1955, pp. 536–537.
3. Engels, Frederick, *Dialectics of Nature, op. cit.,* p. 26; Lenin, V.I., *Selected Works,* Vol. XI, International Publishers, New York, 1943, pp. 16–18.
4. Engels, F., *Ludwig Feuerbach,* International Publishers, New York, 1941, p. 15.
5. Ibid., pp. 44–46.
6. Marx, Karl, *The Economic and Philosophic Manuscripts of 1844,* International Publishers, New York, 1964.
7. Ibid., pp. 110–111.
8. Ibid., pp. 154–155.
9. See Marx, K., and Engels, F., *The German Ideology,* International Publishers, New York, 1939; Engels, F., "On the Role of Labor in the Transition from Ape to Man," *Dialectics of Nature, op. cit.,* Chapter IX.
10. *The German Ideology, ibid.,* pp.6-7.
11. See Cornforth, Maurice, *Historical Materialism,* International Publishers, New York, 1954.
12. Engels, Frederick, *Socialism, Utopian and Scientific,* International Publishers, New York, 1935, p. 26.
13. Lorenz, Konrad, *On Aggression,* Harcourt Brace, New York, 1966.
14. Wilson, Edward O., *Sociobiology: The New Synthesis,* Harvard University Press, Cambridge, 1975; *On Human Nature,* Harvard University Press, Cambridge, 1978.
15. Vygotsky, Lev, *Thought and Language,* John Wiley, New York, 1962; Luria, Alexander, "Speech Development and the Formation of Mental Processes," in *A Handbook of Contemporary Soviet Psychology,* Eds., Cole, Michael and Maltzman, Irving, Basic Books, New York, 1969.
16. Ibid.

1. Freudianism and Neo-Freudianism

1. *New York Times,* February 13, 1971.

2. *New York Times,* January 11, 1970.

3. Hartman, Heinz, in *Psychoanalysis, Scientific Method and Philosophy,* ed. Sidney Hook, New York University Press, New York, 1959, p. 3.

4. Freud, Sigmund, *Collected Papers,* Vol. V, Hogarth Press, London, 1950, p. 337.

5. Ibid., p. 285.

6. *New York Times,* January 22, 1970; see also Lorenz, Konrad, *On Aggression,* Harcourt Brace, New York, 1966.

7. Ardrey, Robert, *The Territorial Imperative,* Atheneum, New York, 1966; *African Genesis,* Dell, New York, 1963.

8. Sears, Robert, *Survey of Objective Studies of Psychoanalytic Concepts,* Social Science Research Council, New York, 1942.

9. Ibid., p. 133.

10. Gedo, John E. *Beyond Interpretation: Toward a Revised Theory of Psychoanalysis,* International Universities Press, New York, 1980.

11. Kohut, Heinz, *The Search for Self: Selected Writings,* Paul H. Ornstein, International Universities Press, New York, 1980.

12. Goldberg Arnold and Tolpin, Marian, *Advances in Self Psychology,* International Universities Press, New York, 1980.

13. Freud, Sigmund, *Interpretation of Dreams,* Modern Library, New York, 1938, p. 542.

14. Munroe, Ruth, *Schools of Psychoanalytic Thought,* Dryden Press, New York, 1955, p. 440.

15. Fromm, Eric, *Escape From Freedom,* Farrar, New York, p. 137.

16. Munroe, op. cit., Chapter 12.

17. Horney, Karen, *The Neurotic Personality of Our Time,* Norton, New York, 1937, p. 289.

18. Fromm, op. cit., p. 137.

19. Ibid., p. 141.

20. Ibid., p. 163.

21. Ibid., Chap. 5.

22. *New York Times,* November 30, 1966.

23. Freud, Sigmund and Bullitt, William C., *Thomas Woodrow Wilson: A Psychological Study,* Houghton Mifflin, Boston, 1966.

24. *New York Times,* July 30, 1971.

25. *New York Times,* July 18, 1971.

26. *New York Times,* July 3, 1971.

27. *New York Times,* July 26, 1971.

28. *New York Times,* January 17, 1971.

29. *New York Times,* January 31, 1971.

30. Grier, William H. and Cobbs, Price M., *Black Rage,* Basic Books, New York, 1968.

31. *Black Scholar,* March 1970.

32. *New York Times Book Review,* January 25, 1970.

33. Fromm, op. cit., pp. 263-4. Soviet author V.I. Dobrenkov writes: "Fromm attempts to 'synthesize' Freudianism with Marxism, subjecting the latter to an anthropological interpretation and thereby profoundly distorting its essence." *Neo-Freudians in Search of "Truth,"* Progress Publishers, Moscow, 1976, p. 10.

34. Marcuse, Herbert, *Eros and Civilization: A Philosophical Inquiry into Freud,* Beacon Press, Boston, 1966, pp. 87-88.

35. Ibid., p. 243.

36. Ibid., p. 239.

37. Fromm, Eric, *Psychoanalysis and Religion,* Yale University Press, New Haven, 1950; *Zen Buddhism and Psychoanalysis,* Harper, New York, 1960.

38. Munroe, op. cit., p. 534.

39. Hook, op. cit.

40. *New York Times,* July 26, 1971.

41. Lenin, N., *Lenin on the Woman Question,* International Publishers, New York, 1934.

42. Marx, Karl and Engels, Frederick, *The German Ideology,* International Publishers, New York, 1939; Engels, Frederick *Dialectics of Nature,* International Publishers, New York, 1940, Chapter IX.

43. Natadze, R.G., "Experimental Foundations of Uznadze's Theory of Set," *Handbook of Contemporary Soviet Psychology,* eds. Cole, Michael and Maltzman, Irving, Basic Books, New York, 1969.

44. Bozhovich, L.I., "The Personality of Schoolchildren and Problems of Education," *Handbook of Contemporary Soviet Psychology,* ibid.

45. *Daily World Magazine,* January 28, 1978.

46. Pavlov, Ivan, *Selected Works,* Foreign Languages Publishing House, Moscow, 1955, p. 206.

47. Porshnev, B., *Social Psychology and History,* Progress Publishers, Moscow, 1970.

48. Lenin, N., *Selected Works,* Vol. XI, International Publishers, New York, 1943, p. 424.

49. Ibid.

50. Jensen, Arthur, "How Much Can We Boost IQ and Scholastic Achievement?" *Harvard Educational Review,* Vol. 39, No. 1, Winter, 1969.

51. Pavlov, op. cit., p. 447.

2. Skinner's Brave New World

1. *New York Times,* March 18, 1972.

2. Ibid.

3. Skinner, B. F., *Beyond Freedom and Dignity,* Knopf, New York, 1971.

4. Ibid., p. 18.

5. Ibid., p. 121.

6. Ibid., p. 94.

7. Ibid., p. 156.

8. *APA Monitor,* July 1977.

9. Skinner, op. cit., p. 196.

10. Ibid., p. 197.

11. Ibid., p. 149.

12. Ibid., p. 24.

13. Ibid., p. 193.

14. Ibid., p. 200.

15. Ibid., p. 211.

16. *APA Monitor,* July 1977.

17. Skinner, op. cit., p. 8.

18. For fuller discussion, see Woodworth, Robert S. and Schlosberg, Harold, *Experimental Psychology,* Holt, Rinehart and Winston, New York, 1954, pp. 547-557.

19. Pavlov, I.P., *Selected Works,* Foreign Languages Publishing House, Moscow, 1955, p. 537.

20. *New York Times,* February 10, 1972.

21. Marx, Karl, "Theses on Feuerbach," in Engels, Frederick, *Ludwig Feuerbach,* International Publishers, New York, 1941, p. 84.

22. Skinner, op. cit., pp. 101-103.

23. Ibid., p. 37.

24. *New York Times,* April 21, 1972.

25. Black, Max, "A Disservice to All", *Center Magazine,* Vol. V, No. 2, March/April 1972.

26. Ibid.

27. *New York Times,* April 21, 1972.

28. Marx, Karl, *The Economic and Philosophic Manuscripts of 1844,* International Publishers, New York, 1964, p. 113.

29. Skinner, B.F., "The Steep and Thorny Way to a Science of Behavior", *American Psychologist,* January 1975.

30. Engels, Frederick, *Anti-Duhring,* International Publishers, New York, 1939, p. 125.

31. Skinner, *Beyond Freedom and Dignity, op. cit.,* p. 151.

32. Skinner, B.F., *Walden Two,* Macmillan, New York, 1962, p. 55.

33. *New York Post,* March 18, 1972.

34. Skinner, *Beyond Freedom and Dignity,* op. cit., p. 157.

35. Ibid.

36. Black, op. cit.

3. Behavior Modification

1. *Psychology Today,* April 1970.

2. Quoted in Tackwood, L., *The Glass House Tapes,* Avon, New York, 1973, p. 223.

3. February 15, 1974.

4. Knopf, New York, 1971.

5. *New York Times,* February 8, 1974.

6. *New York Times,* February 15, 1974.

7. *New York Times,* February 26, 1974.

8. *New York Times,* February 15, 1974.

9. Mitford, Jessica, *Kind and Usual Punishment,* Knopf, New York, 1973, p. 173.

10. *Human Control and Experimentation Digest, February,* 1974, p. 19.

11. Mitford, op. cit., p. 129.

12. Ibid., p. 153.

13. Quoted in *A Proposal for a National Committee to Combat Behavior Modification and Human Experimentation,* United Defense Against Repression, Los Angeles, 1973, p. 4.

14. Breggin, Peter, *Congressional Record,* February 24, 1972.

15. *A UCLA Center for Psychosurgery?,* SDS Pamphlet, Los Angeles, 1973, p. 5.

16. Harper and Row, New York, 1970, p. 57.

17. *Newsletter,* Medical Committee for Human Rights, no date.

18. Box, Steven, "Hyperactivity: The Scandalous Silence," *American Educator,* Vol. 2, No. 2, Summer 1978.

19. Harper and Row, New York, 1969.

20. Ibid., p. 201.

21. Tackwood, op. cit., p. 227.

22. Ibid.

23. January 15, 1972.

24. *New York Times,* February 20, 1974.

25. *New York Times,* February 15, 1974.

26. *New York Times,* July 21, 1977.

27. Hilts, Philip J., *Behavior Mod,* Harper's Magazine Press, 1974.

28. Ibid., p. 59.

29. *New York Post,* March 18, 1972.

30. *Report on the Center for Reduction of Life-Threatening Behavior,* State of California, Department of Health and Welfare, 1973.

31. *Daily World,* February 13, 1974.

32. *New York Times,* February 8, 1974.

33. *Daily World,* December 15, 1978.

34. June 12, 1973.

35. *New York Times,* February 15, 1974.

36. *Human Control and Experimentation Digest,* February 1974, p. 9.

37. Atkins, Burton M. and Glick, Henry R., eds., *Prisons, Protests and Politics,* Prentice-Hall, Englewood Cliffs, N.J., 1972, p. 156.

38. *Congressional Record,* February 24, 1972.

39. *Condemned to Die For Science,* United Defense Against Repression, Los Angeles, October, 1973.

40. *New York Times,* January 2, 1980.

41. *A Proposal for a National Committee to Combat Behavior Modification and Human Experimentation,* op. cit., p. 15.

4. Altered Consciousness

1. Leary, Timothy, "The Principles and Practice of Hedonic Psychology," *Psychology Today,* January 1973.

2. *New York Times,* June 22, 1971.

3. *Daily World,* May 30, 1973.

4. *New York Times,* July 30, 1973.

5. Watts, Alan, *This Is It,* Vintage Books, New York, 1973, p. 93.

6. Weill, Andrew, "The Natural Mind," *Psychology Today,* October 1972, p. 56.

7. Reich, Charles, *The Greening of America,* Bantam Books, New York, 1971, p. 2.

8. Melville, Keith, *Communes in the Counter Culture,* William Morrow, New York, 1972, p. 25.

9. Blum, Richard, *Utopiates,* Atherton Press, New York, 1964, p. xi.

10. *Before Your Kid Tries Drugs,* Public Health Service Publication No. 1947, U.S. Government Printing Office, 1969.

11. Ubell, Earl, *The Television Report—Drugs: A to Z,* Columbia Broadcasting System, New York, 1970.

12. Naranjo, Claudio, *The Healing Journey,* Pantheon Books, New York, 1974.

13. *Before Your Kid Tries Drugs,* op. cit.

14. Blum, op. cit., p. 43.

15. Ibid, pp. 42–43.

16. *Before Your Kid Tries Drugs,* op. cit.

17. Blum, op. cit., p. 59.

18. Melville, op. cit., p. 226.

19. Leary, op. cit.

20. Melville, op. cit., p. 77.

21. *New York Times,* March 23, 1973.

22. *New York Daily News,* August 16, 1973.

23. Rogers, J. Maurice, "Drug Abuse—Just What the Doctor Ordered," *Psychology Today,* September, 1971.

24. Ibid.

25. Ibid.

26. Ibid.

27. Ibid.

28. *New York Times,* June 22, 1971.

29. Blum, op. cit., p. 1.

30. Robbins, Jhan, and Fisher, David, *Tranquility Without Pills,* Peter H. Wyden, New York, 1972, p. 23.

31. *New York Daily News,* April 16, 1974.

32. Ibid.

33. Robbins and Fisher, op. cit., p. 6.

34. *New York Times,* December 11, 1972.

35. *New York Daily News,* April 16, 1974.

36. Robbins and Fisher, op. cit., p. 3.

37. Ibid., p. 14.

38. *Daily World,* May 30, 1973.

39. Pope, Harrison, *The Road East,* Beacon Books, New York, 1974.

40. Watts, Alan, *This Is It,* op. cit., p. 97.

41. Melville, op. cit., p. 226.

42. Weill, Andrew, *The Natural Mind,* Houghton Mifflin, New York, 1972.

43. Weill, Andrew, "The Natural Mind," *Psychology Today,* October 1972, p. 54.

44. Ibid., p. 65.

45. Ibid., p. 61.

46. Reich, op. cit.

47. Ibid., pp. 429–430.

48. Ibid., p. 1.

49. Ibid., pp. 4–7.

50. Ibid., Chap. IV.

51. Ibid., p. 241.

52. Ibid., Chap. IX for all quotes in this paragraph.

53. Melville, op. cit., p. 183.

54. Hoffman, Abbie, *Revolution for the Hell of It,* Dial Press, Inc., New York, 1973. Quoted In *New York Times Magazine,* July 12, 1970.

55. Kemp, Jonathan, ed., *Diderot: Interpreter of Nature,* International Publishers, New York, 1943, p. 213.

5. Sensitivity Training

1. *New York Times,* January 13, 1974.

2. Burton, Arthur, *Encounter,* Jossey-Bassey, San Francisco, 1970, p. 3.

3. *New York Times,* May 3, 1974.

4. Maliver, Bruce, *The Encounter Game,* Stein and Day, New York, 1973, p. 50.

5. Rakstis, Ted J., "Sensitivity Training: Fad, Fraud, or New Frontier?" *Today's Health,* January 1970, p. 22.

6. Maliver, op. cit., p. 216.

7. Ruitenbeek, Hendrik, *The New Group Therapies,* Avon, New York, 1970, p. 29.

8. Gustaitis, Rasa, *Turning On,* Macmillan, New York, 1969, p. xvi.

9. Schein, Edgar, and Bennis, Warren, *Personal and Organizational Growth Through Group Methods: The Laboratory Approach,* John Wiley, New York, 1967, p. 15.

10. Ibid., p. 16.

11. *New York Times,* January 13, 1974.

12. Maliver, op. cit., p. 40.

13. Ruitenbeek, op. cit., pp. 33–34.

14. Gustaitis, op. cit., p. 35.

15. Ibid.

16. Ibid., p. 22.

17. Gunther, Bernard, *Sense Relaxation,* Collier Books, New York, 1968, p. 59.

18. Ruitenbeek, op. cit., p. 191.

19. Bindrim, Paul, "A Report on a Nude Marathon," *Psychotherapy,* Fall, 1968, Vol. 5, No. 3.

20. Maliver, op. cit., p. 52.

21. Ibid., p. 81.

22. Lowen, Alexander, "In Defense of Modesty," *The Journal of Sex Research,* Vol. IV, No. 1, February, 1968, p. 52.

23. Maliver, op. cit., p. 61.

24. Ibid., p. 62.

25 Perls, Fritz, *Gestalt Therapy Verbatim,* Real People's Press, Lafayette, Cal., 1969, p. 47.

26. Maliver, Bruce, "Encounter Groupers Up Against the Wall," *New York Times Magazine,* January 3, 1971.

27. Maliver, *Encounter Game,* op. cit., p. 81.

28. Bach, George R., "The Marathon Group," *Psychological Reports,* Vol. 18, pp. 995–1002.

29. Schutz, William, *Joy,* Grove Press, New York, 1967, p. 140.

30. Maliver, *New York Times Magazine,* January 3, 1971.

31. Maliver, *The Encounter Game,* op. cit., p. 154.

32. Ibid., p. 147.

33. Ibid., p. 151.

34. Ibid., p. 158.

35. Gustaitis, op. cit., pp. 42–43.

36. Maliver, *The Encounter Game,* op. cit., p. 232.

37. Ibid., p. 170.

38. Gustaitis, op. cit., p. 255.

39. Maliver, *The Encounter Game,* op. cit., p. 32.

40. Gustaitis, op. cit., p. 314.

41. Ruitenbeek, op. cit., p. 139.

42. Maliver, *The Encounter Game,* op. cit., p. 232.

43. Ibid., p. 98.

44. Ibid., p. 26.

45. Lieberman, M, Yalom, I., and Miles M., *Encounter Groups: First Facts,* Basic Books, New York, 1973.

46. *New York Times,* January 13, 1974.

47. Burton, op. cit., p. 23.

48. Maliver, *The Encounter Game,* op. cit., p. 182.

49. Ibid.

50. Ibid., p. 45.

51. Gustaitis, op. cit., p. xv.

52. Ibid.

53. Maliver, *The Encounter Game,* op. cit., p. 236.

54. Gustaitis, op. cit., p. 46.

55. *New York Times,* June 2, 1974.

56. Maliver, *The Encounter Game,* op. cit., p. 36.

57. Ibid., p. 39.

58. Ibid., p. 237.

59. Litwak, Leo, "Pay Attention, Turkeys!" *New York Times Magazine,* May 2, 1976.

60. *New York Times,* April 4, 1976.

61. *N.Y. Daily News,* April 15, 1979.

62. Ibid.

63. Brewer, Mark, "The Case Against EST: We're Gonna Tear You Down and Put You Together Again," *Psychology Today,* August 1975.

64. Litwak, op. cit.

65. Brewer, op. cit.

66. Marsh, Richard, "I Am the Cause of My Own World," *Psychology Today,* August 1975.

67. Brewer, op. cit.

68. Ibid.

69. Marsh, op. cit.

70. *Daily World,* July 3, 1976.

71. Campbell, Colin, "Salesman of Serenity," *Psychology Today,* August, 1976.

72. Litwak, op. cit.

73. Gornick, Vivian, *New York Times Book Review,* April 4, 1976.

74. Brewer, op. cit.

75. *New York Times Book Review,* January 25, 1976.

76. Gornick, op. cit.

77. Marsh, op. cit.

78. *Psychology Today,* August 1976.

79. Campbell, op. cit.

80. Brewer, op. cit.

81. *New York Times,* April 24, 1977.

82. Litwak, op. cit.

83. Brewer, op. cit.

84. Rubin, Jerry, *Growing Up at 37,* Evans, New York, 1976.

85. Brewer, op. cit.

6. Primal Scream

1. Goldman, Albert, "Can Primal Therapy Shortcut the Return to Happiness?", *Vogue,* Sept. 1, 1971.

2. *New York Times,* Nov. 19, 1972.

3. Janov, Arthur, *The Primal Scream,* New York, Putnam's 1970, pp. 22-25.

4. Goldman, op. cit.

5. Ibid.

6. Janov, op. cit. p. 206.

7. Goldman, op. cit.

8. Silverman, Lloyd H., "The Primal Experience: Recollection or Reconstruction?", *Psychotherapy and Social Science Review,* Vol. 6, No. 4, 1972, p. 18.

9. Ibid.

10. Quoted in Tiefer, Leonore, Review of *The Anatomy of Mental Illness, Psychology Today,* June 1972.

11. Ibid.

12. Keen, Sam, "Janov and Primal Therapy: The Screaming Cure," *Psychology Today,* Feb. 1972.

13. Tiefer, op. cit.

14. Janov, op. cit., p. 87.

15. Ibid., p. 20.

16. Goldman, op. cit.

17. Keen, op. cit.

18. Ibid.

19. Ibid.

20. Janov, op. cit., p. 154.

21. Ibid., p. 150.

22. Ibid., p. 136.

23. Keen, op. cit.

24. Ibid.

25. Berne, Eric, *What Do You Say After You Say Hello?*, New York, Grove Press, n.d., p. 19.

26. Ibid., p. 20.

27. Ibid., p. 11.

28. Ibid., pp. 11-12.

29. Ibid., p. 12.

30. Berne, *Games People Play*, New York, Grove Press, 1964, p. 15.

31. Berne, *What Do You Say After You Say Hello?*, p. 25.

32. Gregg, Gary, *Psychology Today*, April 1973, p. 51.

33. Berne, *What Do You Say After You Say Hello?*, p. 400.

34. English, Fanita, "T.A.'s Disney-World," *Psychology Today*, April 1973.

35. New York Times, Oct. 1, 1972.

36. Harris, Thomas, *I'm O.K.—You're O.K.*, New York, Harper and Row, 1973.

37. *New York Times*, November 19, 1972.

38. Berne, *Games People Play*, pp. 178-181.

39. Harris, *I'm O.K.—You're O.K.*, p. xvii.

40. *New York Times*, Jan. 7, 1973.

41. Berne, *Games People Play*, p. 126.

42. *New York Times*, Oct. 1, 1972.

43. *New York Times*, June 4, 1967.

44. Ibid.

45. Ibid.

46. Fensterheim, Herbert, *Help Without Psychoanalysis*, New York, Stein and Day, 1971, p. 215.

47. Skinner, B.F., "The Steep and Thorny Way to a Science of Behavior," *American Psychologist*, January 1975, p. 49.

48. Rubin, Richard D. and Cyril M. Franks, *Advances in Behavior Therapy*, New York, Academic Press, 1969, p. ix.

49. *New York Times*, June 4, 1967.

50. Fensterheim, op. cit., p. 215.

51. Ibid., p. 12.

52. Wolpe, Joseph and Arnold A. Lazarus, *Behavior Therapy Techniques*, New York, Pergamon Press, 1966, Ch. V.

53. Fensterheim, op. cit. pp. 148-149.

54. Wolpe and Lazarus, op. cit., p. 152.

55. Trotter, Sharland, "Patuxent: 'Therapeutic' Prison Faces Test," *APA Monitor*, May 1975.

56. *New York Times*, Oct. 29, 1972.

57. Wolpe and Lazarus, op. cit.

58. See Foreword to *Advances in Behavior Therapy*, ed. by Richard D. Rubin, Herbert Fensterheim, Arnold A. Lazarus and Cyril M. Franks, New York, Academic Press, 1971.

59. Skinner, "The Steep and Thorny Way to a Science of Behavior," op. cit., p. 45.

60. Wexler, David B., "Token and Taboo: Behavior Modification, Token Economies, and the Law," *California Law Review*, Vol. 61 No. 1, Jan. 1973, pp. 81-109.

7. Jensen's "Scientific" Racism

1. Quoted in Daniels, Norman, *The Smart White Man's Burden*, Committee Against Racism, Tufts University, Medford, Mass., 1973.

2. Jensen, Arthur, *Genetics and Education*, Harper and Row, New York, 1972, p.12.

3. *The Harvard Educational Review*, Vol. 39, No. 1, Winter, 1969. Included in *Reprint Series No. 2, Harvard Educational Review*, 1969, referred to in these Reference Notes as *HER, No. 2.*

4. *HER, No. 2*, p. 2.

5. Jensen cites a 15-point difference but states that "when gross socioeconomic level is controlled, the average difference reduces to about 11 points." Ibid., p.81.

6. Herrnstein, R.J., "IQ," *The Atlantic*, Sept. 1971.

7. Herrnstein, R.J., *IQ in the Meritocracy*, Little, Brown, Boston, 1974.

8. Eysenck, H.J., *The IQ Argument*, The Library Press, Freeport, N.Y., 1971.

9. Daniels, op. cit.

10. Moos, Elizabeth, *Soviet Education*, National Council of American-Soviet Friendship, N.Y., 1967, p. 13.

11. Ibid.

12. Guilford, J.P., *The Nature of Human Intelligence*, McGraw Hill, New York, 1967, p.37.

13. Klausmeier, Herbert J., and Goodwin, William, *Learning and Human Abilities*, Harper and Row, New York, 1966, p. 35.

14. Morris, Frank, "The Jensen Hypothesis: Social Science Research or Social Science Racism?" *Center Monograph Series No. 2*, UCLA Center for Afro-American Studies, Los Angeles, 1971.

15. Ibid., pp. 29-32.

16. Jensen, *HER, No. 2*, p. 29.

17. Pavlov, I.P., *Selected Works*, ed. Kh. S. Koshtoyants, Foreign Languages Publishing House, Moscow, 1955, p. 447.

18. Dobzhansky, Theodosius, "Differences Are Not Deficits," *Psychology Today*, December 1973.

19. Anastasi, Anne, *Psychological Testing*, Macmillan, New York, 1961, p. 317.

20. *Psychology Today: An Introduction*, no authors listed, CRM Books, Del Mar, Calif., 2nd ed., 1972, p. 397.

21. *New York Times*, October 18, 1979; *Daily World*, October 19, 1979; *Daily World Magazine*, January 31, 1980.

22. *New York Post*, September 4, 1971. Also see Mercer, Jane, "IQ:The Lethal Label," *Psychology Today*, September 1972.

23. Ibid., *N.Y. Post.*

24. *New York Times*, January 22, 1974.

25. *Daily World*, October 15, 1974.

26. Wechsler, David, *Wechsler Intelligence Scale for Children*, The Psychological Corporation, New York, 1949.

27. Garcia, John, "IQ: The Conspiracy," *Psychology Today*, September 1972.

28. Klineberg, Otto, *Race Differences*, Harper, New York, 1935.

29. Garcia, op. cit.

30. Cited in Kagan, Jerome, "Inadequate Evidence and Illogical Conclusions," *HER, No. 2*, pp. 126-129.

31. Watson, Peter, "IQ:The Racial Gap," *Psychology Today*, September 1972.

32. Jensen, Arthur, "The Differences Are Real," *Psychology Today*, December 1973.

33. *The New York Times Magazine*, August 31, 1969.

34. Ibid.

35. Ibid.

36. Dunn, L.C., *Race and Biology,* UNESCO Publications, 1951.

37. Bodmer, Walter, and Cavalli-Sforza, Luigi, "Intelligence and Race," *Readings from Scientific American,* W.H. Freeman, San Francisco, 1971. For a full refutation of Jensen's claim that intelligence is 80 percent heritable, see Lawler, James M., *IQ, Heritability and Racism,* International Publishers, New York, 1978.

38. Jensen, "The Differences Are Real,", op. cit., p. 81.

39. Ibid.

40. Ibid., p. 84.

41. Ibid., p. 81.

42. Aptheker, Herbert, "A Racist Lie Exposed," *Daily World Magazine,* December 18, 1976.

43. *New York Times,* November 28, 1976.

44. John Wiley, New York, 1974.

45. *New York Times,* November 28, 1976.

46. For fuller discussion, see Aptheker, Herbert, "Sterilization, Experimentation and Imperialism," *Political Affairs,* January 1974.

47. Jensen, *HER, No. 2,* p. 95.

48. *New York Times,* May 2, 1974.

49. Aptheker, op. cit., p. 45.

50. Jensen, *HER, No. 2,* p. 37.

51. *New York Times,* March 1, 1980.

52. *New York Times,* August 31, 1969.

53. Jensen, HER, No. 2, p. 237.

54. *New York Times,* July 29, 1979, and December 9, 1979.

55. See Gordon, Edmund, "Compensatory Education in Perspective," *IRCD Bulletin,* Vol. IV, No. 5, Teachers College, Columbia University, New York, 1970.

56. *New York Times,* January 6, 1980.

57. Ibid.

58. Jensen, *HER, No. 2,* p. 117.

59. Williams, Robert L., "Scientific Racism and IQ: The Silent Mugging of the Black Community," *Psychology Today,* May 1974.

60. Ibid.

61. *Amsterdam News,* September 3, 1975.

62. Patterson, William, *We Charge Genocide,* Civil Rights Congress, New York, 1951.

63. *Amsterdam News,* September 3, 1975.

64. Garcia, op. cit.

65. *Daily World Magazine,* October 12, 1974.

66. *Daily World,* March 13, 1973.

67. Ibid.

68. Quoted In Daniels, op. cit.

69. Jensen, Arthur, *Bias in Mental Testing,* The Free Press, New York, 1979.

70. Williams, op. cit.

71. Quoted in *Daily World,* February 15, 1974.

72. *Daily World,* July 16, 1974.

8. Racism in Psychiatry

1. Thomas, Alexander and Sillen, Samuel, *Racism and Psychiatry,* Brunner Mazel, New York, 1972, p. xii.

2. Ibid., p. 2.

3. Ibid., p. 5.

4. Ibid.

5. Jung, Carl G., *Contributions to Analytical Psychology*, Harcourt Brace, New York, 1928; "Your Negroid and Indian Behavior," *Forum*, 1930, 83, pp. 193-199.

6. McDougall, William, *Is America Safe for Democracy?* Scribner, New York, 1921.

7. Thomas and Sillen, *Racism and Psychiatry*, p. 17.

8. *Bulletin of the History of Medicine*, 1944, 15, pp. 469-482.

9. Thomas and Sillen, *Racism and Psychiatry*, p. 18.

10. Ibid.

11. *British Journal of Medical Psychology*, 1953, 26, pp. 278-288.

12. Carothers, A., "Normal and Pathological Psychology of the African," *Ethno-Psychiatric Studies*, 1954; quoted in Fanon, Frantz, *The Wretched of the Earth*, Grove Press, New York, 1963, p. 302.

13. Fanon, ibid., p. 303.

14. Torrey, E. Fuller, *The Death of Psychiatry*, Chilton Book Co., Radnor, Penn., 1974, p. 10.

15. Sharpley, R.H., "A Psychohistorical Perspective of the Negro," *American Journal of Psychiatry*, 1969, 126, pp. 645-650.

16. Hunter, D.M. and Babcock, C.G., "Some Aspects of the Intrapsychic Structure of Certain American Negroes as Viewed in the Intercultural Dynamic," *The Psychoanalytic Study of Society*, Vol. 4, W. and S. Axelrod, Eds., International Universities Press, New York, 1967.

17. McLean, Helen V., "Psychodynamic Factors in Race Relations,"*Annals of the Academy of Political and Social Science*, 1946, 244, pp. 159-166.

18. Thomas and Sillen, *Racism and Psychiatry*, p. 58.

19. Sterba, R., "Some Psychological Factors in Negro Race Hatred and in Anti-Negro Riots," *Psychoanalysis and the Social Sciences*, Vol. I, G. Roheim, Ed., International Universities Press, New York, 1947.

20. Hamilton, J.W., "Some Dynamics of Anti-Negro Prejudice," *Psychoanalytic Review*, 1967, 13, pp. 5-15.

21. Bird, B., "A Consideration of the Etiology of Prejudice," *Journal of the American Psychoanalytic Association*, 1957, 5, pp. 490-513.

22. Robinson, H.A., "Pseudo-therapeutic Benefits from an Adverse Social Phenomenon (Racial Prejudice)," *American Journal of Psychiatry*, 1971, 128, pp. 232-234.

23. *The Black Scholar*, March, 1970, pp. 58-62.

24. Kardiner, A. and Ovesey, L., *The Mark of Oppression*, Meridian (World), New York, 1962.

25. Thomas and Sillen, *Racism and Psychiatry*, p. 49.

26 Ibid.

27. Moynihan, Daniel, *The Negro Family: The Case for National Action*, U.S. Department of Labor, 1965; quoted in Thomas and Sillen, *Racism and Psychiatry*, p. 84 ff.

28. *New York Times*, July 27, 1971.

29. Ibid.

30. Ibid.

31. Staples, Robert, "The Myth of the Black Matriarchy," *The Black Scholar*, January-February, 1970.

32. Ladner, Joyce A., *Tomorrow's Tomorrow: The Black Woman*, Doubleday, New York, 1971.

33. Ibid., pp. xii-xiii.

34. Ibid., pp. xiii-xiv.

35. Ibid., p. xxi,

36. Ibid., p. 3.

37. Ibid., p. xxiv.

38. Ibid., p. 97.

39. Ibid., p. 32.

40. Ibid., p. 49.

41. Ibid., p. 101.

42. Chesler, Phyllis. *Women and Madness,* Doubleday, New York, 1972, p. 216.

43. Ibid., p. 323.

44. Summary based upon Chap. 10, Thomas and Sillen, *Racism and Psychiatry,* and Rogow, Arnold, *The Psychiatrists,* G.P. Putnam, New York, 1971.

45. Chesler, *Women and Madness,* p. 323.

46. Hurvitz, Nathan, "Psychotherapy as a Means of Social Control," *Journal of Consulting and Clinical Psychology,* 1973, 40, No. 2, pp. 232-239.

47. Rogow, *The Psychiatrists,* p. 73.

48. See Chapter 3.

49. *Daily World,* May 14, 1974.

50. Thomas and Sillen, *Racism and Psychiatry,* pp. 146-147.

51. Ibid., p. 147.

9. Women in Psychiatry

1. Freud, Sigmund, "Some Psychological Consequences of the Distinction Between the Sexes," *Collected Papers,* Vol. 5, London, Hogarth Press, 1956. Quoted in *N.Y. Times Magazine, Jan. 31, 1971.*

2. Gilman, Richard, "The FemLib Case Against Sigmund Freud," *New York Times,* January 31, 1971.

3. Ibid.

4. Ibid.

5. Ibid.

6. Ibid.

7. Freud, Sigmund, "Contributions to the Psychology of Love: The Taboo of Virginity," 1918, quoted in Gilman, op. cit.

8. Chesler, Phyllis, *Women and Madness,* New York, Doubleday, 1972, p. 69.

9. *New York Times,* March 5, 1974.

10. Ibid.

11. Morgan, Robin, ed., *Sisterhood is Powerful,* New York, Vintage Books, 1970, p. 235.

12. *New York Times,* January 31, 1971.

13. DeCrow, Karen, *The Young Woman's Guide to Liberation,* New York, Pegasus, 1971, p. 128.

14. Morgan, op. cit., p. 209.

15. *New York Times,* January 31, 1971.

16. Sears, Robert, *Survey of Objective Studies of Psychoanalytic Concepts,* New York, 1942, p. 133.

17. Montagu, Ashley, *The Natural Superiority of Women,* New York, Macmillan, 1953.

18. Quoted in Morgan, op. cit., p. 206.

19. Freud, *New Introductory Lectures in Psychoanalysis,* New York, W.W. Norton, 1933, pp. 134-135.

20. Gilman, op. cit.

21. Greer, Germaine, *The Female Eunuch,* New York, McGraw Hill, 1970, p. 88.

22. Erikson, Erik, "Inner and Outer Space: Reflections on Womanhood," *Daedelus,* 93, 1964.

23. DeCrow, op. cit., p. 135.

24. Grotjahn, Martin, "Sexuality and Humor," *Psychology Today,* July, 1972.

25. Chesler, op. cit., p. 91.

26. Ibid., p. 92.

27. Morgan, op. cit., p. 208.

28. Szasz, Thomas, *The Manufacture of Madness,* New York, Delta, 1970, p. 15.

29. Chesler, op. cit., p. 34.

30. Ibid., p. 118.

31. Ibid., p. 65.

32. Jong, Erica, *Fear of Flying,* New York, Signet, 1973, p. 18.

33. Angrist, Shirley, Mark Lefton, Simon Dinitz and Benjamin Pasamanick, *Women After Treatment,* New York, Appleton, Century, Croft, 1971, p. 11.

34. Ibid., p. 128.

35. Chesler, op. cit., pp. 37, 105.

36. Breggin, Peter, "The Return of Lobotomy and Psychosurgery," *Congressional Record,* February 24, 1972, pp. EL602-1612.

37. Chesler, op. cit., p. 35.

38. Ibid., pp. 35-38.

39. *New York Times,* December 28, 1972.

40. *The Negro Family: The Case for National Action,* U.S. Department of Labor, Washington, D.C., 1965.

41. Staples, Robert, "The Myth of the Black Matriarchy," *The Black Scholar,* January-February 1970, p. 2.

42. *New York Times,* March 11, 1973.

43. Chesler, op. cit., p. 216.

44. Ibid., p. 67.

45. Winston, Fern, "For a Class Approach to the Struggle For Women's Equality," *Daily World,* January 4, 1975.

46. Ibid.

47. Morgan, op. cit., p. 209.

48. Quoted in *Daily World,* March 8, 1974.

49. "Black Delegation Visits the U.S.S.R.," *New World Review,* Vol. 39, No. 3.

50. Ibid.

51. Quoted in *Political Affairs,* March 1971, p. 35.

10. Behavior Research

1. *New York Times,* January 22, 1975.

2. *New York Times,* February 2, 1975.

3. Ibid.

4. Engels, Frederick, *Dialectics of Nature,* International Publishers, New York, 1940, p. 183.

5. *New York Times,* September 11, 1975.

6. Ibid.

7. *New York Times,* August 13, 1975.

8. *New York Times,* August 11, 1975.

9. *New York Times,* September 17, 1975.

10. Warwick, Donald P., "Deceptive Research: Social Scientists Ought to Stop Lying," *Psychology Today,* February 1975.

11. *New York Times,* July 29, 1979, December 9, 1979. *Daily World,* April 5, 1975.

12. Kerlinger, Fred N., *Foundations of Behavioral Research,* Holt, Rinehart and Winston, New York, 1964, p. ix.

13. Ibid., p. 20.

14. Engels, op. cit., pp. 158-159.

15. Caplan, Nathan, and Nelson, Stephen D., "Who's To Blame?" *Psychology Today,* November 1974.

16. Ibid.

17. Ibid.

18. Signorelli, Anthony, "Statistics: Tool or Master of the Psychologist?" *American Psychologist,* October 1974, pp. 774-777.

19. Caplan and Nelson, op. cit.

20. Ibid.

21. Williams, Robert, "The Silent Mugging of the Black Community," *Psychology Today,* May 1974.

22. Gordon, Thomas, "Notes on White and Black Psychology," *Journal of Social Issues,* Vol. 29, No. 1, 1973, pp. 87-95.

23. Thomas, Charles W., "The System-Maintenance Role of the White Psychologist," *Journal of Social Issues,* Vol. 29, No. 1, 1973, pp. 57-65.

24. Cedric X (Clark), "Some Reflexive Comments on the Role of Editor," *Journal of Social Issues,* Vol. 29, No. 1, 1973, pp. 1-9.

25. Campbell, Angus, "The American Way of Mating," *Psychology Today,* May 1975.

26. Signorelli, op. cit.

27. For lack of validity of Rohrschach Test, see Klausmeier, Herbert J. and Goodwin, William, *Learning and Human Abilities,* Harper and Row, New York, 1966, pp. 616-617. Also Hertz, Marguerite R., "Rohrschach: 20 Years After," *Psychological Bulletin,* 1942, *39,* p. 538.

28. *The Piers-Harris Children's Self-Concept Scale,* Counselor Recordings and Tests, Nashville, Tennessee, 1969.

29. *The Intellectual Achievement Responsibility Scale,* Crandall, V., Katovsky, W., and Crandall V., "Children's Beliefs in Their Own Control of Reinforcements in Intellectual Academic Achievement Situations," *Journal of Consulting Psychology,* 1965, *36,* pp. 91-109.

30. Battle, E., and Rotter, J.B., "Children's Feelings of Personal Control as Related to Social Class and Ethnic Group," *Journal of Personality,* 1963, *31,* pp. 482-490.

31. *Psychology Today,* November 1973, p. 13.

32. Caplan and Nelson, op. cit.

33. Williams, op. cit.

34. Ibid.

35. Aptheker, Herbert, "Heavenly Days in Dixie: Or, the Time of Their Lives," *Political Affairs,* June 1974 and July 1974; Fogel, Robert and Engerman, Stanley L., *Time on the Cross: The Economics of Negro Slavery,* Little, Brown, Boston, 1974.

37. Ibid.

38. Daniels, Norman, "The Smart White Man's Burden," *Committee Against Racism,* Tufts University, Medford, Mass., 1973.

39. Lavenhar, Marvin A., "The Drug Abuse Numbers Game," *American Journal of Public Health,* Vol. 63, No. 9, September 1973, pp. 807-809.

40. Gold, David, "Statistical Tests and Substantive Significance," *The American Sociologist,* Vol. 4, No. 1, February 1969, pp. 42-46.

41. Daniels, op. cit.

42. Gold, op. cit.

43. Zitron, Celia, "Racism with a Scholarly Face," *Daily World Magazine,* December 16, 1972.

44. Jensen, Arthur, "The Differences Are Real," *Psychology Today,* December 1973.

45. For a devastating critique of the Kardiner and Ovesey study, see Thomas, Alexander, and Sillen, Samuel, *Racism and Psychiatry,* Brunner Mazel, New York, 1972, Chapter 3.

46. Signorelli, op. cit.

47. Hodes, Robert, *Aims and Methods of Scientific Research,* Occasional Paper #9, American Institute for Marxist Studies, New York, 1968, p. 13.

48. Ibid., pp. 13-14.

49. Ibid., p. 15.

50. Luria, Alexander, *Speech and the Development of Mental Processes in the Child,* Staples Press, London, 1959.

51. Hodes, op. cit., p. 10.

52. Engels, op. cit., p. 183.

53. Quoted in Hodes, op. cit., p. 11.

54. Ibid.

55. *New York Times,* February 2, 1975.

56. Ibid.

57. Caplan and Nelson, op. cit.

58. Thomas, Charles W., "The System-Maintenance Role of the White Psychologist," *Journal of Social Issues,* Vol. 29, No. 1, 1973, pp. 57-65.

59. Brazziel, William, "White Research in Black Communities: Where Solutions Become A Part of the Problem," *Journal of Social Issues,* Vol. 29, No. 1, 1973, pp. 41-44.

60. *Daily World,* November 5, 1975.

61. Brazziel, op. cit.

62. Warwick, op. cit.

11. Psychiatry and Socialism

1. *New York Post,* Nov. 1, 1971.

2. Davidow, Mike, A Question of Concern, *Daily World Magazine,* May 20, 1972.

3. Kiev, Ari, *Psychiatry in the Communist World,* Science House, N.Y., 1968, pp. 12-13.

4. Ibid., p. 16.

5. Ibid., p. 17.

6. Ibid., p. 16.

7. Malis, G. Yu., *Research on the Etiology of Schizophrenia,* Consultants Bureau, N.Y., no date.

8. Kiev, op. cit., p. 12.

9. Ibid., p. 7.

10. Gorman, Mike, *Soviet Psychiatry and the Russian Citizen,* National Committee Against Mental Illness, Washington, D.C., 1968, p. 3.

11. *Daily World,* May 23, 1972.

12. Kiev, op. cit., p. 8.

13. *Daily World,* May 23, 1972.

14. *Psychiatric Spectator,* Sandoz Pharmaceuticals, E. Hanover, N.J., Sept. 1971, pp. 12-13.

15. *Daily World Magazine,* May 20, 1972.

16. *New York Times,* May 18, 1968.

17. *Daily World,* May 23, 1972.

18. Kiev, op. cit., p. 16.

19. Ibid., p. 15.

20. Ibid., p. 14.

21. Crain, Irving J., "Treat a Patient Like a Human Being," *Daily World Magazine*, July 28, 1973.

22. Ziferstein, Isidore, "Group Psychotherapy in the Soviet Union," *New World Review*, 4th Quarter, 1973, p. 59.

23. Ibid., pp. 63–64.

24. Ibid., pp. 64–65.

25. See B.V. Andreev, *Sleep Therapy in the Neuroses*, Consultants Bureau, N.Y., 1960. Also Kiev, op. cit., p. 18.

26. See A.A. Portnov and D.D. Fedotov, *Psychiatry*, Mir Publishers, Moscow, 1969, Ch. XXIII. Also K. Platonov. *The Word as a Physiological and Therapeutic Factor*, Foreign Languages Publishing house, Moscow, 1959.

27. Kiev, op. cit., p. 19.

28. *Daily World*, July 20, 1973.

29. *Village Voice*, Aug. 22, 1974.

30. Gorman, op. cit., p. 11.

31. Ibid., p. 9.

32. Ibid., p. 15.

33. *Daily World*, Oct. 19, 1971.

34. *Psychiatric Spectator*, op. cit. p. 12.

35. *New York Times*, Oct. 24, 1971.

36. *Daily World Magazine*, July 28, 1973.

Index